INDIGENOUS PEOPLES IN LATIN AMERICA

INDIGENOUS PEOPLES IN LATIN AMERICA

The Quest for Self-Determination

Héctor Díaz Polanco

Translated by

Lucia Rayas

WestviewPress

A Division of HarperCollins*Publishers*

Latin American Perspectives

Copyright © 1997 by Westview Press, A Division of HarperCollins Publishers Inc.

Published in 1997 in the United States of America by Westview Press, 5500 Central Avenue, Boulder,
Colorado 80301-2877, and in the United Kingdom by Westview Press, 12 Hid's Copse Road, Cumnor
Hill, Oxford OX2 9JJ

Library of Congress Cataloging-in-Publication Data
Díaz Polanco, Héctor, 1944–
   [Autonomía regional. English]
   Indigenous peoples in Latin America : the quest for self-determination / Héctor Díaz Polanco ;
translated by Lucia Rayas.
      p.   cm.—(Latin American perspectives series ; no. 18)
   Includes bibliographical references and index.
   ISBN 0-8133-8698-5 (hc.)—ISBN 0-8133-8699-3 (pbk.)
   1. Indians—Government relations.   2. Indians—Politics and government.   3. Autonomy.   4.
Pluralism (Social sciences)   5. Latin America—Politics and government.   I. Title.   II. Series.
E59.G6D5213 1997
323.1'19708—dc21   96-39371
                                                                                                CIP

The paper used in this publication meets the requirements of the American National Standard for Per-
manence of Paper for Printed Library Materials Z39.48–1984.

10   9   8   7   6   5   4   3   2

Contents

Preface

In previous works I have dealt with various theoretical problems associated with the ethnic-national question and the complexity of its contribution to the structure of society. Throughout these essays I have emphasized the vital political issues arising from the pluralism of the majority of Latin American nations. From that perspective, I have emphasized a theme that seems of the utmost importance for the future of these countries: the challenges and difficulties of solving the problem of sociocultural inequality and achieving national democracy in the historical context of an enduring colonial legacy and a subsequent period of independence in which insensitivity to diversity persists.

This work examines a sociopolitical policy that in various national contexts has proven to be the most appropriate way of resolving the conflicts and ameliorating the conditions of oppression, discrimination, and inequality that go hand in hand with ethnic-national heterogeneity in Latin American social life. I will call this policy *regional autonomy*. My analysis focuses on indigenous ethnic groups, but it will be evident that many of the questions presented here are also applicable to other collectivities that have their own identities, such as the black and criollo communities, that abound in the region.

The history of the Latin American peoples involves policies explicitly aimed at denying rights to communities considered inferior and incapable of handling their own affairs precisely because they are socioculturally different from the dominant groups. Underlying this characterization of their difference is the intention of depleting their resources, exploiting their labor forces, and dominating them ideologically and politically. Hence, the various class concerns that began to take shape from the very first contact of the European invaders with the aboriginal peoples of America presume the exclusion of any possibility of *self-determination* for these indigenous ethnic groups, thereby placing them in a subordinate position.

In the first section I examine the main features of the historical conditions under which indigenist policies were established as a denial of any kind of autonomy for the various groups with identities of their own.

Indigenous peoples continue to be an important part of the population of many countries in Latin America despite the coordinated action and the more subtle divisive forces that for centuries have operated to make these ethnic groups vanish from the social horizon. In four of these countries (Bolivia, Guatemala, Peru, and Ecuador), indigenous peoples constitute more than 40 percent of the national population, in the first two cases reaching nearly 70 percent. In a dozen countries, including Belize, Honduras, Mexico, and Chile, the indigenous population represents from 5 to 20 percent of the total. All in all, there are more than 50 million people who maintain indigenous lifestyles, and this population is not only growing in absolute terms but in some areas also increasing relatively.

Although quantitative criteria allow us to form an idea of the importance of ethnicity, this is not enough. One must also consider the qualitative significance of indigenous populations even where (as in Nicaragua and Brazil) they are clearly a demographic minority. This qualitative dimension stems from economic considerations such as the resources present in the regions they inhabit, geopolitical considerations (their location in strategic areas such as borders and coasts), and sociocultural considerations such as their being historical reference points and sources of national cohesion. The influence that ethnic communities can exert over national processes in spite of their demographic minority status is evident from the Nicaraguan experience of the 1980s.

Given that the dominant groups are disinclined to concede these groups their rights, being more interested in keeping them true "internal colonies," the sociopolitical premises for their recognition, can be established only through their own struggles. This seems to be the general situation in several Latin American countries, with understandable differences depending on the different national contexts. The particular situations in which such trends appear range from the achievement of a regime of regional autonomy that ethnic groups are struggling to consolidate and preserve to the first attempts to turn renewed ethnic pride into clarity of purpose and organized force. Thus, perhaps for the first time in the history of the continent, the utopian goal of autonomy for indigenous peoples and other ethnic communities seems socially viable. Given this situation, clarifying the characteristics and implications of eventual regimes of regional autonomy in the complex Latin American context is all the more urgent. Some of these questions are addressed in the second part of the book.

I will avoid the temptation to consider autonomy a panacea, instead stressing its strict historical determination. Regional autonomy is not in fact the solution; rather, it is a means for solving problems under particular conditions. Besides, the fact that autonomy may become a suitable arrangement for indigenous peoples depends not on any mysterious categorical imperative or teleological design but on the concrete action of the sociopolitical forces that make it a reality. In this sense, autonomy is only possible, not necessary.

For reasons that may seem obvious, I will approach these topics in terms of their historical context and, particularly, from a regional perspective, with special stress on the Mexican case. Nevertheless, I hope that the ideas and conclusions that stem from this work will benefit both indigenous peoples and scholars from other countries.

The substance of this book and many of its basic theses are inspired by the rich experience of the Nicaraguan people during ten years of popular revolution. That the first constitutionally established regime of regional autonomy in Latin America developed on the Nicaraguan Atlantic Coast is of course no accident. The process launched by the Sandinista government is an experiment with wide-ranging lessons. I am grateful to the Nicaraguan people for their practical demonstration of the extent to which the viability of autonomy depends on active popular participation.

As a professor-researcher at the Centro de Investigaciones y Estudios Superiores en Antropología Social (CIESAS), I have appreciated the supportive working environment and the time granted to me to complete this study. I want to acknowledge both the generous support of the institution's academic authorities and the insightful observations and critical suggestions made in the course of several internal seminars by my colleagues in CIESAS's Area 3. I am also indebted to several colleagues and friends. Above all, the intellectual stimulus I received from Pablo González Casanova was very important in the completion of this study. I am grateful for commentaries and ideas from Felipe Bate, Diego Iturralde, Sergio de la Peña, Enrique Semo, and Roberto Varela. Araceli Burguete, Julieta Haidar, and Gilberto López y Rivas offered useful comments on the bibliography. Lucia Rayas prepared the translation. The constant support and critical opinions of Consuelo Sánchez were invaluable. Naturally, the conception and contents of this book are entirely my own responsibility.

Héctor Díaz Polanco

Translator's Acknowledgments

Richard Wood, sociologist and friend, went through the complete translation of this book with enormous patience and dedication. This work would not exist in this version without his input.

Many other friends and colleagues proofread parts of this work. The comments and suggestions of Stephen Towey, Apen Ruiz, Bill Maurer, Jaana Remes, Andrés Resendes, Mauricio Tenorio, Stefan Helmreich, and Michelle Beatty are included in these pages.

Special thanks go to Michael Kearney, whose constant support and friendship were the beginning of this endeavor, and to George and Jane Collier whose advice invariably led to further learning.

I am also indebted to Héctor Díaz Polanco, who listened to my doubts and cleared them kindly and promptly.

Finally, Federico Besserer led me through the good and bad times during the months it took to translate this book. For his continual presence I thank him and love him, as I do Iván and Andrés. They too were a constant source of encouragement.

Lucia Rayas

PART ONE

■

Excluded Identities

CHAPTER ONE

———— ■ ————

Nation Building and the Ethnic Question

During the past few decades, the theoretical-political tendency to separate ethnic issues from national dynamics and structure has lost its impetus in Latin America. Instead, there has been a revitalization of the Latin American analytic tradition of linking ethnic issues with regional and national development. The discussion that follows falls within this tradition.

Not only are ethnoregional and national issues related but it is impossible to understand the so-called indigenous problem (or any other problem having to do with groups distinguished ethnically) apart from the regional and national contexts (political, economic, and sociocultural) that inform it. This simple principle has important consequences not only epistemologically but also politically, since its acceptance or rejection has an effect on policymaking.

Historically, the importance of ethnicity can be understood only in terms of the processes that have determined the makeup of national societies in Latin America and, in particular, guided the emergence of its nation-states. It is important to note that in using this concept of nation, I am referring not to any sociopolitical organization in particular but to a historically determined form that gives shape to the modern nation-state. The term "nation" is applied to a great variety of sociopolitical formations.[1] This undifferentiated and chaotic use positions the "modern nation" alongside other "nations" (e.g., the Maya, Yaqui or Zapotec). (Here I am speaking of theoretical or scientific usage; the political denominations these peoples apply to themselves are beyond question.)[2] In many cases the main reason for this—to avoid the ranking associated with domination and political oppression—is laudable. However, proceeding in this way obscures the understanding of what is specific to contemporary nationalism and precludes any understanding of the significant relationships (the very basis of domination and oppression) that develop when indigenous "nations" persist within the framework of modern nation-states. As Leonard Tivey has put it, "Although men have always joined together in some kind of unit, their grouping in nation states is a modern characteristic whose full development is certainly an essentially contemporary phenomenon."[3] Disregarding some early forms, nation-states first appeared during the eighteenth and nineteenth centuries; before that there were nationalities or states but no nation-states. According to Cornelia Navari, the nation-state not only expresses continuity with earlier social formations but "implies the process of its own destruction and replacement by new contents, ideas, and kinds of social relations."[4] Its development implies huge transformations that correspond to a given historical stage and that distinguish the nation-state from previous forms of organization of which it is often the *negation*.

Several transformative forces interacted organically in the genesis of the nation-state: (1) *rationalism*, a system of thought that modified the idea of the state, conceiving it as at the service not just of the monarch but of the "citizen" and producing uniform legal systems patterned mainly on the Napoleonic code and the notion of legal equality, among other fundamental innovations; (2) *capitalism*, a complex process of transformations in economic and social relations that created the "free worker" (free to sell her/his labor power), a new culture of efficiency and accumulation, and the framework for the development of modern social classes as well as for the vast linkages of a world economy; and (3) the *state*, which formulated common systems (educational, legal, and so on) and organized bureaucracies capable of rationalizing the functioning of the new sovereign sociopolitical structures. "These are the characteristic features of the modern state, precisely the features that constitute its modernity. But they are also the characteristic features of the nation-state, the ones that helped create it. The modern state and the nation-state are coextensive phenomena. In the development process, modernization and nation building imply the same program."[5] This is not the place to attempt a detailed historical analysis of the genesis of nation-states. Rather, I will examine, from the perspective of the national development process, some aspects of the treatment of sociocultural issues characteristic of Latin America.

With regard to the construction of the majority of nation-states in Latin America and their sociocultural makeup, there are at least two characteristics worthy of detailed analysis. The first is the early reiterated concern, which in some cases has become a political obsession, with the "incomplete" or "inauthentic" character of the nation attributable to the persistence of ethnic groups, and the second, a corollary of the first, is the eager pursuit of a formula that would allow the "completion" or "integration" of societies whose fabric is socioculturally heterogeneous. This heterogeneity is often considered a stigma, a defect to be overcome.

Coincidentally, ethnic heterogeneity as an opprobrious blemish has repeatedly been the subject of discussion among ideologues and scholars in a number of Latin American countries. In contrast, national homogeneity has been presented as a desirable and necessary goal. Manuel Gamio's approach to this issue can be considered paradigmatic. Gamio was an important Mexican intellectual whose ideas were influential throughout Latin America. Until his death in 1960 he was the director of the Instituto Indigenista Interamericano (Inter-American Indigenist Institute), charged with launching a campaign for the integration of indigenous peoples throughout the continent—one of the basic agreements of the first Inter-American Indigenist Congress, held in Mexico City in 1940, in which delegates from nineteen countries participated. From this institutional platform Gamio's ideas expanded to other countries through local indigenist agencies that he himself helped to found.[6]

Gamio developed the idea of a link between the forging of a nation and the elimination of the ethnic heterogeneity that characterizes most Latin American countries.[7] The fact that he was concerned well into the twentieth century with the urgent need "to form a true nation" and that he considered the "ethnic heterogeneity of the population" an obstacle shows the durability of this point of view.[8] This paradigmatic perspective has loyal followers to this day.[9]

ETHNIC-NATIONAL HETEROGENEITY IN EUROPE

As an initial working hypothesis, it can be said that there was generally little concern for the problem of heterogeneity in the Western European countries in which capitalism developed early (e.g., England, France, Holland, Switzerland) or at least no such policy proposals as Gamio's. This is not to be explained in terms of the absence of ethnic-national heterogeneity within the European national formations. On the contrary, the makeup of these nations, a product of the development of modern states, is diverse and protean. Nearly every European national society, even those that achieved a coherent nation-state through fundamentally endogenous processes, includes many ethnic-national groups. The examples of Scotland, Wales, and Ireland (Ulster) in Britain, Aquitaine, Brittany, and Corsica in the French case, and the various sociocultural groups organized in Swiss cantons illustrate that ethnic differences need not be perceived as problematic for nation building and point to differences between Western Europe and Latin America in the processes that led to the formation of nation-states. Generally, it would seem that in this part of Europe a previous unification that in some cases included strong socioeconomic integration, was crucial. This unifying process was determined, among other factors, by the development of an internal market driven by the expansion of market relationships and by the emergence of a new bourgeoisie whose social identity did not rest upon the division into estates as did that of the aristocracy. The bourgeoisie proposed a model of society based not on sociocultural or ethnic differences but on the unity established by "equality" among citizens, free labor, the regulatory action of the market, and open competition. These were the foundations for the nation.

In this context, the ethnic question was not a critical obstacle to the formation of the European nation-states. According to Andrés de Blas Guerrero,

the most complete form of political nation, the nation-state, coincides with the development of the middle classes that have become the reference group for the majority of the population; this is the case in England, Holland, Switzerland, the United States of America, and—with its own peculiarities—France. Ethnic conflict plays a minimal role because there are no ethnic separations between the middle and lower classes, and therefore upward social mobility is not hindered by ethnicity. The national project of these national states therefore emerges free of historical mortgages, dominated by a sense of rationality and empirical concerns. This would explain the success of nation building in societies as intimately divided by cultural factors as Holland or Switzerland or, to a lesser degree, states such as the English, the North American, and the French.[10]

In many cases, European nationalities[11] or "nationality" groups were formed during the eighteenth century, even before the nation as such had appeared in its modern form as the nation-state. The latter was constituted out of that plural reality rather than against it. This does not mean that ethnic-national conflicts were absent, but as a rule solutions to these conflicts were not sought through the total elimination of diversity. Certain sociocultural components allowed the distinction of some ethnic-national groups from others, but these ethnic configurations never became an insurmountable socioeconomic obstacle or a political hindrance to nation building. This tolerance of or, rather, relative indifference to sociocultural variety arose not from the elaborations of ideologues but from transformations originating at the base of society. Structural processes and in particular the expansion of market relations that prepared the way for modern capitalism served as the cement for the political fusing of socioculturally heterogeneous components. They also prevented the establishment of rigid socioeconomic hierarchies stemming from "cultural" differences, particularly with regard to the characterization of the labor force. The hegemonic actions of the bourgeoisie or the aristocracy-turned-bourgeoisie converted these elements, originating in the socioeconomic substratum, into sociopolitical realities: nation-states.

To sum up, these initial economic activities influenced the emergence of a minimal socioeconomic articulation that facilitated the integration of "nationality" groups into a larger national unit, making sociocultural heterogeneity a secondary concern—at least during the stage of modern state building. Thus, the ethnic or linguistic differences that persisted in many regions were not an immediate handicap to the creation of unified nation-states, however multiethnic or, in some cases, even multinational. Thus, the question of ethnic-national heterogeneity did not generate the deep uncertainties about national viability or the acute homogenizing tendencies observed in the Latin American case.

Some of the Western European nation-states date to the end of the eighteenth century, but most of them emerged during the nineteenth century, generally developing from the bottom up. This does not mean that the role of the state during this phase was insignificant. Rather, it means that strong structural processes and the shaping of class systems headed by groups such as the bourgeoisie led to the development of nationalities and the cohesion conducive to nation building. National society was a product of this process, and during that phase of the development of capitalism, with its contradictory tendencies toward both universalization and the requirement of fixed spaces for production and for the realization of profit, it in turn required the structure of a nation-state.

This European process was the basis of the great schemes for explaining the national question. Marxist theory itself is, to a large extent, an outgrowth of this Eurocentric analytical tradition, and this is the source of certain persistent difficulties in comprehending the national processes of capitalism's peripheral regions, particularly in Latin America. Marx's incorrect and unfair judgment of Simón Bolívar, and his struggle for the emancipation of the Latin American colonies is an example of this misunderstanding.[12]

NATION BUILDING AND ETHNIC GROUPS IN LATIN AMERICA

In spite of the great diversity of conditions that have influenced the structure of nation-states in the Latin American framework, certain broad patterns point to important differences from the European process. Among these patterns are that of the non-Hispanic Caribbean countries (English, French, Dutch), which developed out of societies that instead of emerging organically, were organized from the outside as businesses[13] or entrepreneurial ventures (plantation and habitation as a production unit[14]); that of societies in which the plantation economy took root relatively late and the autochthonous population was completely eliminated; and that of formations in which the indigenous population survived the rigors of European invasion and became an important subordinate sector of society in colonial times and after the achievement of political independence (more than a dozen countries fit this description). With these varying patterns in mind, Edelberto Torres Rivas's observation is instructive: "The Latin American countries differ from the outset in terms of the various ways in which conquest, colonialism, and the later republican relations took place, and this makes it difficult for its generic qualities to take precedence over its basic heterogeneity."[15] Without ignoring this historical reality, and adopting a level of generality that is potentially problematic, I will emphasize some elements of the Latin American process that contrast significantly (regarding sociocultural issues) with those of Europe.

National life in colonial Latin America was constructed under conditions very different from those prevailing in Europe. The colonial process, instead of developing a socioeconomic structure and an internal market that would have generated integration, created conditions to prevent this from happening. The restriction of foreign trade to the metropolis and the strict restrictions that hindered economic exchange among the colonial provinces (which were relaxed only with the Bourbon reforms in the twilight of the eighteenth century),[16] the internal monopolies, the intricate and detailed administrative controls of all kinds created in the distant peninsula, the abundant customs and sales taxes, the estates inherited by primogeniture, the benefices, and the various privileges operated as tremendous restraints on the development of capitalism. Practically the entire social fabric was smothered under this heavy colonial cloak whereby the metropolis had exported its own backwardness, aggravated by the harshest despotism.[17]

For a long time the labor force was severely exploited under conditions of slavery and servility. Extraeconomic mechanisms of exploitation and surplus extraction were unequivocal indicators of the immature capitalistic character of social relations. The Spanish monarchy used restrictive measures to seize the wealth created by the Indians through tribute or by the peninsular colonizers and criollos managing to squeeze the last drop from the aboriginal population's labor force. During the first stage of the colonial regime, direct slavery was accompanied by the more subtle de facto slavery constituted by the *encomienda*. By the mid-sixteenth century the forced *repartimiento* (division) of the indigenous labor force among the various sectors of the narrow colonial power circle (*encomenderos*, landholders, wool mill owners, clergy, royal officers, and others) was established. Even though, according to the "New Laws," one had to pay for the Indians' work, this pay was often merely symbolic, and in any case the indigenous worker was forced by the official *repartidor* to provide services. In the provinces where the forced *repartimiento* was later forbidden (as in New Spain), coercion of workers (through slavery or debt servitude) were not outlawed.[18] Beginning in the seventeenth century, a further *repartimiento* (this one commercial in character) became prevalent as a mechanism for exploiting indigenous peoples.

During the more than three hundred years of Spanish colonization, the majority of the labor force was what might be called "ethnicized." By this I mean the sociocultural ascription of the exploited labor force, particularly Indians and slaves. The ethnic stratification was superimposed on the class structure, complicating and reinforcing it. According to the social rationale of the period, the Indians had to pay tribute and work for nothing or practically nothing for the colonizers because they were vassals—that is, because they were Indians. The subordinate character of the Indian towns as communities was based on the same logic.

Colonial society rested upon these sharp differences among its components, differences that often persisted even after independence and inhibited the development of the cohesion among sectors and strata of society that would have contributed to a national identity. One of the tasks of emerging nation-states was precisely to destroy such "caste" systems, attacking the noncapitalist institutions and social relations upon which these systems were based. In the Western European case, as we have seen, this task was accomplished largely by the generalization of market relations; the differences in question had generally been eroded by the structural development of society before the emergence of the modern nation-state.

The construction of the nation-state in Latin America took place in the absence of a well-established bourgeoisie as an expression of capitalist logic. The seeds of burgeoning capitalism were certainly present in the activities of some agricultural entrepreneurs, merchants, and others, representing an incipient criollo bourgeoisie, but they were swamped by the estates, privileges, and other relationships and institutions established by the colonial system.[19] Thus the effort to build a typical capitalist sociopolitical organization was undertaken without a socioeconomic structure in which capitalistic premises predominated. Besides, in several Latin American countries cohesion had to be developed among sectors that were distinct not only economically and politically but also ethnically. When criollo elites became leaders of liberation movements, nationalities were not yet fully formed as collective identities with a clear goal of self-determination, especially in countries with significant sociocultural heterogeneity. This had important consequences with regard to the national role of elites and the emerging state to which I will return.

NATIONAL INTEGRATION VERSUS SOCIOCULTURAL PLURALITY

Given the conditions just described, the leaders of newly independent countries were faced with the fundamental task of creating the political and socioeconomic bases of emerging nation-states. The noncapitalist relationships inherited from the colonial period were colossal obstacles to the integration of this new national base. Among the most visible expressions of these relationships were the servitude and oppression imposed particularly upon indigenous communities, and therefore there was a tendency for leaders to identify the social relations they wanted to annul with the various ethnic configurations that had been formed or restructured during the long colonial period themselves. Thus, by allowing the survival of indigenous ethnic communities, the ruling elite in Latin America embarked upon independent life ratifying economic and sociocultural relations that they considered undesirable (and that directly harmed the groups in question). Liberals in particular considered these groups not only undesirable but also a hindrance to nation building. In the ideology of the learned elites, Indian identities, now differentiated not only from the Spanish but also from the criollo or mestizo, were "colonial." This character was persistently attributed to indigenous ethnic groups up until twentieth-century indigenism.[20]

In other words, the ethnic cohesion of dominated and exploited communities is conceived of as a kind of colonial legacy that must vanish in the process of nation building. The aim was not to annul any relationship that oppressed and exploited colonized Indians (in fact, new oppressive and exploitative relations, later conceptualized as "internal colonialism,"[21] were developed within the framework of the independent states) but to deny the basic identity of the distinctive ethnic groups. To acknowledge such an identity would have implied acceptance of an autonomous way of life for ethnic groups and, especially, respect for their subsistence base, their land and other communal resources, intensely coveted by both conservatives and liberals.

This seems to be one of the roots of the early confrontation or opposition in Latin America between national integration and sociocultural plurality. In protonational Europe, ethnic configurations could not so readily be assimilated to precapitalist relations or "backwardness." The socioeconomic development of the various nationalities in Europe was comparatively more balanced, and there were instances in which a dominated nationality matched or surpassed the dominant one in socioeconomic position (for example, the case of Catalonia vis-à-vis Castile). In Latin America, in contrast, given the conditions imposed on the autochthonous population by colonial domination, there was an almost automatic identification between indigenous ethnic communities and the colonial social relations that had to be eradicated to build national society. The conditions that might have forced an understanding of the distinction between colonial servitude and the sociocultural structures that characterized the indigenous ethnic groups did not exist. Sporadic heroic Indian rebellions did occur, but they were too scattered to be effective.

ELITES, THE STATE, AND ETHNIC GROUPS

It is evident that colonial conditions were determinant in the process of nation building in Latin America. In Europe the development of modern national unity meant the destruction of feudal divisions and privileges; in Latin America the construction of nation-states was linked not only to the suppression of state privileges and servile relations but also to the formal dissolution of colonial bonds. The sequence of events that created the cultural atmosphere in which the revolution for independence developed (among them the crisis of the Spanish monarchy and the irruption of the Napoleonic army into Europe) and, more important, the impact of new ideas (of the Enlightenment and the North American and French revolutions) contributed greatly to the development of libertarian aspirations and desires for self-determination that did not, however, closely correspond to the social and economic development achieved within the confines of colonial society. Hence, as a rule, during the first years of the struggle for independence the national project was the vague goal of a learned elite[22], rather than one of Latin American peoples.[23]

This is not a unique case. The lack of concordance between the embryonic national consciousness of the Latin American criollo elites, on the one hand, and the consciousness and living conditions of the great majority of the people (poor mestizos and mulattos, small landholders and artisans, Indians and slaves), on the other, is similar to that between the elite and the majority in the backward regions of Central and Eastern Europe in contrast to the correspondence between political ideology and socioeconomic reality observed in Western Europe. According to Kohn,

> National consciousness grew as a result of these complex and contradictory elements. So vigorous is the influence of thought that, while the new Western European nationalism corresponded to new social, economic, and political realities, ideas expanded in the central and eastern parts of the same continent much earlier than the correspond-

ing economic and social transformations. The cultural contact among the learned classes of the continent changed in intellectual and moral character while the economic order and the way of life of the vast majority of the people remained unchanged.

However, this phenomenon did not eliminate regional differentiation as the new ideas adapted to the various social matrices into which they sought to fit: "The political and social changes occurring in Western Europe accentuated the deep differences between the two halves of Europe. The new ideas found, in the different nations, a great diversity of institutional and social conditions bequeathed from the past and molded to them."[24]

Thus, it is not surprising that, in Latin America, it was these criollo elites who led the liberation struggles. Many of them constituted a learned stratum, steeped in the ideas of Rousseau, Encyclopedism, and the great ideals of freedom, equality, and democracy advanced by the North American and French revolutions. It is true that, as Jospeh Pérez has shown, one must not exaggerate the penetration of the Enlightenment into the circle of the educated Latin American elite, since one finds in their ideas much of the Hispanic tradition slightly revised.[25] However, the articulation of these renovating ideas with those inspired by the North American Revolution and especially, with the ideological explosion projected by the French Revolution, provoked a dramatic shift in focus for many Latin Americans vis-à-vis the colonial reality. Some, as in the case of Francisco de Miranda and Simón Bolívar, had been to the great centers of political debate (especially London and Paris) and had even directly participated in revolutionary struggles.[26]

It is not surprising that the caudillos and founding fathers played so outstanding a role as leaders and arbiters. This role was the more important the less developed were the foundations for national social cohesion. Revolutionary upheaval naturally provoked extreme centrifugal reactions that could be controlled only with the firm guidance and, in several instances, the rule of these leaders (of whom the archetypical figure would be Bolívar).

According to Ricaurte Soler, during the emancipation stage

the great revolutionary caudillos (not to be confused with local caciques) had the potential and the responsibility for establishing the solidest and most viable bases for national organization. . . . Fundamentally concerned with asserting independence vis-à-vis the metropolis and with internal political stability, they performed a socially moderating function as arbiters that was nationally advanced and both privileged and necessary.[27]

Soler adds that with the caudillos "the process of national structuring is initiated more resolutely by the state. From this point of view, one could not understand their historical importance if it were ascribed to the representation of a given social class. Rather, what characterizes them is the subordination of social consciousness to American national consciousness."[28]

✱ The role of the state in nation building is not original or exclusive to Latin American development. In other regions as well, national development would be incomprehensible without the crucial involvement of the state. It is in this sense that several analysts speak of the state as the "creator" of the nation.[29] However, the dialectic involved in nation building of course implies in turn that the class-based socioeconomic structure resulting from state involvement impacts the state itself. What is distinctive about the Latin American process is its historical environment, the socioeconomic and cultural matrix in which the emerging state realizes its integrating effects. It is in relationship to that economically obsolete and socioculturally diverse matrix (in which no complete nationality yet existed and many indigenous ethnic groups had a limited national perspective) that the articulating role of the state is so striking.

Social and cultural issues were subordinated to the consolidation of the nation-state, still threatened by the assaults of the metropolis and very dependent upon military victories. In this context, ethnic or regional conflicts that might vaguely express sociocultural demands seemed an offense against the fundamental goal of the moment: to ensure independence by maximizing the unity of the nation-state.

In determining the nature of these new nation-states, the idea of a democratic establishment of autonomous regions was either absent or set aside. It is debatable to what extent the tradition of fierce centralism that characterized the Castilian culture dominant in the peninsula influenced Latin America, in contrast with that of a littoral Spain that was more tolerant of difference and inclined toward the development of autonomous institutions within its territorial domain. This typically Castilian tendency to reject any kind of autonomy must not be forgotten. Beneyto mentions that "while littoral Spain is skeptical, inland Spain is dogmatic: while one negotiates, the other imposes. Therefore autonomy is intrinsically inconceivable to the Castilian monarchy: anyone who wants to be ruled in any other way is—just like anyone who wants to think for himself—a heretic."[30] Certainly, the Castilian monarchs systematically looked for ways to impose the strictest centralism in the peninsula itself and extended it practically unrestricted to their domains in America.[31]

Such a fixed tradition of dogmatic and intolerant centralism vis-à-vis any sociocultural difference is not easily cast aside. Indeed, the hypothesis that one can trace the social, economic, and political life of the continent's countries to a persistent centralism is an attractive one. This is the analytical strategy followed by Claudio Véliz, for example, who begins with "the vital importance of the existence, before the emergence of industry of a centralist secular tradition that has been the common denominator of transformations and discernible continuities throughout the economic, social, and political history of the Latin American nations." For Véliz, the origins of this centralism are clear: "The Iberian countries of the western hemisphere entered the modern age as the administrative, legal, and political creations of a Castilian postfeudal monarchy dominated by the principle of central control. The political and administrative structure of Latin America owes its centralism to a resolutely centralist Castile and not to a more or less plural Spain."[32]

The fact remains that centralism was dominant during the construction of the Latin American nation-states. When federal systems were adopted, they were, in reality, groups of "provinces" that were not the expression, in a national context, of autonomous entities with a distinctive sociocultural component. Of course, the absence of ethnic-national groups capable of expressing themselves as political forces at that time was crucial to this result.

During the emancipatory phase, the caudillos and founding fathers favored a continental federation (confederation) but declared themselves firmly antifederalist within their respective national frameworks. The conditions imposed by this historical stage may have offered them no alternative.[33] In sum, there was no room for political recognition of plurality or of the specificities within each national formation. The confederation was a project almost exclusively oriented toward strengthening or asserting the existence of nation-states rather than promoting any kind of plurality within them; it was simply thought that a close alliance would permit the states to defend themselves more efficiently vis-à-vis external threats and to consolidate their independence.

FROM CRIOLLO NATIONALISM
TO LIBERAL CENTRALISM

Throughout the continent (with the exception of Río de la Plata) liberals inclined toward federalism while conservatives were fervent advocates of centralism. In this dispute, however, there was no question of the organization of the state in terms of recognition or rejection of sociocultural plurality; instead, the issue under discussion was the economic and political organization of society. As a rule, the conservatives wanted to maintain economic disarticulation, the forms of property and privileges that ensured them their power, and centralism was consistent with the corporative character of such traditional institutions as the church and the army. Federal decentralization, in contrast, sought to destroy conservative power by developing "urban nuclei" in the various provinces that would operate as allies of the central power in its effort to annul the economic relations and forms of property inherited from the colony.[34]

The process that caused the leaders of the new nation-states to deny the validity of indigenous societies and even consider them a hindrance to national assertion and progress is complex and diverse, but in every case one sees the same adverse attitude toward indigenous peoples and the desire to destroy them as ethnic groups. At first glance, it is as if indigenous societies embodied everything that the new rulers sought to reject in the colonial past. However, it is clear that such attitudes were related more to the conditions existing after independence than to the past. Aversion to the indigenous was directly proportional to what, potentially, their presence meant for the societal projects outlined by the groups competing for control of the new states.

In reality, the indigenous presence was then, as, *mutatis mutandis,* it remains today, a temptation to some to propose democratic initiatives, agrarian and popular, in opposition to the authoritarian and oligarchical inclinations of the elites, and this made indigenous people a threat to the latter. The sectors that valued indigenous people as an element of a possible social project were few and politically weak. Conservatives and liberals alike strenuously opposed them and indeed, any romantic appreciation of the indigenous past that did not include a politically positive formulation for the present.

The Mexican case allows us to observe the conditions of political struggle that made it impossible to set forth a national project without rejecting indigenous ethnic groups. This phenomenon has to do with the history of the criollos' emerging national consciousness, which was incapable of incorporating living Indians into a viable national project. The consciousness of conservatives was attached to Hispanic values, and the liberals became an outspoken enemy of the "heavy yoke of the community."

The first criollo nationalists, even when they developed what David Brading calls a "historical indigenism," focused on the glory of the past Indian civilizations, were not interested in being advocates of the indigenous societies of their day, which they did not trust or respect. Conservatives, for their part, embracing a Hispanism that could not provoke popular enthusiasm, excluded from their project and their nationalist perspective ethnic groups that they did not consider precursors of the Mexican nation. The absence or weakness of a third approach that, by including the demands of indigenous societies, could have led to an agrarian socialism opened the door for the liberal movement.

In Mexico, recognition of indigenous communities came almost a hundred years later, with the popular revolution of the beginning of the twentieth century. Nineteenth-century liberalism, with its social base in small rural producers as well as large landowners, deemed indigenous peoples a colonial residue and was able to summon the strength to condemn them to destruction.[35] It was impossible for indigenous peoples to find a national group with which they could coordinate, and their situation after the fall of the colonial regime prevented them from influencing, by themselves, the course of national events; thus the homogenizing project was imposed upon them naturally.

During the colonial era, the criollos, whose social position depended on Indians' subordination, could not be their allies. The criollos found a basis for their ideals primarily in the exaltation of the conquest. Indeed, after the second half of the sixteenth century they turned for patriotic authority to the conquistadores, who had "legitimately" won American land for their descendants and created the bases for the new homeland.[36] They were interested in emphasizing the achievement of the conquistadores and thereby strengthening their rights vis-à-vis the crown and the "upstart" peninsular Spanish.[37] Incidentally, they made reference to the virtues and capacities of the past native society that their ancestors had subdued at a great cost but took special care to avoid any mention of the relationship between the conquest and the present unfortunate situation of the colonized Indians. When the criollos "defended" the Indians they were almost always defending, in reality, the monopoly over their labor power and control over the tributaries of their *encomiendas*, or their influence and power over them against the increasingly aggressive competition of the royal administrators, other colonizers, or the clergy (especially of the regular orders).

In preinsurgent Mexico the criollos were preparing themselves ideologically to confront Spanish domination, seeking direct support in an idealization of the indigenous past while ignoring flesh-and-blood contemporary indigenous people.[38] Little by little, some members of the intellectual criollo elite sought to reconstruct aspects of their history, stripping it of those elements that justified the conquest and adding ingredients that rejected the colonial regime and legitimized independence. It was the opinion of the Spanish that the paganism of the Indians and the evangelizing work that was therefore necessary to save them from the devil fully justified the conquest. Before this, for example, the patriotic friar Servando Teresa de Mier had defended the far-fetched but efficient hypothesis that the natives had been evangelized before the arrival of the Spanish by Saint Thomas of Mylapore, transfigured in Quetzalcóatl.

De Mier's interpretation included two hypotheses. First, he maintained that Saint Thomas had evangelized in Mexico towards the sixth century, pointing to rituals and beliefs found in ancient Mexican society. He rejected the interpretation of Quetzalcóatl that made the Mexicans "snake worshippers" and any identification of that figure with the Spanish one. In reality, according to De Mier, Quetzalcóatl was not Spanish but a missionary, Saint Thomas. In addition, the friar placed the apparition of the Virgin of Guadalupe ten centuries earlier, robbing the Spanish of any merit regarding this event. Lafaye suggest that "if Mier's hypothesis had triumphed, Guadalupe would have been even more specifically Indian. Linked to the hypothesis of pre-Hispanic evangelization, she would have undermined the main (and even the only) judicial basis for the conquest, the evangelizing mission."

It is not surprising that the Spanish authorities rejected De Mier's daring revisionism, since his intentions and its political implications were obvious: it contradicted, for the Spanish, their self-image as a chosen people carrying divine grace to the American pagans. In contrast, it characterized Mexicans as a chosen people without Spanish mediation. This liberation from "the Spanish messianic tutelage" was, in turn, a formidable impulse toward political autonomy.[39]

De Mier's ideas amounted to giving political meaning to religious ideology in order to buttress a national sentiment that was all the more efficient for its highlighting the negative action that colonization had implied. In effect, the friar made "a retrospective baptism of the indigenous past" that transformed the evangelization claimed by the Spanish into the destruction of a preexisting aboriginal Christianity.[40] Equally, de Mier expressed a new attitude in the criollos, who now saw themselves as the heirs not of the conquistadores but of the missionaries who opposed them. Thus, criollo nationalism recovers clerics such as the friar Bartolomé de las Casas, who had denounced the excesses of the foreign invaders.[41] The recovery of the indigenous past was a powerful weapon against Spanish domination despite its including no recognition for living Indians. This feature of the emerging criollo national consciousness (absent in that social class in other regions, such as Peru) explains, in part, the distinctive character of the Mexican insurgency (popular, *Guadalupana*, with an agrarian element and an element of "caste" struggle against the Spanish). Such "historical indigenism" was also a pool from which a later Mexican nationalism drew valuable cohesive elements. At the same time, however, its sociopolitical distance with regard to the surviving indigenous ethnic groups facilitated the strong anti-indigenous currents (liberal for the most part) that affected Indian communities toward the middle of the nineteenth century throughout Latin America.

During the decades that immediately followed independence, indigenous communities suffered only slight reduction in their agrarian possessions and disruption of their communal structure. This was not because of any protective policy of the new states but because the new class arrangements had not been completed and the socioeconomic conditions that would make these communities' lands and resources coveted had not yet been created.[42] In reality, after independence consensus emerged around the idea that the communal organization of indigenous peoples—"that kind of communism," as it was characterized by a Mexican liberal in 1851—was a social cancer that had to be extirpated. In Mexico this point of view had become so widespread by mid-nineteenth century that it penetrated conservative circles, as is illustrated by the critiques by a group of *hacendados* of certain measures favorable to the Indians and by the change of opinion of the renowned conservative intellectual Lucas Alamán with regard to the indigenous community.[43] Up to that point there had been more talk than action, but "by the mid-nineteenth century there begins, almost everywhere, an assault on Indian lands (in some regions linked to the assault on church-owned lands)."[44]

Liberals were not interested in acknowledging the rights of these ethnic groups as such. On the contrary, they included Indian communities in their notion of the civil corporation, as an obstacle to nation building. Thus the dispute between centralists and federalists placed indigenous people between the devil and the deep blue sea. The main goal of the conservatives was not to destroy indigenous communities but to maintain with some modifications the oppressive conditions and exploitative relations they suffered. The liberals sought to cancel those relations by dismantling the communities. The liberals' true goal was to attack the agrarian and corporative pillars on which conservative power rested, projecting a program that left no room for sociocultural distinctions. Their federalism resulted in new types of centralism. With regard to ethnic composition it was not pluralistic but homogenizing.

In Europe, the economic, political, and sociocultural conditions that accompanied and were favored by capitalist development, especially the inclusion of multiple nationalities within the nation-state, determined that liberalism assumed a certain tolerance toward internal diversity to counteract the disintegrating pull of a strong cultural nationalism (with relativist and historicist roots) that cherished the idea of a state for every nationality. The alternative was clear: either such diversity was accommodated within each nation-state or there was the real risk of an immediate struggle of the nationalities for self-determination that would lead to the organization of states corresponding to particular cultural identities. In reality, both things happened. Where multiethnic states were established, not without conflict, diversity found a less adverse milieu than in Latin America. The distinguished liberal Lord Acton, for example, referring to the European nationalities, called the "existence of different nations under a single sovereignty" a positive development. The unity of the nation-state was not in conflict with plurality. In his opinion, freedom was a diversity-generating factor, and the latter preserved the former: "The coexistence of different nations within the same state is at once the proof and the best guarantee of freedom."[45]

Latin American liberalism displayed a different attitude: in the absence of a national diversity that might establish internal competition for the state or any real possibility of creating a separate sovereignty as a real option, and facing socioeconomic and political restrictions on their capitalist project, they were inclined toward an almost fanatical homogenization. The dominant nationality, criollo-mestizo, confronted not other nationalities with the capacity of disputing state control or negotiating their positions but an archipelago of politically disarticulated communities with little national perspective (indigenous ethnic groups).[46] It is in this historical context that, ideologically, national unity and sociocultural plurality become antithetical.

The liberal project of destroying noncapitalist relations was realized slowly and with great difficulty. Success was achieved as the new states developed greater external dependency. Indigenous tribute, for example, was still being used several decades later in some countries and in the extreme case of Bolivia persisted until the early twentieth century.[47] In other countries debt servitude, colonial in origin, not only continued after independence but became very general in the rural world. With regard to the abolition of the inefficient extensive and "amortized" forms of property, failures were more common than achievements, if in fact ending them was the liberals' real goal. Often, the liberal movement (e.g., in Mexico) fervently defended the interests of the large landholders; their leaders showed a "proprietary mentality" stemming from the fact that they themselves owned large landholdings or aspired to do so.[48] Even though the liberal measures (particularly the Ley Lerdo of 1856 and others after that) stripped many communities of their land, the outcome was not the creation of a society of smallholders. In fact, large landholdings reemerged strengthened, eating up even the corporations' non-"deamortized" plots, and rural land was again concentrated in the hands of new large landholders.[49]

Indigenous ethnic communities were affected and often deeply disrupted or destroyed by the liberal measures, but they showed a greater capacity for resistance than had been expected, favored by the very contradictions of the homogenizing project. Many communities survived the division and privatization of their lands and the homogenizing programs socially, politically, and linguistically. However, no group went through the historical phases unchanged, since ethnicity is not immutable. The ethnic groups that survived this commotion were modified, and new identities were created. Ethnic heterogeneity persisted as a national issue.

Uncertainty about "appropriate" integration remains in the Latin American states to this day, especially where states were established across ethnic or sociocultural divisions. Historically, national life is crisscrossed by strong sociopolitical antinomies—conservatism versus liberalism, centralism versus federalism, nationalism versus Hispanic Americanism—but as a consequence of this unresolved heterogeneity there are also sociocultural tensions, expressions of the ethnic-national problem. To the extent to which indigenous peoples emerge in the national arena (in Guatemala, Nicaragua, Ecuador, Mexico, and elsewhere) as social subjects—as a political force potentially capable of undertaking the project of autonomy within the unity of a new democratic nation—the conditions or premises are created for a solution. Such autonomy must be the result not of a concession but of a conquest by the indigenous ethnic subject (necessarily articulated with other popular subjects). The various indigenisms of Latin America have made every effort to prevent any such conquest.

NOTES

1. Cf. Federico Chabod, *La idea de nación*, Mexico City, Fondo de Cultura Económica, 1987.

2. Indeed, according to their particular contexts and experiences, Latin American ethnic groups call themselves "peoples," "nationalities," or even "nations." These designations, part of the traditions and political strategies of the groups concerned, are perfectly legitimate and have no reason to coincide with analytical concepts, but they must not be confused with them.

3. Leonard Tivey, "Introducción," in L. Tivey (ed.), *El Estado nación*, Barcelona, Ediciones Península, 1987, p. 9.

4. Cornelia Navari, "Los orígenes del Estado nación," in Tivey, *El Estado nación*, 32.

5. Ibid., p. 52.

6. There is an abundant literature on Gamio's activities both as an intellectual and as a public official. See the synopsis of Ángeles González Gamio, "Manuel Gamio," in *Instituto Nacional Indigenista: 40 años*, Mexico City, Instituto Nacional Indigenista, 1988, pp.

442–458, and Eduardo Matos Moctezuma, *Manuel Gamio: La arqueología mexicana*, Mexico City, Universidad Nacional Autónoma de México, 1983.

7. See Héctor Díaz Polanco, "Lo nacional y lo étnico en México: El misterio de los proyectos," *Cuadernos Políticos*, no. 52, December-October 1987, pp. 33–34.

8. See Manuel Gamio, *Forjando patria*, 2nd edition, Mexico City, Editorial Porrúa, 1960, p. 93; and M. Gamio, *Antología*, ed. Juan Comas, Mexico City, Universidad Nacional Autónoma de México, 1975, p. 35.

9. The same concern with "diversity" and a similar impatience to "achieve the necessary homogeneity" for Mexico "to establish the solid foundations of a nationality" are found in the works of Gonzalo Aguirre Beltrán, an anthropologist who dominated the indigenist scene for decades. See Gonzalo Aguirre Beltrán, *Formas de gobierno indígena*, Mexico City, Fondo de Cultura Económica, 1991, pp. 15ff.

10. Andrés de Blas Guerrero, *Nacionalismo e ideologías políticas contemporáneas*, Madrid, Espasa-Calpe, 1984, p. 34.

11. For a definition of "nationality," see Héctor Díaz Polanco, *La cuestión étnico-nacional*, 2nd edition, Mexico City, Fontamara, 1988.

12. For a critical synthesis of Marx's interpretations of the Latin American process, particularly his judgments on Bolívar, and explanations thereof, see José Aricó, "Marx y América Latina," *Nueva Sociedad*, no. 66, May-June 1983, and his book by the same title, 2nd edition, Mexico City, Alianza Editorial Mexicana, 1982.

13. As Manuel Moreno Fraginals has observed, in the non-Hispanic Caribbean "we have a historical development that differs entirely from European history in a key sense: the social structure of the Caribbean did not emerge spontaneously. No: This Caribbean society constitutes the first case in the world, on a large scale, of implanted societies created by modern entrepreneurial activity. For almost two centuries, 80 percent or more of the population has been subordinated to the original entrepreneurial ends, which shape the demographic characteristics of the society." Manuel Moreno Fraginals, "Entrevista," *Cuadernos de Nuestra América*, 3, no. 6, July-December 1986, p. 295.

14. See Alain Yacou, "La esclavitud en las Antillas francesas y españolas en vísperas de la Revolución francesa: Estudio comparativo," in *La América española en la época de las luces*, Madrid, Ediciones de Cultura Hispánica, 1988, pp. 327ff.

15. Edelberto Torres Rivas, "La nación: Problemas teóricos e históricos," in E. Torres Rivas and Julio César Pinto, *Problemas en la formación del Estado nacional en Centroamérica*, San José, Instituto Centroamericano de Administaración Pública, 1983, p. 164. Another intellectual, Marcos Kaplan (*Formación del Estado nacional en América Latina*, Buenos Aires, Amorrortu Editores, 1976, p. 121), points to "a great regional diversity regarding the origins, relative importance of the causes, rhythm, characteristics, and results of the emancipating process."

16. See Eduardo Arcila Farías, *Reformas económicas del siglo XVIII en Nueva España, 1. Ideas económicas, comercio y régimen de comercio libre*, SEPSetentas 117, 1974, pp. 124–125.

17. "Just as England passed on to North America its liberal and enlightened traditions, Spain imposed on Middle and Central America its despotism and backwardness. Every communication between its American possessions and Europe went through Spain; education, when there was any, lay in the hands of the clergy; modern science and its points of view, let alone autonomous government institutions, remained unknown." Hans Kohn, *Historia del nacionalismo*, Mexico City, Fondo de Cultura Económica, 1949, p. 407.

18. Silvio Zavala, *Estudios acerca de la historia del trabajo en México*, (ed.) Elías Trabulse, Mexico City, El Colegio de México, 1988.

19. "The development of a Hispanic American sector of planters and *hacendados* in the process of becoming bourgeois, not linked to estates inherited by primogeniture and more dependent on market production, together with a dynamic group of nonmonopolist criollo merchants and an incipient petite bourgeoisie—artisans, intellectuals, and others—introduced a protocapitalist component into the class conflicts of the final colonial stage. Hence the increase in the number of petitions for greater commercial liberalization so as to have access to the overseas market beyond the realm of Spanish and Portuguese intermediaries. Prosperity for the majority of these groups depended on increasing their links with the international economy." Sergio Guerra Vilaboy, "Los movimientos populares y la problemática de la revolución burguesa en América Latina," *Instituto de Investigaciones Históricas Antropológicas y Arqueológicas Estudios,* 3, no. 2/88, November 1988, p. 6.

20. Cf. Gonzalo Aguirre Beltrán *Obra polémica*, Mexico City, Secretaría de Educación Pública/Instituto Nacional de Antropología e Historia, 1976, p. 226: "In truth, the cultures we call indigenous are configurations of ideas and sets of behavior peculiar to the colonial social formations, because that is where they come from." This view of ethnic groups as a colonial "residue" is shared by much of Latin American leftist thought.

21. The most comprehensive formulation of the concept of "internal colonialism" is found in Pablo González Casanova, *Sociología de la explotación*, 11th edition, Mexico City, Siglo XXI, 1987, pp. 223–250.

22. For a while the leaders commonly showed vacillation or confusion with regard to the goal of building their own national states, as is evident in the adherence to the "legitimate" monarch Fernando VII, successor of the monarch deposed by Napoleon.

23. With regard to the composition and orientation of the insurgent movement, the insurrection led by Miguel Hidalgo and continued by José María Morelos in Mexico is the exception that proves the rule.

24. Kohn, *Historia del nacionalismo*, pp. 380–381.

25. Joseph Pérez, "Tradición e innovación en la América del siglo XVIII," in *La América española en la época de las luces*, Madrid, Ediciones de Cultura Hispánica, 1988, pp. 267–279.

26. Gerhard Masur, *Simón Bolívar*, Caracas, Ediciones de la Presidencia de la República, Academia Nacional de la Historia, 1987, pt 1. Besides its critical rigor, this biography has the rare virtue of amenity. See also J. L. Salcedo-Bastardo, *Bolívar: Un continente y un destino*, Caracas, Ediciones de la Biblioteca, Universidad Central de Venezuela, 1982, and Augusto Mijares, *El libertador*, Caracas, Ediciones de la Presidencia de la República, Academia Nacional de la Historia, 1987.

27. Ricaurte Soler, *Idea y cuestión nacional latinoamericanas: De la independencia a la emergencia del imperialismo*, Mexico City, Siglo XXI, 1980, p. 73.

28. Ibid.

29. "In a great many cases the state comes to be the creator of the nation not only in the European context but also in the case of first America (both in the U.S.A. and in Iberian America) and later of Asia and Africa." Blas Guerrero, *Nacionalismo e ideologías*, p. 28.

30. Juan Beneyto, *Las autonomías: El poder regional en España*, Madrid, Siglo XXI de España Editores, 1980, pp. 4–5.

31. "Institutions capable of maintaining autonomy are a reality in Overseas Aragon, while in Overseas Castile they do not appear even exceptionally. One is reminded of the example of the parliaments, so powerful in Italy and unknown and rejected in the Indies." Ibid., p. 216.

32. Claudio Véliz, *La tradición centralista de América Latina*, Barcelona, Editorial Ariel, 1984, pp. 18 and 27.

33. In support of the need to adopt this approach, it has been argued that "during the stage of the emancipation wars this was the alternative better suited to the structuring of emerging nationalities. It was, in effect, a situation in which the conciliation of internal social contradictions had to give way to the main objective of building the state free from the colonial yoke." Soler, *Idea y cuestión nacional* p. 147.

34. Ibid., pp. 148–149.

35. David Brading, *Los orígenes del nacionalismo mexicano*, Mexico City, Editorial Era, 1988.

36. These criollos' heroes describe, in their chronicles, how they "won" the American territory. Bernal Díaz del Castillo, Cortés's companion in many incursions subduing Mesoamerican peoples, describes in his famous chronicle "the heroic feats and deeds we undertook when we gained the New Spain." *Historia verdadera de la conquista de la Nueva España*, 8th edition, Madrid, Espasa-Calpe, 1989, p. 25.

37. See, for example, the analysis of criollo patriotism done by Severo Martínez Peláez in the context of the kingdom of Guatemala, on the basis of the work of the chronicler Francisco Antonio de Fuentes y Guzmán: "to enhance the conquest's merits was a way to strengthen the rights and claims to commendation of the descendants of the *conquistadores*." Severo Martínez Peláez, *La patria del criollo: Ensayo de interpretación de la realidad colonial guatemalteca*, 5th edition, San José, Editorial Universitaria Centroamericana, 1979, pp. 53–54.

38. For example, in Mexico Francisco Javier Clavijero expressed an identification with the pre-Hispanic past in his work (1780) and, at the same time mentioned "the lack of understanding among the Indians of his day. He took over the role of their protector and, as such, expropriated their history for his own patriotic ends. His work foreshadowed the insurgent attempt at denying the immediate past by vehemently reclaiming an idealized indigenous antiquity." Brading, *Los orígenes del nacionalismo mexicano*, p. 40. See Francisco Javier Clavijero, *Historia antigua de México*, 8th edition, Mexico City, Editorial Porrúa, 1987.

39. Jacques Lafaye, *Quetzalcóatl y Guadalupe: La formación de la conciencia nacional en México*, Mexico City, Fondo de Cultura Económica, 1985, pp. 280–281.

40. Brading, *Los orígenes del nacionalismo mexicano*, p. 52.

41. Ibid., p. 71; also, Lafaye, *Quetzalcóatl y Guadeloupe*, p. 283.

42. As Tulio Halperin Donghi indicates, "Rather than any tutelary intention of the new authorities (who, on the contrary, in the majority of cases were, in principle, hostile to communal organization) it was the situation that defended archaic rural organization: the weakening of the upper urban sectors and the lack, in new nations with large indigenous populations, of the expansion of internal consumption and, above all, of agricultural exports that would make the Indian lands immediately coveted explain why these lands remained in the hands of rural communities that were atrociously poor, incapable of defending themselves against expropriation, and often lacking recorded ownership of their land."

Tulio Halperin Donghi, *Historia contemporánea de América Latina*, Madrid, Alianza Editorial, 1972, pp. 139–140.

43. Donald J. Fraser, "La política de desamortización en las comunidades indígenas, 1856–1872," in Various authors, *Los pueblos indios y las comunidades*, Mexico City, El Colegio de México, 1991, pp. 229–231.

44. Halperin Donghi, *Historia contemporánea*, p. 211.

45. Quoted by Blas Guerrero, *Nacionalismo e ideologías*, p. 50.

46. Díaz Polanco, *La cuestión étnico-nacional*, pp. 102ff.

47. Soler, *Idea e cuestión nacional*, pp. 125 and 145.

48. T. G. Powell, *El liberalismo y el campesinado en el centro de México (1850–1876)*, Mexico City, SEPSetentas 122, 1974, pp. 69–70.

49. On the deamortization of church property, see Jan Bazant, *Los bienes de la iglesia en México (1856–1875): Aspectos económicos y sociales de la revolución liberal*, Mexico City, El Colegio de México, 1971, and Robert J. Knowlton, *Los bienes del clero y la Reforma mexicana, 1856–1910*, Mexico City, Fondo de Cultura Económica, 1985. For regional studies on the Mexican reform, see Charles R. Berry, *La reforma en Oaxaca: Una microhistoria de la revolución liberal, 1856–1876*, Mexico City, Ediciones Era, 1989; R. J. Knowlton, "La individualización de la propiedad corporativa civil en el siglo 19: Notas sobre Jalisco," in Various authors, *Los pueblos indios y las comunidades*; Héctor Díaz Polanco and Laurent Guye Montandon, *Agricultura y sociedad en el Bajío (siglo 19)*, Mexico City, Juan Pablos Editor, 1984, chap 2.

CHAPTER TWO

■

Colonial Policy and Slavery

The various indigenist policies that have operated throughout history are the reflection and, in many ways, the cause of the Latin American nation-states' unresolved heterogeneity. "Indigenism" as a common usage can be distinguished from "indigenism" as a theoretical concept. In its common usage indigenism includes attitudes, expressions, or practices vaguely associated with appreciating or even defending the Indian. In this sense, "indigenist" can be used to describe the fervor and frenetic activity of Friar Bartolomé de las Casas during the sixteenth century and of the people who defend Indians' human rights today, or the contemporary musicians, writers, or painters who are interested in the life or culture of indigenous groups. As a theoretical concept, in contrast, indigenism is a *sociological category* that refers to the relationship among sociocultural groups in given economic, social, and political contexts. In this sense it implies subordination and conflict. The presence of dominated (Indians) and dominators (non-Indians) within the framework of a state makes it possible for the latter to use the instruments and institutions of power to impose their will on the former. Such indigenism is often simultaneously an ideology, a more or less formalized anthropological topic, and a practice that tends to serve as state policy.

In reality, especially when state policy is paternalistic, indigenisms in the two meanings just explained tend to mix; that is, indigenism as state ideology and practice seeks to convey the positive connotations and the idealism of indigenism in its common usage. But since the former is, in fact, antithetical to the latter, it is useful to distinguish between them.

Therefore, the indigenism we are concerned with here involves policies that have been thought out and designed by non-Indians to be applied to others. It does not assume any consideration of the points of view and interests of those others. Rather, it assumes a more or less blatant denial that these others have anything to say about their own affairs and destiny. The various indigenisms of this kind are at once alien (with regard to ethnic groups) and extremely homogenizing. And when exclusionary sociocultural patterns become the platform of a

23

given national organization, indigenism becomes a strategic vehicle for antide-
mocratic and conservative projects.[1]

Past indigenisms have often systematically and even deliberately precluded any
kind of autonomy for distinctive sociocultural groups. Indigenism employed as
state policy may go as far as genocide, ethnocide, ethnophagy, or a combination of
these, or it may modify ethnic diversity and even make it more complex, but it
never resolves the tensions and conflicts of diversity. In any event, the solution to
the ethnic problem lies not in identifying "good" as opposed to "negative" indigenism but in escaping *the very logic of any indigenism*. Indigenism is not the solution to the ethnic-national question; it is part of the problem.

As we have seen, the colonial regime was in general an immense cauldron in
which new mixtures formed from preexisting sociocultural ingredients as a consequence of a painful brewing. But the result was not an undifferentiated or homogeneous society. Later, during the nineteenth century and the first decades of
the twentieth, policies deliberately sought the homogenization of society in the
criollo-mestizo sociocultural mold. These policies did not meet their goal of extermination but did provoke transformations in the ethnic composition of the society. In the twentieth century, the question of persistent ethnic diversity remained a policy "problem" whose resolution lay in the hands of modern
"integrationist" indigenists.

Three phases of indigenism can be distinguished:[2] (1) the indigenism of the
first three centuries of the colonial regime, (2) the postindependence indigenism
of the nineteenth and early twentieth centuries that liberals conceived and effected, and (3) the indigenism of modern Latin American states, developed particularly since the mid–twentieth century.[3]

Some researchers have identified the policy applied during the colonial phase[4]
with the "segregationist"—better described as corporatist—modality that was
characteristic of nearly all of the Spanish dominions in America during the second
half of the sixteenth century. Corporatist measures were designed to differentiate
(though not properly to separate structurally) native groups from the rest of the
population in the economic, sociocultural, and political spheres. During the sixteenth century the Spanish crown concentrated the scattered native populations in
their original areas of settlement or, more frequently, in new places (called Indian
towns). Religious and civil authorities often selected these sites with a view to facil-
itating direct control (ideological, political, economic, social, administrative) over
the settlements. Structurally, this divided colonial society into two systems that,
nevertheless, were kept closely articulated. The resulting "republic of the Indians
and republic of the Spanish"[5] gave rise to a model of socioeconomic and ethnic
barriers later called "castes."

INDIAN SLAVERY

Colonial policy toward ethnic groups did not simply take the form of segregationism or corporatism, although this modality dominated the more advanced

phase of the regime. The enslavement of natives was widespread during the early colonial era. Indeed, it is sometimes forgotten that trafficking in slaves began not in the Old World-New World direction but in the opposite one. A few years after the Europeans arrived, the first contingent of Indian slaves, captured at Hispaniola, was sent to Spain.[6] In addition, Indians were used as slave labor on their own land after the invasion. Thus, it was the Indians and not the Africans who where the first to suffer the yoke of slavery in America. Later, as the native population quickly perished under the harshness of this exploitative regime and as a consequence of the illnesses brought by the Europeans, black slaves imported on a large scale began to supply labor for the heavy tasks of production in the new possessions.[7] Before that, however, the Spanish sought to provide labor for the islands by exploiting Indian slaves brought from other parts of America (natives of the so-called useless islands and the mainland coasts).

Because the islands of the Antilles, particularly La Española or Hispaniola,[8] were the initial site of the conquest and colonization of the Americas,[9] the indigenous peoples there were the first victims of slavery. Only four years after the "discovery," in 1496, a third of the indigenous population of Hispaniola had already perished.[10] Less than two decades later, in 1510, when the Spanish monarch was considering the introduction of Indian slaves into Castile, "the extraordinary decline of the Indians in Hispaniola forced the king to change his mind."[11] The rapid extermination of the island's indigenous peoples was merely a prelude to the regional demographic disaster that was to come: The autochthonous population of the other islands was also decimated in a short period. Already by this stage, slave labor was essential to the exploitation of the gold deposits or placers discovered in several parts of the new lands.

During the first third of the sixteenth century, Indian slavery had been broadly extended throughout subjugated America. Indians were enslaved in their own homelands and exploited in the process of Spanish production. Spanish troops in sailing vessels would capture the aboriginal people of the mainland and transport them to the Antilles, especially Hispaniola and Cuba. Because of transport conditions, ill-treatment, inadequate food, and so on, many prisoners died during these journeys. Some sources report that hundreds of corpses were thrown into the sea.

THE *REQUERIMIENTO* AND THE "JUST WAR" AGAINST THE INDIANS

Indian slavery required some justification that, at least according to the interpretations of those days, could resolve the conflict between the autochthonous population's captivity and the dominant culture's ethical precepts, particularly those of Catholicism. To construct such rationalizations and to define an adequate *modus operandi* compatible with Christian principles (all ironies apart), the most outstanding theologians, canonists, and legal experts were consulted. The so-called doctrine of the just war emerged from the thinking of these intellectuals.[12]

In essence, this doctrine declared that it was legitimate to capture and enslave Indians who forcefully "resisted" the conquerors and refused to accept the Catholic faith. According to the accepted precepts of "natural law," members of the human species were considered free, but in time of war, "the peoples' natural law" accepted captivity because it was more humane than killing defeated enemies. Thus, the general principle of human freedom was made compatible with the exception accorded cases of "just war."[13]

What was necessary, therefore, was to be sure that warfare was "just," giving the natives the opportunity to remain peacefully under Spanish rule. With this objective, at the beginning of the sixteenth century a renowned Castilian jurist, Doctor Juan López de Palacios Rubios, adviser to the king, Ferdinand the Catholic, wrote what Saco describes as "one of the most unusual and extraordinary documents ever produced by history. Before the Castilians took possession of the lands and the Indians, they were to read the document, the *Requerimiento,* written in the Castilian language which, if the Indians could ever understand in words, through interpreters, they would never be able to comprehend,"[14] since the document addressed questions completely foreign to the Indians worldviews and sociocultural systems.

The document "explained" that God created heaven and earth and made Saint Peter, the first pope, the lord of all humans, that Saint Peter had jurisdiction over all the world's people, that a successor of his had given the islands and mainland of the Atlantic Ocean to the king and queen of Spain, and that, therefore, all the inhabitants of those territories should submit to those monarchs and accept the Catholic faith without resistance. Leaving no options and permitting no discussion of any of its premises, this unusual text ended with the following threat:

> If you would not be willing, and if with malice you would be slow to submit, I certify that with God's help we shall powerfully assail you and make war against you from every side and in every way, and we shall subject you to the yoke and obedience of the Church and Their Highnesses, and we shall take your persons and those of your women and children and enslave you and sell you and dispose of you at Their Highnesses' command, and take your goods and inflict upon you all the injury and hardship we can as vassals who neither obey nor want to receive their lord and resist and contradict him; and we declare that you shall be accountable for the death and injuries that ensue and that Their Highnesses, ourselves, or these knights who come with us shall not be culpable.[15]

One can easily understand that this *Requerimiento* served as a simple pretext for the Spanish army to take many Indians as slaves, arguing they had been captured under conditions of "just war" and for "just reasons." This is, without any doubt, one of best illustrations of the hypocritical use of religion to justify vile deeds.[16] Several centuries distant from us, this rambling may seem an exercise in black comedy, but it was quite seriously used to support horrendous excesses. There are many accounts of instances in which indigenous people, who could not comprehend the exact contents of the document, did not have to show that they would not comply with it or even display any sort of hostility toward the recently arrived foreigners for violence to fall upon them. Peaceful aboriginal groups who accepted the foreigners and who wanted to please them were assaulted, captured on the pretext of having "resisted," and, finally, enslaved.

Often the military did not even concern themselves with communicating the message (if such an address could be called a message, since, as Las Casas said, to the Indians it would have been the same if "it had been Latin or jabbering"). The Spanish read the document at a great distance from Indian villages and even in the loneliness of the fields, where they had no visible interlocutor. Afterwards, the army moved on to capture the malicious "rebels."[17]

The *bachiller* Anciso, sent to Cenú territory by Pedrarias de Ávila, describes the reaction to the *Requerimiento* of two caciques:

> They answered that in that which I said, that there was not but one God and that he governed heaven and earth, and that he was the Lord of everything, that it seemed all right to them and that that was the way it should be, but that in what I said about the pope being the lord of the universe, in God's place, and that he had given that land to the king of Castile, they said that the pope must have been drunk when he did that, since he was giving away what was not his, and that the king, who asked for and took things at will, must be a lunatic, because he was asking for what belonged to others. . . and they said that they were lords of their lands and there was no need for another lord. I asked again for their submission; if not granted, I said, I would make war against them. . . . we took their lands by force; . . . and later I captured another of their caciques in a different place and found him to be a man of truth who kept his word and who found wrong what was wrong and right what was right; and there, almost all wars are made in this way.

Las Casas, who transcribed this passage, thought that it also demonstrated how unjust warfare was initiated, but he considered what Anciso claimed to be the response of the Indian chiefs pure "fable," since they could not have comprehended the concepts of the *Requerimiento* and there was mutual ignorance of each other's language.[18] If so, the reported responses of the caciques are even more interesting, since they may be the expression of the doubts that plagued the conquerors about the legitimacy and rationality of their arguments and activities.

There were, of course, other "legitimate" means of enslaving Indians. Especially in New Spain (where, in contrast to Peru, capture played a large role), another cause for slavery was *rescate*—the "rescuing" of indigenous people who had been slaves under the pre-Hispanic system and in turn had become slaves under Spanish rule. The caciques and *principales* (indigenous authorities) also gave the Spanish indigenous people as slaves as part of their tribute payments.[19]

The Spanish conquerors argued that it was legal to enslave at least some Indians because in pre-Hispanic societies (particularly the highly developed groups of Mesoamerica) the institution of slavery already existed. However, there is reason to believe that in this case, as in others regarding contact between two cultures, there was misinterpretation, whether with malice or not, of an institution that did not precisely match its European counterpart.

Indeed, what the Spanish called "slavery" among the Indians was not slavery in the sense in which the relationship was understood in Europe. The Spanish chroniclers noted the substantial differences between the two institutions. It was mentioned, for example, that neither the existence of so-called pre-Hispanic slavery nor its causes could be compared with their European counterparts. In the indigenous societies the causes for slavery could be extremely trivial, and the condition of indigenous "slaves" in their own society was nearly identical to that of "free men" in the European system. Indigenous slaves could have possessions and even slaves of their own; service to the master was occasional and not fundamentally oriented toward production; "it often happened that male slaves married their women masters and female slaves their male masters," reported López de Gómara. Whereas in Europe the children of slaves were born into slavery, in the pre-Hispanic system they were born free.[20] Motolinía, who observed the Spanish practice of enslaving Indians who had been "slaves" under the autochthonous regime in exchange for tribute, considered that "according to [indigenous] law and truth, almost no one is a slave." And in relation to their condition in the communities, he clarified that

> these Indians do not use the services of their slaves with the servitude and labor that the Spanish do, because they have them as almost free, in their ranches and estates, where they farm a certain part for their masters and another portion for themselves, and they have their homes, wives, and children, in such a way that they do not have so much obligation that they would run away from their condition or from their masters.[21]

THE ABOLITION OF INDIAN SLAVERY

Beginning in the 1530s, measures were adopted to abolish the slavery of the American Indian population. This process was influenced in particular by the denunciations of slavery by the friars. The Spanish crown's attitude oscillated because of the contradictory considerations involved: It received income on the basis of slavery, but, from another perspective, slaves did not pay tribute to the monarch, and at the same time slavery reduced the Indian population. In time the arguments in opposition to Indian slavery became overwhelming. A document issued on August 2, 1530, prohibited the enslavement of Indians even if they were captured in the course of a "just war." The *rescate* was also abolished.

The colonizers opposed these measures, arguing that the military actions taken in America were a *private* matter paid for by captains and soldiers rather than by the state and the main benefit these men had from their incursions was the appropriation as slaves of the prisoners. Besides, it was said, it was no help to the natives themselves to forbid slavery, because more indigenous people would be killed in battle if the soldiers had no incentive to take men as prisoners. Slavery via *rescate* was justified, according to the colonizers, because in becoming slaves of the Spanish instead of the caciques the enslaved Indians would "benefit" by learning Christian doctrine and, eventually, avoiding being sacrificed in pagan religious rites. Partly because of these arguments but, more important, because of the effective pressure of the colonizers and the royal interests themselves, on February 20, 1534, Charles V abrogated the prohibition on enslaving Indians and allowed the resumption of enslavement by war and by *rescate*.

Nevertheless, protests against slavery continued to be raised. Now better situated to impose its will, the crown issued New Laws in 1542 of which chapter 21 prohibited Indian slavery in any form. The *Recopilación de Leyes de los Reinos de las Indias* (1681) incorporated this prohibition.[22]

In spite of these resolutions, certain forms of enslavement of natives persisted for a long time in several areas of the New World. One of these forms was a court sentence to forced labor. It was not uncommon for Spanish magistrates to condemn Indians to work in a mine or a mill for life. After the Indian rebellion in the province of Tehuantepec in 1660,[23] which expanded into other provinces and districts of the bishopric of Oaxaca (Villa Alta, Nexapa, and Ixtepeji), the punitive judge sent by the viceroy (the Count of Baños) sentenced the indigenous leaders to serve "all their lives in a mill whose service is sold" in favor of "His Majesty's court."[24] In fact, the Indians being sentenced were practically sold to Spanish entrepreneurs who kept them locked up under severe conditions that included excessive labor and little food.

Slavery also resulted from the constant warfare waged by the criollos against Indian villages that resisted colonial expansion, for example, the peoples generically called Chichimecas in the northern part of Mexico. The great Chichimec War took place from 1550 to 1600. The Chichimecs were nomadic groups of northern New Spain. Whereas the sedentary indigenous ethnic groups of the central New Spain were easy prey for the Europeans, the northern groups for decades resisted repeated attempts at conquest (or "pacification," as the crown preferred to call it). As in the central territories (where the Tlaxcaltec were used in the subjugation of Moctezuma's empire), in the north the Spanish astutely used the military strength of some indigenous groups to subdue others. In this case it was the Mexicas, Tarascos, and Otomís who spearheaded the annihilation of Chichimec resistance.[25]

The Caribs of the Antilles, the Araucanians (Mapuches) of the southern part of the continent, and the Mindanao in the Philippines also suffered warfare and slavery. Indian slavery gradually ceased to be a central method of domination of the autochthonous population as other mechanisms and institutions whose objective was to secure a stable labor force gained strength.

THE MISERY OF THE INDIGENOUS PEOPLES

Discussion of the effects of slavery, the brutality of the *encomienda* (legalized in Hispaniola in 1503), and the cruelty of the conquistadores on the aboriginal population of the islands of the so-called West Indies continues to this day. In these passionate debates it has routinely been asserted that the true "executioners of the conquest were not the conquistadores" but the pathogenic microbes brought from Europe, which caused enormous mortality among the indigenous population. To deny the effect of the great epidemics would be absurd, but it cannot be overlooked that the microbes operated within the social framework created by colonization and that many other factors brought about by colonial relations were the direct and fundamental cause of the destruction of the autochthonous Caribbean population. These same conditions later put the survival of the mainland's native societies at risk.

During the initial phase of colonization in Hispaniola, as Frank Moya Pons stresses, natives "were put to work in the mines, and in Columbus's time they were treated as an inexhaustible natural resource that one need not feed or look after because there were always villages waiting to be conquered." After Columbus was dismissed, the Indians had it no better under Francisco Bobadilla and Nicolás de Ovando. The consumption of Indians that these governors allowed and even encouraged at the beginning of the sixteenth century "finally destroyed the island's aboriginal ecological balance." The shattering of their social system and subsistence as well as the harshness of the work imposed upon them made the desperate Indians commit mass suicide (eating the poison of the bitter cassava, killing their children, and provoking self-induced abortions).[26]

Silvio Zavala and José Miranda note the diverse and complex causes (among them, of course, epidemics) of the drastic decline of the Indian population of the Antilles.[27] The account of Friar Toribio Motolinía, a member of the Franciscan mission of "the twelve" that arrived in Mexico in 1524, of what he called the "ten work plagues" that fell especially upon the Indians is well known: (1) illnesses, (2) the "conquest of this New Spain;" (3) the famine that followed the capture of Mexico City, (4) the excesses imposed upon the *calpixques* or servants that the conquistadores placed in their *repartimientos* and towns, (5) "the great tributes and services that the Indians rendered," (6) work in the gold mines, because the Spanish treated this metal "like another lamb adored by God," (7) the building of Mexico City, during which "many Indians" perished, (8) slavery, a plague that "is not taken to be the lesser of them," (9) the effects of providing labor for the mines (especially carrying the cargo long distances), and (10) dissent among the Spanish that had as a consequence the execution of many Indian nobles (Cuauhtémoc among them).[28]

According to Sempat Assadourian, the chroniclers of Peru emphasize as causes of the population's collapse "the indigenous mortality produced by the wars of conquest and, among the members of the Spanish army themselves, the periods of hunger resulting from those wars and from the greedy disorder of the Europeans in their struggle to obtain gold and silver. To these we could add death brought about by the war of succession between Huáscar and Atahualpa. A recent analysis of indigenous sources has confirmed these demographic observations."[29]

Regarding the Antilles, several elements, including the aforementioned epidemics, coalesced in what has been called the "Antillean demographic disaster." The aboriginal population in the Antilles was relatively small compared with that in other territories (e.g., the central part of Mesoamerica and the Andean region) and the Caribbean social groups were relatively fragile (hunter-gatherer societies or, at most, egalitarian or cacique-stage tribal systems) and collapsed soon after the early colonial impact.[30] These peoples had not reached the degree of political and productive organization or the sociocultural complexity characteristic of other regions at the moment of the clash with the invaders. Thus, this population was even less well prepared to face the exhausting labor regime, the new productive relations, and the destruction of communal order introduced by the Europeans.

The Antillean region, being the first center of European settlement in the New World and a strategic point from which the conquest radiated toward the mainland during the crucial first phase, bore the heavy burden of contributing the goods and capital necessary to finance much of the rest of the colonizing enterprise. Thus, its indigenous population was literally exploited to the point of exhaustion, especially in mining but also in food production and in the provision of certain services.[31]

Within a few decades the indigenous population of the islands had been practically annihilated. For example, it is estimated that when the Europeans arrived there were about 1 million Indians in Hispaniola,[33] but by 1508 only some 60,000 survived, and this figure had diminished to about 11,000 by 1518. As Carl Sauer points out:

> [Alonso] Zuazo correctly foresaw the end of the aboriginal people by the last years of the century's second decade, a date valid for Jamaica and Puerto Rico, too, and closely approximate for Cuba as well. Occasionally small groups survived in scattered mountain refuges, perhaps to disappear by mixing with future immigrants. In less than twenty years from the founding of La Isabela [the first city, established by Columbus toward the end of 1493], the imminent extinction of the aboriginal people was evident, and within ten more years it had been fully accomplished.[33]

The final result was total extinction: by 1570 only some five hundred indigenous people had survived the devastating impact of the conquest.[34] The extent of the catastrophe cannot be measured by the initial population of natives in the scholars' estimates. There is no difference, in principle, between a process that causes the elimination of hundreds of thousands of human beings and one that causes the extinction of millions. Speaking of the controversies surrounding the original number of Indians in the various American regions, Nocolás Sánchez-Alborñoz asserts that this alters only in relative terms the question of the abrupt decline in the population. Thus, "by 1570 there were several hundred Indians in Hispaniola. What is being discussed, then, is whether they had diminished from an original population of several million or several hundreds of thousands," but whatever their initial number, the result is "equally catastrophic."[35]

During the first half of the sixteenth century, the Spanish colonizers attempted to deal with the increasing scarcity of labor by immigrating themselves and importing indigenous people captured in other areas of America. The first option was a failure, and the second had no future because it soon became clear that the real problem lay in colonial policy with regard to the indigenous labor force, a policy characterized by incredible clumsiness. Given the increasing difficulty in introducing Indian slaves from other parts of the continent and the scarcity of labor in the Antilles, the introduction of black slaves acquired momentum.[36] It began on a small scale at the beginning of the sixteenth century, when Africans were brought in first from the peninsula itself and, later, massively, from the African coast.[37]

The Antillean drama was extraordinarily important for the ensuing stages of colonization in the vast and densely populated territories of the mainland. The holocaust that resulted from the first large-scale colonizing experience in American lands "was so horrifying and unproductive for the Spanish themselves that they tried to create more orderly and judicious systems of exploitation on the mainland."[38] In their own way, they achieved this goal. When it seemed that the Europeans were about to repeat the same disaster in the new colonies (killing the indigenous population on whose tribute and labor they fundamentally depended), the example of the Antillean experience prompted them to mend their ways.

The case of New Spain illustrates the process. Cook and Borah estimate that by 1518 there were in central Mexico alone some 25 million Indians; thirty years later (in 1548) the autochthonous population had diminished to a fourth of that (6.3 million) and two decades later (in 1568) to a tenth of its original size (approximately 2.5 million).[39] The combination of the reckless exploitation of the Indian communities and the frequent epidemics they suffered was decimating the native population much as it had in the Antilles.[40] During the first years of the sixteenth century there continued to be a significant reduction of the native population, which had decreased to less than 1 million by 1620. Cook and Borah conclude that "by 1620–1625, the Indian population of central Mexico, under the effects of the arrival of the Europeans, had diminished to approximately 3 percent of the size it was when the Europeans first landed on the beaches of Veracruz."[41]

The Spanish were heading toward a second total destruction of aboriginal peoples, but this time they had the experience, the conditions, and the time to make the goals of colonization and the survival of sufficient numbers of autochthonous people compatible. As a matter of fact, Borah explains;

> On the mainland, in contrast to what happened in the West Indies, there was time to experiment. In spite of the serious decline suffered by the Indians during the decades following the conquest, considerable nuclei survived in the majority of regions, especially in the highlands. They lasted long enough for the conquerors to realize that these problems existed and, by a process of experimentation and reexamination, try to implement solutions.[42]

Thus, by mid-sixteenth century the collapse had been averted and a certain stability had been achieved; then, by the end of the century, there was a perceptible increase in population that continued throughout the eighteenth century. The moment at which the Indian population of central Mexico reached its nadir is debatable, but regional and local variations were evident and must not be overlooked.[43] Apparently, the inflection point in the demographic curve must be located around 1650.[44]

Demographics influenced the course of the colonial process. The organization and management of Indian communities, together with the gradual consolidation of the European system of domination and exploitation, had perceptible effects on the demographic tendencies that prevailed for more than one and a half centuries.

The various measures adopted by the crown, especially during the second half of the sixteenth century, shaped the colonial regime's indigenist policy. Meticulous legislation, not always rigorously observed, and the creation of a series of economic, administrative, and judicial institutions were enough to allow the colonial government to work with a modicum of effectiveness (which, of course, says nothing about the fairness of the system) in avoiding the destruction of the Indian population.

It is important to clarify that the goal was not to impose any constraint on the exploitation of indigenous people; rather, it was to regulate and rationalize this exploitation in such a way that the wealth created by the native population and their labor could be appropriated in the most orderly way possible by the various sectors involved in colonization. Colonial policy toward Indians, precisely because of the drastic decline in the autochthonous population and the parallel increase of the non-Indian population and its demands for tribute and services, caused a relative increase in the burden on these communities, particularly during the seventeenth century. In other words, disorderly exploitation and senseless destruction was avoided while, at the same time colonial indigenism sought to exact the most out of the surviving Indian population. Exactions did not, however, decline in proportion to the decline in the Indian population.[45] What has been called "the economic benefit policy" meant, in brief, the extraction of the largest possible amount of wealth from the New World.[46]

Since a great variety of sectors were fighting over much diminished booty, it was necessary to refine the methods of political and ideological control. Although sporadic outbursts of indigenous rebellion were not avoided, the Spanish were able to prevent an explosion that would totally undermine the system. Certainly, all the non-Indian social groups (excluding slaves and other workers) and even the indigenous "nobility" that was incorporated into the colonial system of domination, depended on the natives' labor. The *encomenderos*, the settlers, the clergy, the growing bureaucracy, and the Indian caciques and *principales* all participated in an organization that offered each and every one of them the space and opportunity to exploit, to the same degree, the bulk of the indigenous people.[47] The Spanish crown, favored by the arrangement and the system's new cohesiveness, was in charge of regulating its functioning so that the common source of benefits would not be extinguished.

NOTES

1. Elsewhere I have pointed out that "indigenist variants have the common feature of being essentially politically alien conceptions with regard to the ethnic groups themselves. They are aimed at understanding or justifying the policies (the practice) imposed upon 'others' by non-Indians. From the point of view of their goals, these indigenist variants are definitions of what must change so that everything (or, at least, everything important for maintaining the logic of the system) will remain the same." Héctor Díaz Polanco, *Etnia, nación y política*, 2nd edition, Mexico City, Juan Pablos Editor, 1990, p. 28.

2. My intention is to provide a broad survey of the main issues that frame these indigenist policies, and thus forces me to omit many details and peculiarities, doubtless important, that go beyond my purpose.

3. The indigenist anthropologist Gonzalo Aguirre Beltrán has called the policies that correspond to these phases *segregation, incorporation,* and *integration.* Cf. Gonzalo Aguirre Beltrán, "Un postulado de política indigenista," in *Obra polémica*, Mexico City, Secretaría de Educación Pública/ Instituto Nacional de Antropologiá e Historia, 1975, pp. 21–28.

4. I shall continue this analysis in the following chapter and will leave the nineteenth and twentieth centuries for chapter 4.

5. Enrique Semo, *Historia del capitalismo en México*, Mexico City, Era, 1973, pp. 69 ff.

6. On February 24, 1495, Christopher Columbus sent to Seville in four ships 500 Indian slaves that he had captured at Hispaniola. In June 1496 another cargo of 300 Indians left for Spain. Silvio Zavala, "Los trabajadores antillanos en el siglo XVI," *Revista de Historia de América*, no. 2, 1938, p. 32.

7. José Antonio Saco, *Historia de la esclavitud de los indios en el Nuevo Mundo, seguida de la historia de los repartimientos y encomiendas*, Havana, Editora Cultural, 1932, p. 112.

8. Now Santo Domingo Island, shared by the Dominican Republic and Haiti.

9. "During this period [1492–1520], America's economic and political center was at Hispaniola, and Santo Domingo was for many years its capital. The island became a real laboratory for relationships between the Europeans and the American Indians, as well as an experimentation center for the acclimatization of the Europeans and their animals and plants. . . . From 1492 to 1518, the majority of the Spanish emigrants passed through Santo Domingo; very important individuals (Fernández de Enciso, Hojeda, Francisco Pizarro, Diego Velázquez, Vasco Núñez de Balboa, Juan Ponce de León, Hernán Cortés, Pedro de Alvarado) and also people who became not only chiefs or soldiers but writers or critics of the conquest (Las Casas) went there." Francisco de Solano, "El conquistador hispano: Señas de identidad," en Francisco de Solano et al., *Proceso histórico al conquistador*, Madrid, Alianza Editorial, 1988, pp. 21–22. The Spanish learned to name many American things in these islands before going on to the mainland, which explains why some terms of the extinct *Taino* language (of the Arawakan family) spoken by those aboriginal people are among the most abundant in Castilian today.

10. Saco, *Historia de la esclavitud*, p. 113.

11. Ibid. p. 157.

12. Silvio Zavala, *La colonización española en América*, Mexico City, SepSetentas, 1972, chap. 4.

13. Ibid.

14. Saco, *Historia de la esclavitud*, p. 149.

15. Fray Bartolomé de las Casas, *Historia de las Indias*, vol. 3, 2nd edition, Mexico City, Fondo de Cultura Económica,1965, pp. 26–27.

16. Lewis Hanke, "The 'requerimiento' and its interpreters," in *Revista de Historia de América*, no. 2, 1938, pp. 25–34.

17. In chap. 58 of his *Historia* Las Casas refutes each of the arguments included in the document I am discussing, as well as the "great and reprehensible deceit" in it that shows "how unjust, impious, scandalous, irrational, and absurd such *requerimiento* was."

18. Ibid., p. 46.

19. Zavala, *La colonización,* p. 77. More information can be found in the book by the same author, *Los esclavos indios en Nueva España*, 2nd edition, Mexico City, El Colegio Nacional, 1981.

20. Francisco López de Gómara, *Historia general de las Indias*, vol. 2, *Conquista de México*, Barcelona, Ediciones Orbis, 1985, p. 313; Zavala, *La colonización,* pp. 79–80.

21. Fray Toribio Motolinía, *Historia de los indios de la Nueva España*, ed. Edmundo O'-Gorman, 4th edition, Mexico City, Editorial Porrúa, 1984, pp. 17 and 94.

22. See Alberto Sarmiento Donate (ed.), *De las leyes de indias (Antología de la recopilación de 1681)*, Mexico City, Secretaría de Educación Pública, 1988, book 6, title 2, law 1. Cf. Silvio Zavala, "Los trabajadores antillanos en el siglo XVI" *Revista de Historia de América*, no. 2, 1938, pp. 37–39; see also *La colonización,* vi.

23. There is detailed information about this rebellion, credited as being the most important Indian uprising against the government of New Spain during the seventeenth century, in Héctor Díaz Polanco and Carlos Manzo (eds.), *Documentos sobre las rebeliones indias de Tehuantepec y Nexapa (1660–1661)*, Mexico City, Centro de Investigaciones y Estudias Superiores in Antropología Social, 1992.

24. Two chronicles written by Spanish officials (that of Juan de Torres Castillo about the Nexapa, Ixtepeji, and Villa Alta revolts and that of Cristóbal Manso de Contreras about the rebellion in Tehuantepec) may be found in Genaro García, *Documentos inéditos o muy raros para la historia de México*, 3rd edition, Mexico City, Editorial Porrúa, 1982, pp. 273–368.

25. Phillip W. Powell says, "As in almost all phases of the Spanish conquest of Mexico, the Indians were the bulk of the belligerent forces against the Chichimec warriors from north of the viceregal capital. As warriors, interpreters, explorers, and messengers, the pacified aboriginals of New Spain performed important, often indispensable, roles in subduing and civilizing Chichimec country. Sometimes armies made up entirely of other indigenous warriors (particularly Otomís) marauded the war zones to seek out, conquer, and help Christianize the hostile northern nomads. . . . Afterwards, as the penetration of the Great Chichimeca advanced, the recently pacified chichimecs joined the belligerent effort of the white men and were used to conquer other tribes." Philip W. Powell, *La guerra chichimeca (1550–1600)*, Mexico City, Secretaría de Educación Pública, 1984, p. 165; see also *Capitán mestizo: Miguel Caldera y la frontera norteña; La pacificación de los chichimecas (1548–1597)*, Mexico City, Fondo de Cultura Económica, 1980.

26. Frank Moya Pons, *Historia colonial de Santo Domingo*, Santiago, Universidad Católica Madre y Maestra, 1974, pp. 61–62.

27. "Most notable about this course or evolution was the great [population] decline that took place between the time of the conquest and the twilight of the sixteenth century, a decline mainly determined by the following factors: (a) the conquest itself, during which many Indians were sacrificed, and, in addition to warfare, during the exhausting expeditions to faraway lands such as those of Cortés and Nuño de Guzmán, in which Indians had to carry cargo or perform other auxiliary services; (b) slavery, which enormously harmed the Indians, the mining and transportation tasks being terribly harsh and the nourishment given them very deficient; (c) personal service, for the same reasons as slavery; (d) epidemics, above all those of 1545 and 1546, which caused great devastation in al most all the indigenous villages, and (e) famines (whether or not they coincided with epidemics) in years of poor harvest and under the initial economic disorganization. The mortality rate increased considerably among the natives." Silvio Zavala and José Miranda, "Instituciones indígenas en la colonia," in Alfonso Caso et al., *La política indigenista en México: Métodos y resultados,* 3rd edition, Mexico City, *Instituto Nacional Indígenista,* 1981.

28. Motolinía, *Historia de los indios,* pp. 13–18.

29. Carlos Sempat Assadourian, "La despoblación indígena en Perú y Nueva España durante el siglo XVI y la formación de la economía colonial," *Historia Mexicana,* 38, no. 3, January-March 1989, p. 420.

30. For an approach to these social systems, see Luis F. Bate, "El modo de producción cazador recolector o la economía del salvajismo," in *Boletín de Antopología Americana,* no. 13, July 1986; Iraida Vargas, "La formación económica social tribal," in *Boletín de Antopología Americana,* no. 15, July 1987; Mario Sanoja, *Los hombres de la yuca y el maíz,* Caracas, Monte Ávila Editores, 1981, pp. 195ff.

31. Rolando Mellafe, *Breve historia de la esclavitud en América Latina,* Mexico City, SepSetentas, 1974, pp. 21–22.

32. Estimates vary with the author, but the most common version of those days was that Hispaniola had over a million inhabitants." Carl Ortwin Sauer, *Descubrimiento y dominación española del Caribe,* Mexico City, Fondo de Cultura Económica, 1984, p. 106. Cook and Borah's studies consider the island's population to have been much larger. "For Hispaniola island we found that, in 1492, there was a population of approximately eight million people. This huge human reserve was reduced, in ten years, to less than a tenth, and within three decades it was virtually extinct. W. Borah, "La Europa renacentista y la población de América," in Sherburne F. Cook and Woodrow Borah, *El pasado de México: Aspectos sociodemográficos,* Mexico City, Fondo de Cultura Económica, 1989, p. 416.

33. Ibid., p. 307.

34. Mellafe, *Breve hisotría,* p. 22.

35. Nicolás Sánchez-Albornoz, "Las migraciones anteriores al siglo XIX," in Brigitta Leander (ed.), *Europa, Asia y Africa en América Latina y el Caribe: Migraciones "libres" en los siglos XIX y XX y sus efectos culturales,* Mexico City, Siglo XXI/UNESCO, 1989, pp. 63–64.

36. With elegant irony Jorge Luis Borges wrote, "In 1517 Friar Bartolomé de las Casas took pity on the Indians who were languishing in the arduous hells of the Antillean gold mines and proposed to the emperor, Charles V, the importation of black people to languish in the arduous hells of the Antillean gold mines." Jorge Luis Borges, "Historia universal de la infamia," in *Obras completas,* vol. 1, 1923–1972, Buenos Aires, Emecé Editores, 1989, p. 295.

37. On the enslavement of Africans, see José Antonio Saco, *Historia de la esclavitud de la raza africana en el Nuevo Mundo y en especial en los países américo-hispanos*, 2 vols. Havana, Editora Cultural, 1938; Javier Malagón Barceló, *Código negro carolino (1784)*, Santo Domingo, Ediciones de Taller, 1974; Fernando Ortiz, *Los negros esclavos*, Havana, Editorial de Ciencias Sociales, 1988; Hugo Tolentino, *Raza e historia en Santo Domingo: Los orígenes del prejuicio racial en América*, vol. 1, Santo Domingo, Universidad Autonoma de Santo Domingo, 1974; Carlos Esteban Deive, *La esclavitud del negro en Santo Domingo (1492–1844)*, 2 vols., Santo Domingo, Museo del Hombre Dominicano, 1980; José L. Franco, *Historia de la revolución de Haití*, Santo Domingo, Editora Nacional, 1971; Rubén Silié, *Economía, esclavitud y población*, Santo Domingo, Universidad Autónoma de Santo Domingo, 1976; Franklin Franco, *Los negros, los mulatos y la nación dominicana*, Santo Domingo, Editora Nacional, 1969; Jean Price-Mars, *La República de Haití y la República Dominicana*, vol. 1, Puerto Príncipe, 1953; Ricardo Alegría, "Notas sobre la procedencia cultural de los esclavos negros de Puerto Rico durante la segunda mitad del siglo XVI," in *Encuentro*, no. 2, San Juan, Comisión Puertorriqueña para la Celebración del Quinto Centenario del Descubrimiento de América y Puerto Rico, 1990; Miguel Acosta Saignes, *Vida de los esclavos negros en Venezuela*, Caracas, Hespérides, 1967; Luis A. Diez Castillo, *Los cimarrones y la esclavitud en Panamá*, Panama, Editorial Litográfica, 1968.

38. Woodrow Borah, *El juzgado general de indios en la Nueva España*, Mexico City, Fondo de Cultura Económica, 1985, p. 37.

39. Sherburne F. Cook and Woodrow Borah, *Ensayos sobre historia de la población: México y California*, 3, Mexico City, Siglo XXI, 1980, p. 13.

40. A record of the major epidemics suffered by the population of the Valley of Mexico can be found in Charles Gibson, *Los aztecas bajo el dominio español*, Mexico City, Siglo XXI, 1975, pp. 460–463.

41. Cook and Borah, *Ensayos sobre historia de la población* p. 100.

42. Borah, *El juzgado general*, p.37.

43. For example, Miranda asserts that population growth began well before 1650 (between 1620 and 1630) in the bishoprics of México, Michoacán, and Puebla. These estimates are based on the settlement (or liquidation of debts) of the *medio real* that the Indians paid those jurisdictions to build cathedrals during the second half of the seventeenth century. José Miranda, "La población indígena de México en el siglo XVII," in *Historia Mexicana*, 30, no. 4, April–June 1981, pp. 569–570.

44. José Carlos Chiaramonte, "En torno a la recuperación demográfica y la depresión económica novohispana durante el siglo XVII," *Historia Mexicana*, 30, no. 4, April–June 1981, pp. 569–570.

45. W. Borah, *El siglo de la depresión de la Nueva España*, Mexico City, Ediciones Era, 1982, p. 19.

46. Sempat Assadourian, "La despoblación indígena," pp. 425ff.

47. For a description of this situation, particularly during the sixteenth and seventeenth centuries, see Jonathan I. Israel, *Razas, clases sociales y vida política en el México colonial (1610–1670)*, Mexico City, Fondo de Cultura Económica, 1980, introduction and chap. 1.

CHAPTER THREE

———————— ■ ————————

Colonial Indigenism

Despite the consensus on the necessity and legitimacy of subduing the Indians to further the colonial enterprise, a serious difference of opinion emerged about how this should be organized. On the one hand, the conquistadores, their descendants the *encomenderos*, and the first settlers wanted to colonize the American lands as a private enterprise, with the monarchy's blessing but without the intervention of royal power, to perpetuate the enormous privileges and authority they had achieved during the conquest. Opposing them was the faction led by the crown, which included official and religious sectors that defended the Indians and sought to place public interests over the private interests of the conquistadores, and their followers and descendants—that is, to assert the king's power over the colonial process and to increase their share of the American treasure.

OPPOSING INTERESTS

Although the aim of the *encomenderos* and first settlers was expressed in an extreme and destructive exploitation of the native population, the crown's interest coincided with the need for protection of the indigenous people against practices that squandered its major source of wealth. The crown found justification for adopting a series of reforms in the eloquent reports of the friars on the abuses and excesses perpetrated by the Spanish against the Indians. The Dominican order, led by men such as Pedro de Córdova, Antón de Montesinos, and Bartolomé de las Casas, favored reforms to eliminate the most gruesome aspects of colonialism. On Advent Sunday in 1511, on Santo Domingo Island, Friar Montesinos delivered one of the most formidable denunciations of the Spanish colonizers and raised serious doubts about the right of conquest. This noteworthy sermon harshly rebuked the colonizers and royal officials:

> Tell me, what right have you, and on what justice do you rely, to maintain these Indians in such cruel and horrible servitude? What authority has been bestowed upon you to have made such hateful warfare on these peoples, who were in their lands, mild and

peaceful, and an infinity of whom you have extinguished with deaths and unheard-of excesses? How can you keep them so oppressed and exhausted, without feeding them or curing them of the illnesses they get from the immoderate work you give them, that they die? More correctly said, you kill them to obtain and acquire gold each day. . . . Are these not men? Do they not have rational souls? Are you not obliged to love them as you love yourselves? Do you not understand this? Do you not feel this?[1]

These arguments were not the efficient cause of the changes undertaken by the crown, but they provided the ideological and moral support to carry out the adjustments it sought and needed. This does not in the least diminish the merit of the struggle carried on by many friars against the colonizers' excesses, but these praiseworthy efforts were occurring in a sociopolitical context of opposing forces. Behind the agitated theological, legal, and moral disputes of the early sixteenth century, strong contending economic and political interests were in conflict. Within this context, the friars became valuable allies of the crown. Their constant appeals and reports to the court, their chronicles of the terrible crimes perpetrated by the conquistadores,[2] and their theological and moral elaborations were powerful ideological ammunition for the king in reclaiming power that, according to the state, had been unduly appropriated by the pioneers.

CRIOLLO SEDITION

Until the mid-sixteenth century, the Spanish crown had not been in a position to impose its sovereignty over the American territory; the private nature of the colonizing enterprise had not allowed it. Moreover, during this historical phase the conquistadores, and their followers and descendants were granted the concessions and privileges necessary to continue the subjugation of the native population. Once that goal was accomplished, the crown intervened decisively to establish a public order involving a multiplicity of professional bureaucrats, officials, jurists, and clerics. To meet the crown's aims, this army of intellectuals provided efficient discipline, administrative ability, and the authority to achieve consensus.

The statutes of November 1542 known as the New Laws were the first significant changes introduced by the emperor. The *encomenderos* and their followers, seeing their interests threatened, organized protests and mutinies in several provinces. In spite of their resistance—in some cases violent—and the postponement of the measures' full implementation, the crown finally achieved observance of the New Laws. It was eventually able to limit the almost absolute local power of the *encomenderos* and to appropriate a more substantial share of Indian goods and tribute.

The most serious and bloodiest reaction to the new decrees took place in Peru, where, according to Francisco López de Gómara, those affected "howled on reading [the new statutes]." The spokesmen for the groups openly opposed to the sovereign's resolutions publicly questioned their legitimacy:

There were some learned men who asserted that they were not being disloyal nor were they committing a crime by not obeying them . . . ; that they were not laws, and neither were those made by kings compelling when they lacked the common consent of the kingdoms that gave them authority and that neither could the emperor have made those laws without first informing those, who constituted the whole of Peru's kingdoms.[3]

To enforce the new statutes, the emperor sent Blasco Núñez Vela to Peru as viceroy. Núñez Vela was energetic but shortsighted and apparently dim. Very soon the emperor began hearing protests from the settlers: "The conquistadores complained that, having spent their fortunes and spilled their blood in conquering Peru for the emperor, the few vassals that were granted them were now being taken away." The soldiers warned "that they would not go to conquer other territories because the hope of having vassals was being denied them." Royal officials "became very offended when they were deprived of their *repartimientos* when they had not treated the Indians badly," and even clerics complained that "they would not be able to make a living or to serve the church if the peoples were taken away from them." A friar from the order of Our Lady of Mercy wrote that "all those laws smelled more of interest than of sanctity, because they were taking away the slaves they sold without returning the money, and because they took the people for the king, removing them from the monasteries, churches, hospitals, and conquistadores that had earned them."[4]

The viceroy's chain of absurdities and errors of judgment, aggravated by the conflicts he had with members of his own royal tribunal and with the charismatic leader of the *encomenderos*, Gonzalo Pizarro, contributed to a rebellion against royal authority and to his imprisonment and tragic death. Pizarro, considered "the father of his country," became governor of Peru and, encouraged by his followers to name himself king, was able to postpone the crown's reforms. Afterward, in the words of López de Gomara, the emperor "sent a fox because the lion had failed." Pedro Lagasca, an astute man and a discreet and superb organizer, once in Peru, cunningly began to entice Pizarro's followers away from him (thus taking control over Pizarro's vital fleet), gathered support and military forces from other provinces (Nicaragua, New Spain, Santo Domingo, and others), and prepared to face the rebels. Lagasca's political ability was of great advantage to the emperor, whereas Pizarro, in contrast, "was more concerned with making weapons than with making adepts," as the chronicler shrewdly notes. This explains Lagasca's triumph over Pizarro during the crucial confrontation of 1548, in which a large number of men deserted the rebel army in favor of the emperor without real armed conflict. The lion succumbed to the fox, who was able to exploit the regal mentality of the insurrectionists. Pizarro and his captains were imprisoned, accused of treason, and executed.

Thus the most serious defiance of the king's authority, carried out by men who were convinced that they were defending legitimately acquired rights, came to an end. It was the first open and belligerent demonstration of the aspirations to autonomy that would become very strong among the criollos. When Pizarro was taken to Lagasca as a prisoner, Lagasca rebuked him for having rebelled against the emperor, and Pizarro replied: "My Lord, I and my brothers earned this land at our own expense and in wanting to govern it as His Majesty had said I did not think I was mistaken."[5]

ENCOMIENDA, REPARTIMIENTO, AND DEBT SERVITUDE

During the fist half of the sixteenth century, the Spanish were practically free to enslave Indians. However, along with slavery, the *encomienda* had similar practical effects for the indigenous population. Legally, there was a distinction between slavery and *encomienda* (which in theory affected Indians considered to be "free subjects"), but no substantial difference existed between the two.[6]

The *encomienda* was originally a gift from the crown to certain Spanish subjects who had distinguished themselves during the conquest or through other royal services. It consisted of assigning them indigenous caciques and their Indians as laborers and servants. The *encomendero* was in almost exclusive charge of the Christian education of the Indians under his *encomienda*. He could demand tribute and labor from them, but they were not formally considered his property; he had been granted only the use of them. The *encomienda* was inalienable and, in principle, could not be inherited; once vacated, for whatever reason, its Indians paid tribute to the monarch.[7] The *encomenderos*, looking for ways to extend the institution's life, pressed to make it heritable and even proposed its purchase from the king in perpetuity.

The *encomiendas* or *repartimientos* turned into the most obvious expression of the great power of the conquistadores during the first stage of the colonial regime. The military leaders and soldiers of fortune received many Indians through the *encomienda* once the "pacification" of the native peoples was complete. The outstanding example in New Spain is that of Hernán Cortés himself, who obtained a great estate (the Marquesado del Valle) that included several villages and 23,000 indigenous vassals.[8]

Because the *encomienda* had a limited lifespan, it allowed incredible excesses. While it lasted, the *encomendero* tried to obtain as many benefits as possible. In the Antilles, coupled with slavery, it was the cause of the population's devastation. On the mainland, the *encomenderos'* greed and voracity multiplied with the larger population of natives and greater wealth. The degree to which *encomenderos* enriched themselves was limited only by their capacity to exploit, in the least amount of time, their *encomendados*. The level of tribute was established, in principle, by the *encomenderos* themselves, and therefore was raised at their whim. The spiritual responsibilities of teaching Christian doctrine to the Indians became more a justification for the *encomienda* and less a "duty" with any practical effect. This did not stop the *encomenderos* from emphasizing the important "Christianizing" role of the *encomienda* when defending their privileges vis-à-vis the crown.[9]

In the mid-sixteenth century the Peruvian *encomenderos* took a daring step. Knowing that the king faced economic hardship, they offered him 5 million gold ducats in exchange for the concession of *encomiendas,* including civil and criminal jurisdiction, in perpetuity. Had it been accepted, this contract would have dramatically modified the course of events in the New World, creating a group with feudal power. Las Casas and his followers firmly opposed the proposal, while an annoyed Council of the Indies warned that it contradicted the interests of the crown and represented the danger that, with time, the *encomenderos* might renounce the monarch and rise against him. To counteract the *encomenderos'* offer, Las Casas promised a similar amount in the name of the Peruvian Indian nobles for refusing to sell the vassals to the Spanish and keeping all the vacant *encomiendas* perpetually under the crown. Taking advantage of the moment, the Las Casas proposal also included a reduction in the tributes, the restitution of ethnic organizations, and recognition of the authority of the indigenous government (including among other things the prerogatives of those who governed, and consultation with and participation by the people in matters that interested them). The Peruvian royal officials objected to the *encomenderos'* proposal and outlined a program whereby *encomiendas* would be used to increase the crown's power but without instituting a "party of the Indians" that could have led to the strengthening of the ethnic nobles (and the clerics as well). This would in the officials' view, have amounted to sponsorship of "disorder."[10] The *encomenderos'* proposal failed, and instead indigenous councils were created and Spanish bureaucratic agencies were established to control the communities and guarantee an increase in royal revenues.

Gradually, the Spanish government limited the *encomenderos'* vast powers, and in the mid-sixteenth century the *encomienda* underwent a significant transformation. Not only were the Indians of *encomiendas* that became vacant required to pay tribute to the crown, but there was pressure to reduce the number of Indians an *encomendero* could be assigned and limits were placed on the amount of tribute.[11] The number of valid heirs to an *encomienda* was also restricted. The royal decree of February 1549 that reduced the *encomienda* to merely collecting a tribute, suppressed personal service, and ordered that the Indians be paid for their work meant a qualitative change. In some areas, such as Chile, the decree was not obeyed; in others, such as New Spain, there was diligent compliance. The new reality in which the *encomienda*'s beneficiary could not freely and without payment make use of an indigenous labor force not only substantially changed the relationship between *encomenderos* and Indians but "completely altered the indigenous labor panorama."[12]

Control over the labor force passed to the government from that moment on. *Encomenderos* had to request permission from royal officials to use Indian labor on their own *encomiendas*. Those benefiting from the workers' toil had to pay them whether they belonged to their *encomiendas* or not. Officials more actively intervened in the regulation of tributes and working conditions. All of these changes benefited the king, who extended his socioeconomic and political control over the colonial society and increased the number of persons offering him tribute.

In theory, these changes should have created a system in which the Indians paid tribute to the crown because they were vassals but now could freely sell their labor. The extraeconomic coercion of native workers should have disappeared. However, since the vast majority of the Indians had not been totally separated from the system of production in their communities or towns, it was improbable that they would have an interest in entering the labor market. "The aim was free labor, paid for and moderate, but foreseeing that the Indians would not seek it voluntarily, the authorities hastened to order that, through the royal courts, workers were to be given to colonizers who needed them."[13] Thus was born the *repartimiento,* literally the distribution of forced labor, known as *cuatequil* in New Spain and as *mita* in Peru.[14] The "distributing" officials received requests from the *encomenderos,* the colonizers, the clergy, the royal authorities, and even the caciques and *principales* and then recruited Indian workers to be assigned to agriculture, mining, public works, and domestic service. The *repartimiento* operated as a quota system; in Peru it included approximately 15 percent of the adult labor force of the villages for six months out of the year.

In spite of other attempts to free indigenous labor such as hiring indigenous people in the plazas, the colonial regime never managed to avoid coercing the Indians. Even after *repartimientos* for agricultural labor were suspended in New Spain in 1632,[15] farm owners still sent their foremen (*mayordomos*) to the villages to recruit workers against their will. In addition, the public authorities intervened to force the Indians to work on private estates.[16]

The 1549 reforms provoked a fierce struggle for the appropriation of indigenous labor force, by then quite diminished. The *encomenderos,* particularly those who depended exclusively on tribute, were now interested in preserving the people and therefore began to support the demands that the Indians presented to the viceroy.[17] They also routinely came into conflict with the royal officials and other colonizers who used the Indians of their *encomiendas* as workers or took them to their properties as permanent workers. Changing interests defined the guidelines for the *encomenderos'* new alliances.[18] The friars of New Spain also faced turbulent disputes with the colonizers since the latter were attracting more and more indigenous people onto their estates, threatening the existence of the Indian communities. However, it was not unusual that in given situations the friars, tending to their material or political interests, identified with the colonizers against the Indians or, under other circumstances, with royal officials against the colonizers. Hacienda and mill owners in need of labor were not content with the numbers of Indians assigned them and sought to obtain their own workers, incorporating Indians into a permanent labor force. Similarly, the colonizers (including the *encomenderos* as proprietors of haciendas and estates) fought among themselves for workers.

The indigenous authorities looked for support to missionaries and royal officials when the colonizers threatened their communities and their interests, but around 1560 the alliance that had been established between the native nobles and the Spanish state began to break down both in Peru and in New Spain.[19] This was often expressed as hostility toward the preeminence of the native nobles but also took the form of withholding some of the prerogatives of communities and ordinary Indians. The gradual expansion of the state's power weakened not only the *encomenderos'* position but also that of the villages. Facing this plethora of hostile agents, it is not surprising that indigenous people generally saw non-Indians as a source of danger, often referring to them as *coyotes* and other such names.[20]

In New Spain the most serious threat to indigenous people came from *hacendados*. To acquire a labor force without depending exclusively on the *repartimiento*, they fostered the settlement of indigenous people on their lands and then used indebtedness to create a new kind of servitude. The spread of this phenomenon throughout New Spain explains why the elimination of the *repartimiento* did not present great difficulties for landowners, who depended on labor linked to their estates. However, the Indians who escaped the community's control made first the *repartimiento* and later the payment of tribute to the crown or to the *encomendero* a heavier burden on the community. The indigenous authorities were in charge of its levying. Often, members of the Indian government, supported by the friars, would go to the estates to collect the dues and/or to return the workers to the villages, provoking conflict with the owners of the estates, who claimed that the Indians could not leave until they had paid their debts. In time, employers began paying the tribute owed by the Indians in their service, adding that amount to the total of the workers' debt. This practice solidified a servitude based on debt, and the attachment of workers to the haciendas was practically institutionalized.

The authorities introduced measures to lessen the oppressive effect of debt, limiting the amount to the equivalent of a specific number of months' salary. However, debt servitude was retained as a common coercive mechanism to bind indigenous workers to haciendas throughout the colony and, in some countries, throughout the nineteenth century and into the twentieth.

Oppressive and coercive uses of the indigenous population, however softened on occasion, never disappeared during the colonial regime. The various debates and agreements of the Courts of Cádiz (1810–1813) on the abolition or prohibition of tribute, *repartimientos* (in their commercial modality), flogging, imprisonment, and other acts committed against the Indians, personal services (e.g., the *mita*), and so on, reveal the variety of methods used toward the end of the colonial regime.[21] Tribute, for example, was not abolished until the dawn of independence.[22]

SEGREGATIONISM AND ASSIMILATIONISM

The legal and institutional tools that regulated the exploitation of indigenous labor were preceded or accompanied by theoretical elaborations about the shape that colonial organization should take in America. The debate included the proposal of a quasi-autonomous regime for the Indian peoples through a scheme of separation between indigenous and Spanish people as well as the assimilation of the natives. Borah has synthesized the enormous diversity of opinions in terms of "three schools of thought,"[23] a scheme that does not present the entire variety of propositions and the subtlety of certain formulations with total fairness but remains a useful exposition. These three positions can be summarized as (1) autonomy, (2) two separate republics, and (3) assimilation.

1. Francisco de Vitoria, contended that before the Europeans arrived the New World had legitimate indigenous leadership and that indigenous societies should have the right to retain their own institutions and laws without detriment to the introduction of Christianity. Indeed, in his lectures Vitoria concluded, "Before the Spanish arrived, they [the Indians] were true lords, in public as well as in private." He questioned with lively arguments some of the reasons that were accepted by several theologians and jurists as a "legitimate" basis for the conquest and dominion of Spain over America, such as the temporal authority of the pope, the right of discovery, and the sins of the aboriginals.[24]

Nevertheless, it is doubtful that a proposal of autonomy can be derived from the spirit of Vitoria's work. Even a mind as open as his was influenced by the ideas and political interests of his time. Hence, this scholar and counselor to the emperor Charles V accepted as "legitimate" certain reasons (such as the preaching of the gospel) that efficiently sanctioned the conquest and the sovereignty of the Spanish crown over the autochthonous peoples.[25] Vitoria's *Relecciones* (particularly "De indis" and "De indis, relectio posterior") not only opposed illegitimate reasons for the domination of native peoples but also provided seven "legitimate reasons" for European domination. It might be said that in Vitoria's work the Spanish crown found strong arguments for creating its empire.[26]

It is in the perspective of Bartolomé de las Casas, whom Borah does not include as part of this school, that we find a systematic discourse identifying the possible bases for self-determination and Indian autonomy. Rivera-Pagán has correctly summarized the basic elements of Las Casas's thought:

> His imperial paradigm is paternalistic and beneficial. It does not deny the indigenous people's freedom; rather, it is founded on their condition as free beings, both individually and collectively, as autonomous peoples. The relationship of these free peoples with the crown should be similar to that of the free cities that in Europe and in Spain recognized the emperor as their ultimate sovereign without that authority's canceling their capacities for autonomy and self-determination.[27]

In brief, the aboriginals should retain, with the benevolent protection of their new European monarch, their sociopolitical structure (rulers, and institutions) and habits (with the exception of pagan ritual and idolatry). Theoretically, this opened up the possibility of establishing in the colonial possessions a type of "autonomy" for indigenous society.

Again, however, it would be inappropriate to deduce an anticolonial orientation from the proposals of Las Casas. In spite of panegyrical interpretations that make him a radical anticolonialist, the truth is that Las Casas never doubted the legitimacy of the Spanish domination of America. It is true that he advocated humane treatment of the Indians, that he fought for recognition of contractual indigenous self-determination as a matter of natural right, and that he opposed compulsory evangelization and advocated the use of persuasion to convert the natives. But in the face of the evidence that Spanish power was imposed without any consideration of Indian self-determination and without the mediation of any pact, Las Casas did not grasp the obvious consequence: that such domination was illegitimate or invalid.[28]

In any event, the arguments of Las Casas clashed with the primary interests of the colonial regime and the centralist propensity that characterized Castilian political history and mentality. Besides, his perspective was by far the closest to the aspiration to autonomy of the peoples involved, and the Indian elites realized that an indigenous government might fit within the framework of his proposal.[29]

2. The second school of thought proposed the creation of "two separate republics, each with its own laws, customs, and governmental systems." This was enthusiastically recommended by some friars.[30] In New Spain, missionaries such as Friar Gerónimo de Mendieta and Friar Pedro de Gante and colonizers and officials, such as Alonso de Zorita thought that the Indians might constitute an almost perfect Christian society if their traditional organization (with its "natural" elites) were preserved and if they were kept segregated, that is, if prolonged contact with other sectors (Spanish, black, and others), which perverted them, were prohibited.[31] The Indian past was glorified, particularly the alleged golden age that had been the first three decades of the society of New Spain, before the "greed" of the Spanish government was imposed on it in the early 1560s. The goal of this faction was to maintain the ancient values of the indigenous government under the tutelage of the priests.[32] Although these priests favored the ways of life and habits of the Indians in their "republic," certain transformations were considered necessary to ensure good government: the introduction of Christianity and the abolition of anything that was not compatible with it. This position, resolute in its intention to protect indigenous society by means of separation or isolation from other sectors, is perhaps the earliest forerunner of the radical ethnicist perspectives that acquired strength in the twentieth century.[33]

3. There were also those who rejected any plurality and simply advocated a unitary republic. "That meant absolute indigenous assimilation to the institutions, laws, and procedures of Castile. Castilian law would be applied to the Indians in

all its rigor. Their own customs and institutions would be assimilated by the Christian and European ones without any restriction or special arrangement."[34] This direction was the most compatible with the colonizers' interests, and it also fit the crown's practices within Spain itself (with regard to the different regions of the peninsula and the cultural minorities). Such resolute assimilationism has survived in some indigenist perspectives in a more ideologically sophisticated form.

This last perspective was imposed throughout the colonial process, albeit tempered by the inclusion of elements from the other two ideological positions. Some analysts have emphasized the mitigating elements of assimilationism and others the elements that differentiate the population, but the greater historical visibility of the latter has characterized the period as one of "segregation." This segregation varied depending on the labor regime that predominated in each phase of the colonial process. The Europeans had to adapt to American particularities. In the complex and oscillating course of colonial indigenist policy, however, a centralist perspective and an assimilationist practice are evident.[35] The accession of Philip II signaled the ascendancy of this project.[36]

It was inevitable that the colonial regime would include some elements of the first two proposals in the basic assimilationist project. At first glance perhaps the most impressive recognition of the peculiarities of indigenous society was the preservation or restructuring of the Indian hierarchy within the native communities. The Spanish authorities recognized the high-status members of the pre-Hispanic hierarchy who had survived the conquest and showed an inclination to adapt to the new order as caciques or *curacas* and those of lesser status as *principales*. In the chaos of the first years, some ordinary Indians were included in the category of principales. Rather than the basis for an indigenous self-government this was indirect control by an essentially centralist regime. The aim of the Spanish was not to create a system for Indian autonomy but to facilitate control of the communities. Even the most resolute adherents of limiting the power of the indigenous elite concluded that it was too difficult to rule over the conquered peoples without the collaboration of indigenous administrators. They had a specific interest in expediting the collection of tribute and the forced distribution of the native labor force. Thus, the caciques and *principales*, aided by a team of local officials (governors, mayors, councilmen, and so on) and strictly supervised by the Spanish authorities, were in charge of collecting tribute and turning it over to the *encomendero* (or the crown) and of guaranteeing that there were indigenous workers available for the productive enterprises of the colonizers (agricultural estates, mines, and mills), public works, and domestic service.

Although these indigenous authorities were entitled to preserve traditional norms and to administer the affairs of the members of the community, their power was local and legally restricted (any affair that involved a Spaniard was dealt with by a Spanish judge or official), and in time it gradually diminished because of the interference of Spanish officials and provincial governors. Royal officers and magistrates, who were supposed to consider indigenous traditions in the

resolution of issues that involved indigenous people, developed their own interpretations of these practices and simply applied Castilian law.

Although Castilian principles were naturally influenced by the characteristics
of the sociocultural and economic milieu of the colonies, in a relatively short time
the Spanish system was imposed as the universally dominant legal framework.
The indigenous government system was always subordinate to the Spanish government. Besides collecting tribute, organizing the recruitment of forced labor,
and keeping order in the communities, it made business (such as the profitable
repartimientos) manageable for regional oligarchies. As Indian officials of the "republic" took over the functions of the traditional elite, the importance of the indigenous nobility diminished and, in some places, disappeared.[37]

The situation for this stratum of Indians, oscillating between their adherence to
indigenous traditions and their attraction to the new system of power, became
more and more difficult. The information available suggests that during the first
years of the colony members of the indigenous nobility maintained a paternalistic
attitude toward their people, often acting as "protectors" of their communities
and displaying the dignity and prudence of rulers. But as they fell under more severe subjugation by the Spanish they suffered a kind of degradation, and the majority of them turned into executioners in their communities. Once their authority and prestige had been diminished by Spanish domination, the power they
managed to preserve depended on their conformity and even affinity with the
colonial government. Prospero's seduction triumphed over Caliban's loyalty.[38]

From that moment on, in several regions, the vast majority of ordinary Indians
had little reasons to see their vital interests as being represented or protected vis-
à-vis the Spanish by the native nobility. There are innumerable historical references to the extraordinary zeal with which the native caciques and *principales* accomplished the tasks the colonizers gave them, but the severe reprisals of the
Europeans certainly helped explain this compliance.[39]

By the mid-sixteenth century the Indian nobles of the two main American
kingdoms (the caciques in New Spain and the *curacas* in Peru) were often charged
with being the real exploiters of their peoples. In many cases these charges came
from royal officials and the secular clergy as part of a campaign to weaken the
power of the traditional authorities. The former sought to increase the king's income (raising the rates and broadening the base of Indian tribute to include the
Indian nobles themselves), and the latter hoped to limit the main source of the
friars' power in the communities as well as to augment their own income.[40] However, the charges often came from the *macehuales* (the Indians who delivered their
labor force) themselves, who complained of being abused—of excessive tribute
and other injuries.[41] Thus, the excesses of the native high officials often contended
with those of the Spanish. This partly explained why many indigenous people of
New Spain chose to run away from their villages to the towns and cities of the
Spanish "republic" or the workers' settlements established around the haciendas.
Those who deserted were escaping the huge obligations of the community or pur-

suing their own advantage, but they were also avoiding the despotism and the exactions of the Indian authorities.

In many regions the Indian nobles emulated Hispanic culture (dress, household style, norms, etc.), including some economic activities,[42] and of course this hispanicization widened the gap between the upper strata and the ordinary people. This assimilation (which generally made it difficult for most indigenous people to identify with the heads of the government of their "republic") was, without any doubt, one of the most beneficial achievements of the Europeans for the maintenance of the colonial regime. When the Indians rebelled against the regime, the latter often found worthy allies among the indigenous peoples themselves. It is understandable, therefore, that where there was rebellion, one of the first acts of the dissenters was to discharge and punish indigenous officials who had collaborated with the Spanish.[43] Only when there was "a significant reduction in the differences of rank and social position within the rural Indian communities"[44] (as the indigenous nobility eventually lost most of its privileges and internal power) did the traditional Indian authorities become a more stable part of the ethnic cohesion that gradually emerged.

THE POLITICAL AND IDEOLOGICAL
ROLE OF RELIGION

The friars soon understood that their evangelizing activity was more effective if they showed a cautious respect for certain practices and beliefs of the natives and spoke their languages. The missionaries' approach coincided with the crown's interest in respecting as much as possible (i.e., to the degree to which it was politically and socially accepted) certain indigenous "usages and customs." This intention was limited by the incompatibility of Indian rites with "our Christian religion." Obviously, in spite of the sincere sympathy many friars felt for the aboriginals, it was impossible to foster an unqualified respect for their religious beliefs and worldview, since they often contradicted the rigid and intolerant Hispanic Catholic ideology of the time. For the Spanish, absolute certitude about the demonic character of aboriginal rites and beliefs was practically unanimous among the participants in the colonization process, and this view was sometimes shared even by vehement Indian supporters.

The clerics were unable to eradicate the "pagan" practices of indigenous communities because of their unyielding resistance to these pressures. Besides, the rigorous secrecy with which the Indians surrounded the location of their sacred sites and the performance of their rituals made control by the priests very difficult. In some regions the resulting syncretism was more "pagan" (pre-Columbian) than Christian, partly because of the role played by Indian high officials in fostering and even participating in them as officiating priests. During the second half of the sixteenth century and well into the following one, the Spanish realized that, while publicly showing their adherence to Christianity, in private many indigenous authorities were taking part in ancient rites and ceremonies. Perhaps the loss of prestige of these Indian nobles prompted them to seek compensation and recognition through a renewed association with the indigenous religious system.[45]

The colonial authorities clearly sought to demolish the foundations of indigenous religions, and the categorical decrees of the crown officially sanctioned the suppression of local religious practices, calling for the destruction of indigenous temples and idols. In 1538, for example, the Spanish monarch warned New Spain's viceroy "that the natives of that land still use their heathen rites, usually those related to superstitions, idolatries, and sacrifices, only not publicly, as they used to. At night they go to their places of worship and temples that have not been totally obliterated." Since this practice was equivalent to "disdain for God Our Lord," the king ordered "that as soon as this dispatch is received, you must have all places of worship and idol temples in New Spain . . . crushed and removed; once done, see that the stone left over is used to build churches and monasteries."[46]

In many locales the priests undertook a frantic search for sites of worship and "idols" and persecuted indigenous priests and believers, sometimes using as spies the native wardens of churches and convents. The Indians' sacred objects were smashed with outraged fervor, and harsh punishments were inflicted upon transgressors. Most often the outcome of the evangelization was the demolition of the beliefs and rituals that formed the indigenous religious system and the construction of another system that had little to do with the former despite retaining some of its features. The natives' sociocultural system, intimately associated with the religious realm, suffered serious disruption even though they managed to reorganize their identity with the cultural elements imposed upon them. An example of this syncretic solution was the development of a whole religious regime based upon the veneration of saints. To maintain it, complex systems of duties and institutions such as the confraternities were created.[47]

The evangelizing project, as not only a religious mission but also a sociocultural one (which, in this sense, is the remote predecessor of the "civilizing mission" that ideologically supported colonial expansion during the nineteenth century), was the most powerful justification for the European colonial domination of America. The goal of spreading Christianity was among the elements that justified the conquest (in the *requerimiento*, for example) and slavery (because the enslaved would have Christian instruction). Teaching the gospel also justified the *congregaciones* (the forced concentration of Indian communities and populations).

The clergy played a very important role in the consolidation of colonial society. During the early period, the secular clergy, with a stronger criollo presence, more closely associated with the colonizers' power and in constant conflict with the towns' priests, could be distinguished from the friars, who were deeply committed to the preservation of the communal Indian organization and shared and tried to understand the Indian languages and customs as much as they could. Over time, however, these attitudes changed; the humanist and evangelizing impetus of the first missionaries, for example, diminished as the colonial regime developed. By the end of the seventeenth century they had really distanced themselves from the indigenous peoples.[48] However, the very important tasks of acculturation, to the colonial regime performed by members of the religious orders in the villages must not be forgotten. It is no exaggeration to assert that the Christianization and Westernization of the indigenous elite and their children during the years of the consolidation were as vital a foundation for the European project in Mesoamerica as the military victories.[49] The evangelizing effort among the aboriginals, which eroded the ethical and cultural superstructure of the native groups and almost completely substituted one worldview for another, consummated the task. Overall, the activity of the clergy during the colonial period amounted to a very efficient continuation of warfare, through other means, against the indigenous sociocultural system.

Thanks to the clergy, the domination of the colonies could rely more on hegemonic consensus than on military strength, and this is how the crown managed to maintain its control over a large population with only a limited military force primarily charged with patrolling the borders. As Brading puts it, "It was the church and not the military that kept the peace in New Spain and united the diverse races of the colony into a single flock of adherents." The church's influence throughout all sociopolitical sectors and its penetration into the interstices of civil society favored such a role. "As a result of this intimate contact both with the rank-and-file of the people and with the elite, the priests had the opportunity of mediating conflicts among classes. In colonial Mexico, when the populace rebelled it was the clergy and not the army that took to the streets to argue with the mob and to calm it."[50]

Often the regular clergy had to confront not only certain royal officials but the colonizers and the secular clergy who threatened their preeminent positions in the communities and therefore the source of their authority and their livelihood. But it so happened that the very commitment of the friars to protect the Indians from the destructive actions of the colonizers and, at the beginning, of the viceregal officials created a constellation of interests against them. This, in turn, drove them to seek alliances with sectors of the Spanish exploiters themselves so as to prevent the dissolution of their communities and thus of their own power.

A bloody conflict over control of more of the labor power and the wealth created by the indigenous people began and not even the missionaries, no one within the narrow colonial circle of power could remain on the sidelines. Whether they liked it or not, the friars were part of the scramble.

During the sixteenth century the friars constantly clashed with the officials of the viceroyalty (particularly against the governors, mayors, or magistrates) because of the latter's insatiable rapacity and the excesses they inflicted upon the Indians, which threatened the position of the missionaries who lived in indigenous villages. The friars were often in conflict with such officials even during the viceroyalty of the marquis of Montesclaros (1603–1607), but a remarkable change took place when his rule ended:

> Seeing that their position was threatened—not so much by the viceregal officers as by the criollos' dissatisfaction and the secular clergy's anger—the friars stopped complaining about the methods used by the magistrates and accepted them as partners in the domination of the Indians. The magistrates, who were also under pressure from the same forces, no longer considered the friars their rivals and began to understand how convenient it was to ally themselves with them in the struggle against the colonizers. Thus emerged a united bureaucratic front of viceregal officials, indigenous officials and mendicant friars. From the time of the viceroyalty of the marquis of Guadalcázar [1612–1621], friars and government walked hand in hand in political matters.[51]

In other situations, such as Guatemala during the second half of the seventeenth century, the clergy defended the criollos and the colonizers vis-à-vis the royal authorities' attempt at terminating the Indian *repartimiento*. When the royal tribunal attorney of Guatemala proposed the abolition of forced labor in 1663, alarm spread, and the colonizers angrily rejected the petition. In concert with them, the regular clergy of the order of Our Lady of Mercy, the Dominicans, the Augustinians, and the Jesuits wrote to Spain in favor of continuing of the *repartimiento*. The only exception was the Franciscans, who accused the others of defending an institution from which they benefited in that Indian workers cultivated their rural properties. The *repartimiento* regime was maintained.[52]

In contrast, during the same years some high–ranking members of the secular clergy defended the Indians in confrontations with the provincial governors. In New Spain in the seventeenth century, conflicts concerning Indian exploitation between the followers of the bishop-viceroy Juan de Palafox y Mendoza and the Spanish bureaucracy were well known.[53]

INDIAN TOWNS AND NEW IDENTITY

The colonial process had other crucial consequences for the Indian peoples. With the creation of more or less stable Indian governments and towns, the pre-Hispanic political organization and the territoriality associated with it suffered. Thus, the subjects of the "self-government" recognized by the colonial regime were not the ethnic and political-territorial divisions (empires, city-states or *seigniories, caciquil* systems, and so on) that the Europeans found upon their arrival but other entities that they had created.

 Indeed, one of the more remarkable results of the process of colonial domination was the re-creation of the *community* as a sociocultural nucleus in which new and multiple identities found shelter. The *congregaciones* and *reducciones* (Indian villages converted to Christianity) and the political organization supported by the Spanish gave way to "Indian towns" conceived of as Indian republics. But these republics broke down into disarticulated communities—that is, they initiated the ethnic and political fragmentation of indigenous societies that had once been organized at a higher level. This change, part of a larger project of redefinition of space and relocation of populations conducive to ensuring control over native groups, led to a new entity; the Indian community.

There had been Indian communities prior to the colonial regime, but they were dramatically modified by it. The shift consisted of turning the communal nucleus into the single milieu of Indian ethnicity, given the elimination of preexisting higher levels of political, socioeconomic, and cultural organization and the reduction of their territoriality. The jurisdiction of the Indian hierarchy (nobles and other members of the town councils) was limited to a narrower and narrower communal world. Each separate nucleus established its own links to Spanish power, without the mediation of any intermediate political structure as the expression of a supracommunal authority.

In Mesoamerica and the Andes, as among the lowland Mayas, the Spanish found quite complex sociopolitical and economic organizations into which the basic communal type nuclei were integrated. These large hierarchical kingdoms and provinces facilitated the conquest. However, according to Nancy Farris,

> The consolidation of the benefits obtained through military conquest required a certain basic modification of the indigenous system. In particular, it was considered unwise to maintain the hierarchical organization of provinces and states that had facilitated the imposition of colonial domination . . . To consolidate their rule the Spanish had to divide the more stable indigenous structures through which unrest and resistance could have been channeled into smaller, more easily controllable units.[54]

This was exactly what the colonial regime brought about. In the early phase, the *encomienda* system destroyed political and ethnic units as colonial beneficiaries were assigned individual Indian villages, separating each village from the broader structure to which it belonged.[55] During the second half of the sixteenth century, when as happened in Peru the native nobles demanded recognition of their prerogatives, they mentioned the atomization caused by the *encomiendas* as one of the greater affronts they had suffered and the cause of great sadness for their people.

The administrative organization imposed by the Spanish in the next phase, had the same atomizing effect. By reducing the ancient dominions to isolated communal units and negotiating separately with each local council, they quickly destroyed the old hierarchical structures.[56] Without any doubt, one of the great successes of the Spanish was "to fragment the larger indigenous units and fracture the former Indian spatial identity as a category for ethnic allocation. From this point on, indigenous people were sheltered only in the atomized jurisdiction of the separate communities into which the seigniories that formerly made up the great kingdoms were transformed."[57] The provincial organization was maintained in several places for as long as the native nobles lived. As this generation disappeared, however, the caciques and Indian governors administered only a single community each, in the best of cases a *cabecera* or district capital. In some areas of New Spain, supracommunity indigenous units survived longer.[58]

Later the colonial system produced more divisions and reduced the size of indigenous ethnic entities even further. During the first century of domination the Indian towns (the capitals of townships and their subjects) remained organized, but during the seventeenth and eighteenth centuries there was a wave of "separations" in which communities sought and achieved the status of independent towns with their own councils. This situation, brought about by the colonial dynamic imposed on the communities, was allowed by the Spanish authorities, who soon found more advantages than disadvantages in its development. By the end of the eighteenth century previously enormous jurisdictions had become numerous small towns independent of one another.[59]

Spalding emphasizes the transformation of "Andean society into a myriad of small mutually suspicious communities reduced to competing among themselves for constantly diminishing land and labor." The cause of this process was the struggle of Spanish authorities against the Indians' "idolatry." Campaigns against the indigenous peoples' religious systems accentuated fragmentation in that they attacked "those community rituals which limited, restrained, or even eliminated social conflict and lack of cooperation among larger social units. These campaigns managed to do away with the large-scale social rites that reaffirmed the unity, in space and time, of the local group."[60]

The atomization that the Spanish promoted was not random; there were guidelines requiring a prior stage of concentration of population. There is ample historical evidence that the civil authorities and the Spanish clergy considered the pattern of scattered indigenous settlements in the countryside a threat. For example, they linked geographical isolation with licentious activity and the persistence of pagan rituals, whereas life in villages or towns was identified with positive ideas and an orderly existence. Europeans found that scattered rural settlements hindered their economic plans, political control, and religious work.[61] The great epidemics that plagued the Indians in the sixteenth century intensified the isolation of some communities and left large areas empty or semideserted. The authorities supported groups that sought to create dense settlements. Indians who lived in small hamlets and villages were forced to move to towns designed by the Spanish.

In New Spain the dispersion of indigenous peasants persisted until mid-sixteenth century. It was followed by the programs of population concentration known as *congregaciones* or *reducciones*. The Spanish selected sites for the new towns, favoring flat areas to the hilly ones on which the Indians located their ceremonial and political centers, and merged in them the villages and hamlets close to these center, or integrated several such centers into one. When the congregated population could not be entirely relocated in a capital, estates, subject towns, or neighborhoods were created around it. Each entity was assigned land for cultivation. In the capitals the streets were organized according to the grid design familiar to the Spanish, with government buildings and a church surrounding a central plaza.

The concentration of the Indians of New Spain was accomplished in two stages, each preceded by a huge epidemic. The first stage, between 1550 and 1564, was preceded by the 1545–1548 plague, which reduced the native population to a fifth of its original size. As Gerhard has shown, this first experiment was quite successful from the Spanish point of view: "By the end of Velasco's rule [1564], rural Mexican towns had the concentrated appearance they have today in almost all of the area affected by the Spanish."[62] The second wave of *congregaciones* took place between 1595 and 1605, after the plague of 1576–1580. As a consequence, great expanses of territory were left uninhabited. These lands were part of prior ethnic units that still belonged to the Indians, but the authorities conferred control over these lands on private individuals. The Indian towns that emerged from these *congregaciones* opened the way for the ethnic and territorial divisions previously described.

In order to establish Indian governments for these towns the Spanish supervised the creation and performance of local councils and gave them jurisdiction, as "predominant justice," over the provinces into which groups of communities were assembled. Elective Indian posts such as governor, mayor, councilman, constable, and many others were created. The persons who held these positions had to be elected annually. For a while the old caciques seized the highest positions on these councils, and the others were taken by the *principales*. Only nobles and *principales* could vote. Although *curacas* were prohibited form holding the highest posts in the councils of Peru, they maintained an indisputable influence over these councils.

In time there was a gradual separation, both in New Spain and in Peru, between traditional power and the Indian government created by the colonial system. The councils became more important, and ordinary Indians achieved a definite role in the election of the authorities. In this way, a succession system based on a hereditary principle was transformed into one based on elections.[63] Furthermore, as the habit of making *principales* of the councils' former heads was instituted, blood as the foundation of the Indian nobility came to coexist with another source, occupation.[64]

The debate about the nature of the Indian councils is ongoing. Contending opinions range from emphasizing discontinuity and, therefore, the eminently colonial character of the councils to stressing some continuity of the style of Indian government prior to European domination. The truth most certainly lies between these extremes. Although the council was an institution based on a Spanish pattern, in theory and practice it had indigenous characteristics.[65] Indian communities tried to adapt the municipal regime imposed on them to their traditional norms, and, particularly in the lower levels of the new system, they made an effort to maintain old privileges. Regardless, it must be recognized that the *principales* (council officials) had to adjust to the new functions assigned them by those in power and that in general the ancient roles and their meanings remained the same in name only. In summary, the transformation was so complete that it is difficult to identify any substantial continuity, at least within the sphere of the council. It is also impossible not to see in the indigenous municipality one of the most important institutions of Spanish domination. In this regard, the Indian council cannot be separated from another typically colonial institution; the *alcaldía mayor* or *corregimiento*.[66]

The *corregidores* were, strictly speaking, regional governors They appeared in New Spain by a royal decree of 1550, whereby the authorities were instructed to assign "the most neighboring towns" to each *corregimiento* and to delegate to the *corregidor* the task of hearing all the suits, both civil and criminal, between Indians and Spanish, Spanish and Spanish, and Indians and Indians. From this point on the *corregimientos* stopped being only "for Indians" and "became full territorial jurisdictions on a local, that is subprovincial scale."[67] This position was introduced in Peru in 1556. The *corregidor* was turned into a Spanish official with governmental and judicial functions on a regional scale whose jurisdiction included both Spanish cities and Indian towns and their councils.

These regional governors not only intervened in the functioning of the Indian councils (for example, in the election and confirmation of their members) and closely linked native rule to colonial command but also were vital initiators of the most important changes experienced by the communities—their entry into commercial life. Indeed, taking advantage of their almost absolute regional power, the *corregidores* became traders and created the complex *repartimiento* system that placed the Indians fully within the commercial circuit.[68] The *repartimiento* turned the natives into "buyers" of merchandise provided by the officials and "sellers" of their products to the governor, who had advanced them money or raw materials. In both cases the Indians were forced into transactions in which prices (and therefore the amount of profit) were set by the *corregidores* and "captain general's lieutenants," who normally expected substantial rewards from such transactions. These relationships and mechanisms created a market for European products and allowed the purchase of Indian products at prices convenient for the Spanish.

Since the Spanish governor's activities were supported by the purchase price, from which he would obtain a profit beyond his salary, and since regional merchants and powerful consulate members (as well as officials at every level, including royal court magistrates and the viceroy himself) were involved in his dealings, the authorities pretended not to notice such maneuvers.[69] Besides, commerce locally sustained by *corregidores* became an indispensable support for the economic development of regional colonial administrations. The "perversion" of regional rule allowed by the monarch expressed more than private interest; it was state-sponsored enterprise based on the socioeconomic subordination of the Indian peoples.[70]

The so-called Indian republics can now be evaluated with more precision. Like other proposals for the formation of a more plural system, the segregationist project of dividing colonial society into two separate "republics" was a failure. Although during the sixteenth century the crown adopted measures to keep the Spanish and other groups (blacks, mulattos, and others) away from the Indian communities, these gave shape to a particular spatial organization of indigenous populations rather than creating any isolated entity. In fact, Indian towns and neighborhoods remained firmly linked to the rest of the system throughout the colonial regime. It could not be otherwise, since separation was thwarted by the very logic of the colonial regime.

One of the main reasons separation was impossible was that indigenous "government" was established to facilitate access to tribute, servitude, or forced labor, to maintain of internal order, and to support commercial transactions that were as illegal as they were indispensable. In the towns there was a virtual army of clergy who, in spite of the variety of their evangelizing methods, sought to establish the pattern of beliefs, values and worldview of "Christian society" among the Indians. In brief, economic, social, political, and cultural factors, all of them emerging from colonial imperatives, obstructed, in practice, the coexistence of two "republics" each with its own foundations or functioning logic. The so-called Indian republic was an immense archipelago of communities, converted for the most part into payers of tribute, exploitable labor, and a captive market. This is why, in the long run, the prohibition against residence of the Spanish and "the castes" in Indian towns and the efforts to prevent Indians from living with the non-Indians were ineffective. The colonial system's socioeconomic foundations made it inevitable that many Spanish would take up residence in the towns and, after the seventeenth century, that the number of Indians relocated near Spanish and criollo settlements would constantly increase.[71]

Neither the *encomienda* in its primitive version nor the *repartimientos* and other aspects of the labor regime caused indigenous ethnic groups to disappear. The segregationist policy founded on the relocation of indigenous populations made it possible for indigenous peoples to create, develop, and reproduce identities of their own. This must be seen as a typical unanticipated consequence. In fostering organization into towns and neighborhoods, the aim of the crown was not to maintain or reproduce particular identities but to promote its own material interests and achieve certain sociopolitical goals. Furthermore, the colonial regime made every possible effort to destroy the pre-Hispanic sociocultural cohesion and succeeded. The dialectics of history produced, as a result, communal forms of life (town councils, ejidos, communal lands, religious cults and festivities, and so on) and gave birth to new sociocultural symbols of a renewed identity that continues to be modified and restructured.

Although elements from the past and a latent historical memory served as raw materials for the new ethnicities, there was never an authentic return to the past. This was impossible to achieve given the irreversible catastrophic effect of the conquest and the colonial dynamics in which indigenous groups were involved for centuries. Nevertheless, denied the chance to recover their old identities, the Indian peoples constructed new ones that proved to be even more resistant. These new identities became socioculturally cohesive systems but they did not reflect the "preservation" of pre-Columbian elements. Rather, they were constructed under the new conditions in which the colonial regime had placed the Indians. It is in this sense that it can be said that the colonial system created the Indian.[72]

The strategy of differentiation and its coercive labor regime created relationships of subordination that deeply marked indigenous people. The characteristics that thenceforth distinguished indigenous ethnic groups did not come from the pre-Hispanic period but for the most part were born during colonial times, particularly in the Indian towns. Of all their features, the atomization of peoples or communities is most important. A multiplicity of socioeconomic processes produced parochial identities in a process of disarticulation and articulation that continues to this day.

Later indigenisms attempted to erase or destroy these parochial identities, especially during the nineteenth century. In the twentieth century efforts were made to atomize indigenous ethnic groups to prevent them, at all costs, from achieving any broader articulation (regional or national) capable of generating a sociopolitical force that defied exploitation and subordination. Therefore struggles against oppression and exploitation have historically been linked to the recovery of a unity of purpose that transcends the communal and parochial world in which indigenous peoples were submerged by the colonial regime. But before approaching this objective—even outlining it—the Indian peoples had to confront the indigenisms of independent national life: the liberal liquidationism of the nineteenth century and the integrationism of the twentieth.

NOTES

1. Fray Antón de Montesinos, "Ego vox clamantis in deserto," in *Boletín de Antropología Americana,* no. 6 December 1982, pp. 147–161. The full story of the battle of the Dominicans of La Española against Indian slavery can be found in Bartolomé de las Casas, *Historia de las Indias,* vol. 2, 2nd edition, Mexico City, Fondo de Cultura Económica, 1965, pp. 438–458.

2. For the strongest and most complete account of the massacres, injustices, and excesses perpetrated by the Spanish against the native population, see Bartolomé de las Casas, *Brevísima relación de la destrucción de las Indias,* 4th edition, Mexico City, Editorial Fontamara, 1989.

3. López de Gómara, *Historia general de las Indias* vol. 1, p. 221.

4. Ibid., p. 223.

5. Ibid., p. 267. Lagasca also confronted the rebellion led by the Contreras brothers in Nicaragua, who had assassinated the bishop and seized goods belonging to the king. He vanquished the rioters and had them executed. Lagasca returned to Spain in 1550, and as a reward the emperor "made him Palencia's bishop." A rebellion organized in New Spain with the same motivation found a cohesive symbol in Martín Cortés, Hernán Cortés's son. The main instigators were imprisoned and killed in 1566, and the heir of the marquis of the Valley was deported to Spain. Bloody repression of the criollo community followed.

6. Peggy K. Liss, *Orígenes de la nacionalidad mexicana,* 1521–1556: *La formación de una nueva sociedad,* Mexico City, Fondo de Cultura Económica, 1986. p. 255.

7. Gibson, *Los aztecas bajo el domino español,* p. 63.

8. By royal decree on July 6, 1529, Cortés was made a present of the villages and towns "with their subjects and hamlets and districts and vassals and civil and criminal jurisdiction," an exceptional gift considering its size. However, the monarch kept the gold and silver mines "and the salt mines there might be in said territory," as well as "the sovereignty of our royal justice," (which included hearing appeals of rulings by the Marquis and his *alcaldes mayores*) and, generally, "all those other issues pertaining to the royal dominion that cannot and should not be overlooked." Archivo General de la Nación, Mexico City, Hospital de Jesús, docket 412, dossier 1, 4 pp.

9. An example of the excesses and cruelties is that of Tepetlaoztoc in the Valley of Mexico. This *encomienda* first belonged to Cortés and then passed to two of his followers, who subjected the Indians to drastic exactions. Later, Gonzalo de Salazar was indescribably voracious and cruel; he increased tributes at will, expropriated the lands of the natives, took over Indian public works vital to the community, and punished and humiliated the cacique, among other injustices. To this *encomendero*, the Indians were lower than animals. When Salazar traveled to Spain in 1530, Gibson writes, "more than two hundred Indians from Tepetlaoztoc died carrying his belongings to Veracruz to be shipped." Gibson, *Los aztecas bajo el dominio español,* pp. 83–84.

10. Carlos Sempat Assadourian, "Los señores étnicos y los corregidores indios en la conformación del estado colonial," *Anuario de Estudios Americanos,* 44, 1987, pp. 15–16.

11. Archivo General de la Nación, *El libro de las tasaciones de pueblos de la Nueva España* (Siglo 16), Mexico, City 1952.

12. Silvio Zavala, "La evolución del régimen de trabajo," in *Estudios acerca de la historia del trabajo en México,* ed. Elías Trabulse, Mexico City, El Colegio de México, 1988, p. 27.

13. Ibid., p. 28.

14. The term *repartimiento* was used variously to refer first to the Indian *encomiendas* and later to forced labor and the illegal trade of the provincial governors that reached its climax during the seventeenth and eighteenth centuries.

15. In other provinces, such as Guatemala, the colonizers successfully opposed the abolition of the *repartimiento*, which persisted throughout colonial times.

16. Zavala records for the late seventeenth century and the first half of the eighteenth "a persistence of the habit of using public power to make workers from the villages go to the haciendas." Silvio Zavala, "Orígenes coloniales del peonaje en México," in *Estudios acerca de la historia del trabajo,* pp. 44–45.

17. Zavala notes, "Naturally, the *encomenderos* were interested in conserving those who paid tribute to them. Therefore it was common for *encomenderos* to appear before the viceroy defending points of view similar to those of the indigenous peoples whenever third parties attracted *encomienda* Indians to their properties. Nevertheless, there are examples in which the viceroy supported Indians against *encomenderos* in disputes about farm labor." Ibid., p. 42.

18. Sempat Assadourian says for Peru, "Up until 1564, the religious people of the Indian party and the chiefs (*curacas*) maintained an alliance against the *encomenderos* and certain officials; in 1566 the *encomenderos* seemed to participate in a united front with their previous adversaries to defeat a governor who sought to impose royal power on ethnic territory." Sempat Assadourian, "Los señores étnicos y los corregidores, pp. 50–51.

19. Carlos Sempat Assadourian, "Dominio colonial y señores étnicos en el espacio andino," *Hisla*, no. 1, 1983, p. 11.

20. Brigitte B. de Lameiras, *Indios de México y viajeros extranjeros (siglo XIX)*, Mexico City, SepSetentas, 1973, p. 161.

21. For a selection of the issues that concerned Indians during the sessions of the Courts of Cadiz, see Cesáreo de Armellada, *La causa indígena americana en las Cortes de Cádiz*, Caracas, Universidad Católica Andrés Bello, Instituto de Investigaciones Históricas, 1979.

22. Francisco Xavier Venegas, the viceroy, ordered on October 5, 1810, "that all Indians be freed from tribute, with express prohibition of their Indian governors, caciques and *encomenderos* from demanding the smallest amount of them as tribute." The measure was extended to "the castes of mulattos, negroes, and others." However, the viceroy reestablished the odious *repartimiento* of native merchandise practiced by royal officials. These measures were obviously oriented toward limiting support for the independence movement, as Guridi Alcocer, deputy to the Courts of Cadiz and representative of New Spain, noted: "I must say, honoring truth and New Spain's viceroy, that his proclamation expresses his wishes to calm the unrest, trying to please the Indians by eliminating tribute and pleasing his employees by offering them the *repartimiento* they so long for." Ibid., p.29; for Venegas's order, see pp. 70–72.

23. Borah, *El juzgado general de indios*, pp. 40–41.

24. Francisco de Vitoria, *Relecciones: Del estado, de los indios y del derecho de la guerra*, 2nd edition, Mexico City, Editorial Porrúa, 1985, p. 36 and passim.

25. I agree with Luis N. Rivera Pagán who observes in Vitoria's thought "an obvious coincidence between the state's reasoning and a Catholic missionary sense." Ultimately, Vitoria's elaborations "legitimize Spanish sovereignty and generally declare warfare against riotous Indians just." Luis N. Rivera Pagán, *Evangelización y violencia: La conquista de América*, San Juan, Editorial Cemi, 1990, p. 129.

26. Noam Chomsky has called attention to the legitimization for European domination found in Vitoria's arguments. Noam Chomsky, "El sistema de los 500 años y el nuevo orden mundial," *América: La patria grande*, no. 9, October-December 1991, p.26.

27. Rivera-Pagán, *Evangelización y violencia*, p. 105.

28. Besides, like the rest of the Spanish, Las Casas considered the autochthonous belief systems pagan rites that should be radically extirpated. He was distinguished from the majority of his contemporaries by the method he recommended—conversion without violence or peaceful preaching—but he accepted the idea that Indian religions were the work of Satan. One should notice the dreadful consequences of this ideocentric perspective throughout the colonial period. Las Casas was a man of his time, and it is inappropriate to try to make him into a man of our era through an interpretation that transmutes him into a sort of modern relativist anthropologist.

29. The preexisting elite of Peru, Sempat Assadourian says, by 1567 had a reason to identify with Las Casas's project: It was "akin to the lifestyles of the elite, to their preeminence and ancient authority, and to their ideas about the prestige and functions that corresponded to them, even as subjects of the Catholic king." Sempat Assadourian, "Los señores étnicos y los corregidores," p. 67.

30. Borah, *El juzgado general de indios*, p. 41.

31. Israel, *Razas, Clases sociales*, p. 25.

32. Patricia Nettel, *La utopía franciscana en la Nueva España: El apostolado de fray Gerónimo de Mendieta*, Mexico City, Universidad Autónoma de México–Xochimilco, 1989,

pp. 18 and 27. The same complaints that the priests expressed about the colonial government's politics vis-à-vis the Indians in New Spain beginning in 1560 were voiced in Peru by the orders' provincial priests; cf. Sempat Assadourian, "Los señores étnicos y los corregidores," pp. 37–38.

33. On this outlook, see chap. 4.

34. Borah, *El juzgado general de indios,* p. 40.

35. Among the more characteristic features of Indianist law Ots Capdequí notes an "assimilating and uniformist tendency." He explains: "From the metropolis there were attempts, first by the monarchs of the House of Austria and even more by those of the House of Bourbon, to structure the legal life of these territories with a uniformist vision, to assimilate them to the old peninsular conceptions." J. M. Ots Capdequí, *El estado español en las Indias,* Mexico City, Fondo de Cultura Económica, 1986, p.12.

36. "During the rule of Philip II, the conception of a territory and society founded on economic utility was imposed on the Indies, whereby what was 'useful' for the royal estate was identified with what was 'fair' for the Indians. Because of this false consciousness, there was no place in the gradual construction of the colonial state for the prestige and power of the native nobles." Sempat Assadourian, "Las señores étnicos y corregidores," p. 85.

37. In some regions the native nobility was able to remain throughout the colonial period but with reduced powers. In New Spain, the cases of Tlaxcala and the Valley of Oaxaca illustrate these special situations. Charles Gibson, *Tlaxcala en el siglo XVI,* Mexico City, Fondo de Cultura Económica, 1991; and William Taylor, "Cacicazgos coloniales en el Valle de Oaxaca," *Historia Mexicana,* 20, no. 1, July-September 1970.

38. What Gibson says about central Mexico is essentially true for the other regions of New Spain: "The Spanish favored, with privileges and honors, those indigenous rulers who cooperated, reinforcing their positions, confirming their titles, and approving of their possession of land and vassals. The caciques and *principales* showed an open disposition toward this favoritism and asked for benefits. . . . The favors bestowed by kings and viceroys allowed caciques and *principales* to carry swords and fire weapons, to dress Spanish-style, to ride horses or mules with saddle and bridle, or to show their rank within indigenous society in some other way." Gibson, *Los aztecas bajo el dominio español,* pp. 157–158.

39. In relation to the *repartimiento* of indigenous workers, for example, S. Zavala and M. Castelo (*Fuentes para la historia del trabajo en Nueva España,* 2nd edition, Mexico City, Centro de Estudias Históricas y Sociales del Movimiento Obrero, 1980) have compiled materials illustrating the harsh punishment of the indigenous authorities. In a "Notice" in volume 3, they write: "If the Indian rulers and *principales* do not allot the number of workers required of their villages, they suffer penalties including imprisonment. . . . When they do not bring the required number, the constables in charge of assembling workers are forced to perform the task in their place."

40. In Peru the viceroy and other high officials held that "the ethnic nobles were the actual plunderers of the Indians" and that their power should be limited; the archbishop made similar assertions. Sempat Assadourian, "Los señores étnicos y los corregidores," pp. 29 and 69. In New Spain from 1551 on the archbishop complained about the excessive power of the friars over the native authorities. Also, tribute was imposed on the traditional nobles in 1563 when Jerónimo de Valderrama visited; see Nettel, *La utopía franciscana,* pp. 67–68.

41. E.g., *Archivo General de la Nación,* Mexico City, Hospital de Jesús, docket 450, dossier 1, pp. 1–11v, in which *macehuales* complain of the cacique's abuses.

42. Gibson, *Los aztecas bajo el dominio español*, p. 158.

43. This happened, for example, during the Indian rebellions of 1660 in Oaxaca. See Hector Díaz Polanco (ed.), *El fuego de la inobediencia: Autonomía y rebelión en el Obispado de Oaxaca*, Mexico City, Centro de Investigaciones Superiores en Antropología Social, 1992, pp. 67–68.

44. Karen Spalding, "Los escaladores sociales: Patrones cambiantes de movilidad en la sociedad andina bajo el régimen colonial," in *De indio a campesino*, Lima, Instituto de Estudios Peruanos, 1974, p. 86.

45. Spalding, "Los escaladores sociales," p. 81.

46. García, *Documentos inéditos*, pp. 423–424. The Inquisition branch of the Archivo General de la Nación, Mexico City, includes many proceedings against practices considered pagan or sinful that were undoubtedly part of the native sociocultural system.

47. For an analysis of devotion to saints as a strategy for rearranging communal identity among the colonial Yucatec Mayas, see Nancy M. Farris, *La sociedad maya bajo el dominio colonial: La empresa colectiva de la supervivencia*, Madrid, Alianza Editorial, 1992, chap. 11.

48. The Augustinians, for example, showed a lack of interest in the indigenous population at that time and preferred to live in the comfortable convents of the Spanish cities. "The growth of the order and its criollization had radically transformed the situation that had emerged from the evangelizing done during the sixteenth century." Antonio Rubial García, *Una monarquía criolla: La provincia agustina en el siglo XVII*, Mexico City, CNCA, Mexico, 1990, p. 69.

49. Motolinía tells how the friars "took into their homes the children of the lords and *principales*." The children "received the good doctrine in such a good way that they taught it to others. Besides, they helped a great deal because they revealed, for the friars, the rites and idolatries and many secrets of their parents' ceremonies." Motolinía, *Historia de los indios de la Nueva España*, pp. 19 and 182.

50. David A. Brading, *Mineros y comerciantes en el México borbónico (1763–1810)*, Mexico City, Fondo de Cultura Económica, 1983, p. 46.

51. Israel, *Razas, clases sociales*, p. 58.

52. Martínez Peláez, *La patria del criollo*, pp. 222–223.

53. For example, the bishop of Oaxaca under Juan de Palafox y Mendoza, the criollo Alonso de Cuevas Dávalos, was a defender of the Indians who sullenly faced the magistrates and members of the royal tribunal. In 1660, in contradiction to the viceroy himself, he backed the rebellious Chontal, Huave, Mixe, and Zapotec Indians of his jurisdiction before the king. A. de Cuevas Dávalos, "Informe del Obispo de Oaxaca," *Archivo General de Indias*, Seville, México 600, pp. 124v–148v. (Included in Díaz Polanco and Manzo, *Documentos sobre las rebeliones indias*, doc. 11–33, pp. 108–139.)

54. Farris, *La sociedad maya*, pp. 236–237.

55. It was exceptional for several villages and their subjects to be bestowed upon a single *encomendero*. Such was the case of the marquisate awarded to Cortés. François Chevalier, "El Marquesado del Valle: Reflejos medievales," *Historia Mexicana*, 1, no. 1, July-September 1951.

56. Gibson, *Los aztecas bajo el dominio español;* Farris, *La sociedad maya* pp. 238–239. Pedro Carrasco notes that in Mesoamerica the Spanish divided kingdoms and empires, and the seigniories that constituted them "were turned into social units of the indigenous groups in such a way that their social solidarity was fragmented and limited to the level of the local community or, as it was called, the Indian republic." Pedro Carrasco, "La transfor-

mación de la cultura indígena durante la colonia," in B. García Martínez (ed.), *Los pueblos de indios y las comunidades,* Mexico City, El Colegio de México, 1991, p.4.

57. Francisco G. Hermosillo, "Indios en cabildo: Historia de una historiografía sobre la Nueva España," *Historias,* no. 26, 1991, p. 39.

58. Such was the case of the nobles of Tehuantepec, who managed to maintain their influence beyond the township's capital. In 1661 the robed judge sent by the viceroy to punish the rebel Indians found that this dominion had survived and of course recommended its immediate elimination. The clarity with which the judge understood the value of political and ethnic fragmentation is surprising: "I have also noticed another great inconvenience that requires an effective solution for the tranquillity and public order of these provinces; in some of them the governors of the capitals are governors of the whole province and command all of the Indians in it, which is not our aim, especially during these days, [because it would not be easy for the governor to rule] when not all the towns are under his authority, because they would not be compelled to obey him and thus each town would have its own judgment." J. F. de Montemayor de Cuenca, "Copia del despacho hecho al señor virrey," *Archivo General de Indias,* Seville, México 600, no page number. (Included in Díaz Polanco and Manzo, *Documentos sobre las rebeliones,* document II-50 pp. 183–184).

59. The capital town of Tlapa, studied by Dehouve, for example, had six subjects by 1579 and by the end of the eighteenth century had turned into some sixty scattered towns. Danièle Dehouve, "Las separaciones de pueblos en la región de Tlapa (siglo XVIII)" in various authors, *Los pueblos de indios y las comunidades,* p. 104.

60. K. Spalding, "La red desintegrante," in *De indio a campesino,* pp. 115 and 121.

61. Such was the situation in New Spain: "By 1519, south of the Chichimec border, aside from a small number of urban concentrations there was peasants' land. They lived close to their fields in single units or in places with just a few houses." Peter Gerhard, "Congregaciones de indios en la Nueva España antes de 1570," *Historia Mexicana,* 26 no. 3, January-March 1977, p. 348.

62. P. Gerhard, "La evolución del pueblo rural mexicano: 1519–1975," *Historia Mexicana,* 24, no. 4, April-June 1975, p. 572.

63. Hermosillo, *"Indios en cabildo,"* p. 29. Especially during the sixteenth century, traditional chiefs in several areas managed to retain their influence in the council through kin or political contacts. Nevertheless, with time the council won preeminence over traditional government almost everywhere. See, for example, Juan Manuel Pérez Zevallos, "El gobierno indígena colonial en Xochimilco (16th century)," *Historia Mexicana,* 33, no. 4, April-June 1984, pp. 456–457.

64. Hermosillo, *"Indios en cabildo,"* p. 35. From the seventeenth century on, occupation became the source of authority and prestige in the community.

65. José María Ots Capdequi, "Apuntes para la historia del municipio hispanoamericano del período colonial," *Anuario de Historia de América,* 1, 1924, pp. 93–126.

66. The terms *alcalde mayor* and *corregidor* were applied in the New World to the same regional official. The former was favored in New Spain, especially in the seventeenth century, and the latter in the viceroyalty of Peru. Carlos Molina Argüello, "Gobernaciones, alcaldías mayores y corregimientos en el reino de Guatemala," *Anuario de Estudios Americanos,* 17, 1960, p. 107.

67. Alberto Yalí Román, "Sobre alcaldías mayores y corregimientos en Indias: Un ensayo de interpretación," *Jahrbuch für Geschichte von Staat, Wirtschaft und Gesellschaft Lateinamerikas*, 9, 1972, pp. 18–19.

68. Rodolfo Pastor, "El repartimiento de mercancías y los alcaldes mayores novohispanos: Un sistema de explotación, de sus orígenes a la crisis de 1810," in Woodrow Borah (ed.), El gobierno provincial en la Nueva España (1570–1787), Mexico City, Instituto de Investigaciones Históricas–Universidad Nacional Autónoma de México, 1985, pp. 201–202.

69. See W. Borah, "El gobernador novohispano (alcalde mayor/corregidor): Consecución del puesto y aspectos económicos," in Borah, *El gobierno provincial en la Nueva España (1570–1787)*, pp. 37–38.

70. Sempat Assadourian has observed that the indolence of the state with regard to the governors' activities was due to "the fact that this intermediate ruling apparatus in ethnic territory became one of the most important factors of peasant mobilization for mercantile production and had a great influence on the development of the mercantile system. This element must be the central reference in analyzing the role of the *corregidores* within colonial power systems." Sempat Assadourian, "Dominio colonial y señores étnicos," p. 15.

71. Borah summarizes: "In practice, of course, the separation was impossible to achieve because the Spanish needs for tribute and labor required considerable and constant contact between them and the Indians, with the result that, even if the two groups remained in separate settlements, there could be no real isolation. Actually, there was considerable exchange, since many Spanish established themselves in the Indian towns to open up businesses and look after their properties, and a large number of Indians were attracted into Spanish homes as permanent and semipermanent workers." Borah, *El juzgado general de indios*, p. 44.

72. This must not, however, be interpreted in such a way as to make the Indian a colonial phenomenon, since present-day ethnic groups are also the product of processes that took place during the nineteenth century and are still ongoing within the framework of the various nation-states. Therefore, although it has an obvious historical origin, the so-called ethnic question is a fully contemporary issue.

CHAPTER FOUR

■

Indigenism After Independence

I have examined the social, economic, and political circumstances that conditioned the new dominant groups' attitudes vis-à-vis the diverse and protean sociocultural landscape framed by the emerging nation-state. I shall now analyze the ideological sources that nourished the homogenizing policy of the nineteenth century, with its serious socioeconomic implications, the integrationism that followed the Mexican Revolution, and, finally, the situation of recent decades.

THE LIBERALS' LIQUIDATIONIST INDIGENISM

The establishment of an independent nation-state created new conditions that led to a policy of suppression of ethnic diversity (some scholars call it "incorporation"). This indigenist perspective was a response to the urgency of consolidating the positions of the emergent economic groups as a new foundation for the political system and was founded upon a critique of the divisiveness of "caste" and the dangerous potential of any "corporateness" within the nation. This policy developed in several Latin American countries influenced by liberal thought.

The ideological sources of criollo liberalism can be found in the positivism and evolutionism in vogue at the time in the metropolitan countries. European thought, stemming from the rationalist optimism of the Age of Enlightenment, in the nineteenth century embraced a one-sided positivist sociology and an evolutionist anthropology, both determined to identify the necessary laws of human progress. The other great European tendency, German romantic historicism, which exalted relativism, plurality, and the values of popular culture,[1] did not meet with comparable success in the American countries until much later, filtered through the culturalist school of North American anthropology.[2]

Evolutionism held that human society had passed through certain necessary and sequentially ordered stages on an ascending scale. Advancement through that evolutionary line expressed the fulfillment of the *laws of progress* that writers such as Claude-Henri de Saint-Simon and Auguste Comte, on philosophical and sociological grounds, and Lewis H. Morgan, from an anthropological perspective, sought to establish.[3] By the mid-nineteenth century, faith in *progress*[4] had become the predominant mind-set among the bourgeoisie of the advanced Western European countries and also influenced an important sector of the Latin American intelligentsia. Evolutionism, especially in the positivist form elaborated by Comte, spread throughout "the ruling groups and intellectuals of almost all the continent's nations—Chile, Argentina, Peru, Brazil (whose national flags exhibit the motto "Order and Progress," etc.). . . and, on occasion, there were serious attempts to realize its directives."[5]

The evolutionist perspective offered a convenient rationale for the homogenizing tendencies of the Latin American elites, viewing indigenous ethnic communities as primitive societies representing stages of "savagery" or "barbarism" compared with the Western capitalist system, which was regarded as the crystallization of the last phase of human development, "civilization."[6] National leaders thought that if history expressed a rational development subject to laws and manifest in homogeneous, inevitable, and necessary human progress (and there was no doubt that it did), then all societies—including the indigenous ones—should strive to emulate the Western model.

Thus, in turn, the sociocultural complexes of indigenous ethnic groups were viewed, as a whole, as an expression of "backwardness." It was thought that their culture was responsible for their failure to advance toward civilization. It was no surprise, therefore, that liberal governments established a policy of including Indians in national life but without their cultural characteristics. Indigenist policy in this case was liquidationist and, as such, ethnocidal.[7] In this period the objective was not to obstruct any kind of autonomy for the surviving indigenous ethnic groups but to transform their very existence. Incorporation into the nation became incompatible with the possession of characteristics that shaped an identity different from the criollo-mestizo one then being formed. The solution to "the problem" of the Indians was their disappearance as differentiated identities.[8] Indians were to become merely members of the national society, without any exemption or "privilege." In the legal-political field, they were proclaimed "citizens" and formally equal vis-à-vis the law as part of a sustained effort to erase the Indian from the national horizon.[9]

The destructive effects of the liberal initiatives for most of the indigenous communities can best be observed in the arena of socioeconomic policy. Indian towns were supposed to enter into a system of free competition and adopt the principles of profit and private property. To achieve this goal, it was necessary to modify the communal subsistence base of these ethnic groups. Liberals considered these ethnic communities civil corporations that hindered the free flow of property. Thus, while during the colonial regime Indians' access to private property was restricted (disregarding the particular cases of traditional nobles and *principales* and the later Bourbonist measures), during this period there was intense pressure to privatize communal land, and Indians were ordered to turn their collective possessions into private property.

In the Mexican case, the large-scale alienation of indigenous communal lands occurred simultaneously with the "disentailment" of the property of the ecclesiastical corporations. The monopolistic estate of the Catholic church, the largest landholder in the country and the major credit bank, was equated under the law with the communal lands of the impoverished Indian communities. The Lerdo Law of June 25, 1856, forced "corporations" to sell their land, favoring those who were leasing it.[10] Although this law constitutes a landmark, it must be understood, as Knowlton has observed, as part of a process that began at the end of the colonial regime and continued through the first decades of independence: "There were legal precedents during the last colonial stage, as well as in some national and state laws subsequent to independence, particularly regarding the lands of Indian towns. Besides, the Lerdo Law was not unique in Mexico's history regarding urban municipal property."[11] The immediate effect of this legislation was the massive dispossession of many ethnic communities of their land which was often then leased to individuals in order to meet community needs that were not being satisfied by the central state.[12]

Lands not being leased could be claimed by individuals and then appropriated according to the legal purchase procedure (article 11). Often this procedure was carried out in complicity with the government officials who implemented the law. The political authorities and the judges were key players in the schemes employed for the dispossession of the indigenous people. Powell mentions that many officials "connived with hacienda owners and speculators to strip the Indians of their lands, preventing them from learning about the Lerdo Law until they themselves had claimed and bought the lands in question."[13]

Plunder and excess did not end during the conservative interlude: The law affecting the clergy was annulled, but the one affecting indigenous people was left in force. Similarly, during the ephemeral empire of Maximilian, abuse of the Indians did not end despite its Board of Protection for the Needy Classes, which was impotent in the face of *hacendados* and officials and therefore practically ineffective. The communities' demands for justice were not satisfied. There were indigenous peasant riots and uprisings (such as those in the state of Hidalgo during 1869–1870), but they lacked the strength and articulation to eliminate legal abuses.

The irony of this historical period is that a movement that recommended small landholdings instead encouraged the already persistent latifundium and even larger monopolies, the formation of which was the most significant result of the measures against indigenous communities.[14] The group that seized power during the authoritarian lapse called the Porfiriato (1870–1910), openly advocating a vernacular version of positivism ("freedom, order, and progress"), carried the work begun by their predecessors of the Reform period to its conclusion, thus stimulating considerable indigenous resistance. Latifundia spread and became general as the dominant economic nucleus in rural society.

The extreme actions undertaken by the liberal regimes caused the dissolution of many communities. Moreover, the practice of nineteenth-century governments—the labor regime they imposed, the criollo-mestizo cultural patterns they actively promoted, the contempt for Indian values they demonstrated—undoubtedly influenced peoples' ethnicity. But the ethnic identity of numerous groups, whose members added up to millions, was not altered. At the end of the Porfiriato the indigenous population of Mexico was still considerable: At least one of every three Mexicans considered him/herself indigenous. The great popular revolution that shattered the country's foundations during the second decade of the twentieth century recognized the reality of the surviving Indian communities.

INTEGRATIONIST INDIGENISM: FROM ETHNOCIDE TO ETHNOPHAGY

During the first Interamerican Indigenist Congress, which took place in Mexico (in Pátzcuaro, Michoacán) in 1940,[15] contemporary integrationist indigenism assumed its identity and adopted its theoretical orientation. According to Gonzalo Aguirre Beltrán, one of the major proponents of this perspective, integrationism aimed at "correcting" the ethnocentric ideas of the previous policy and introducing "an element of social justice" into indigenist policy. The components of indigenous cultures (languages, beliefs, customs, sociopolitical organizational forms, etc.) were, in principle, accepted as valid: The policy was to be "integration of the Indians into national society, respecting their values, cultures, and human dignity."

Therefore, in contrast to the previous liberal-evolutionist position, this indigenism accepted the compatibility of integration of indigenous people into national life and conservation of their cultural foundations. The new policy advocated the integration of the Indians, with their cultural baggage, into the national society, providing them with the necessary tools of civilization for their articulation within that society.[16] The proposed policy did not include the elimination of autochthonous culture; there was a demonstration of respect for indigenous cultures, and at the same time "communities were invited to invest their own efforts to achieve their own betterment and their integration into the nation so that they effectively become a part of it."[17]

Was integrationism successful in Latin America? There is every indication that it was not. Certainly it achieved notable results, but none of them guaranteed the original goal of integrating ethnic groups into the national society at the same time as respecting their sociocultural specificities. On the contrary, this indigenism left behind it a tragic trail of cultural dissolution, destruction of identities, political repression, and ethnic-national conflict.

Integrationist indigenism contained a serious contradiction from the beginning. Seeking to overcome the difficulties of the previous evolutionist policy and to avoid the charges of ethnocentrism and ethnocide that had been leveled at it (clearly incompatible with the postulates of equality, democracy, and social justice it proclaimed),[18] indigenists resorted to the principles of another anthropological theory: cultural relativism, an influential perspective originating in North America, where it had displaced the diachronic-evolutionary perspective favored by Latin American scholars.

Relativism or culturalism was based on the vehement rejection of the idea of linear sequences and of the application of the normative criteria of superiority and inferiority in the analysis of cultural systems. Inspired by a romantic historicism, culturalism posited different cultures but not higher or lower ones arguing that to envision what is different (e.g., the Indian ethnic groups) as inferior inevitably led to the most deplorable ethnocentrism.[19] But this position, carried to its logical extreme, presupposed respect for different cultural systems; that is, it encouraged the free development of societies without intervention by another that considered itself superior. This encouragement was contrary to the integrating purposes that had always inspired anthropologists and indigenist officials.

Integrationists did not wish to abandon the goal of "including" the Indians in national society. The most lucid of them perceived the conflict between the relativist postulate of unconditional respect for ethnic groups and the need to integrate them into national society. What began as a mere obstacle turned into an open contradiction until culturalism was rejected and its major tenets abandoned. Ironically, the so-called classical indigenisms had to return to the foundations of the old unilinear evolutionism.

Of the congress at Pátzcuaro, Aguirre Beltrán wrote,

> The postulates of cultural relativism that demand respect for cultures under siege were taken seriously, but in order that the proposed integration not become sterile [it was necessary to adopt, as] an additional principle, that of social justice, establishing a charter of rights and obligations for the Indians without any discriminating barriers derived from racial, social, and cultural differences.[20] [Indigenists felt that Indians had to be integrated so that they could have access to better living conditions, abandoning certain aspects of their cultures "incompatible" with civilization and modernity. Indigenists defined this incompatibility from the position of power provided by the state.[21] Thus the ethnocentrism to be overcome was reestablished.]

Indigenists attempted to forge an agreement between contradictory theoretical sources, separating the positive aspects of indigenous cultures (therefore compatible with civilization) from others that should disappear because they were contrary to progress and nation building. The determination of this "positive" or "negative" character lay in the hands of these indigenists. But the problematic distinction provided by Manuel Gamio[22] did not prevent the assimilationist tendency from gradually taking over.

Integrationism was increasingly forced toward the evolutionist postulates that had served as a basis for the policies of the liberals. The school of indigenist thought that proposed respect for ethnic cultural features eventually vanished in practical terms. According to Aguirre Beltrán,

> Cultural relativism. . . dogmatically considered calls the ideas of progress and evolution into question; it supports the need to evaluate each culture in its own context rather than that of Western civilization, which is ethnocentric and supposedly higher. According to that point of view, indigenous cultures are considered not backward but simply different responses to existential problems and should be respected and understood. . . . However, the pluralist thesis sterilizes indigenist action, since it removes the foundations for its intervention as a movement intended to modify an undesirable situation. As a matter of fact, if Indian cultures represent not surviving groups in the evolutionary sequence but finished products of different evolutionary lines, there is no reason to seek their modernization, since they are modern cultures but distinct from modern Western culture.[23]

What this statement implies is that "Indian cultures" are surviving forms (socioculturally "backward" or "barbaric" forms, in the words of the liberals) and not simply different systems but unfinished structures that must be modernized, societies that, as the incorporationists asserted, had to be pushed toward "progress."

The outcome was that integrationism converted its original relativist content into ideological discourse (in the very ostentatious ideological facade of the inter-American indigenist system) while it based its practice on an evolutionism that imputed superiority to all aspects of the so-called national culture. To reinforce this practice, integrationism made use of the technical-scientific arsenal (community study, systems analysis, field techniques, and so on) offered by the structural-functionalist school of thought. Taking this alchemy into account, this indigenism was formed not as an anthropological theory proper but as an eclectic synthesis of elements from evolutionism, cultural relativism, and structural-functionalism that was offered as a solution for the "undesirable" ethnic heterogeneity of a number of Latin American countries.[24]

Integrationism thus constituted officially became the indigenist policy of the Latin American nation states. Its success was such that it soon became an internationally accepted approach to the solution of the "tribal" and indigenous "problem." For example, the International Labor Conference adopted two documents in 1957: an Indigenous and Tribal Populations Convention (No. 107), and a Recommendation (No. 104). Convention No. 107 of the International Labor Organization (ILO) explicitly accepted the basic postulates of integrationism, giving governments an international basis for their homogenizing policies. In 1988 the ILO formulated an explicit criticism of the integrationist perspective of its Convention No. 107 and reassessed it.[25] The result was Convention No. 169 "on indigenous and tribal peoples in independent countries."[26]

Equipped with a rationalizing discourse in which relativist concepts remained merely rhetorical, governments created the conditions for dismantling every aspect of indigenous cultures that, according to the indigenists, was incompatible with the strategic foundations of national culture. In practice, these incompatible aspects were the majority of the elements that defined ethnic identities. Originally, integrationists considered autochthonous languages as deserving of respect, but very soon there were educational programs throughout the continent aimed at promoting uniformity in the use of the Spanish language without any respect for Indian languages, claiming that their purpose was to foster national unity. The few "cultural features" that were truly respected were visible rather than essential aspects and were transformed into objects of folkloric curiosity or subjected to a ferocious political manipulation and commercialization that ended up demeaning the Indians.

In the integrationist dialectic, the synthesis did not presume to abandon evolutionist and centralist theses. Rather, they appeared in a different guise, and this brought about an important modification in indigenist policies. Integrationist indigenism was the beginning of a new approach to the Indian "problem" that must be evaluated from the point of view of the dominant homogenizing ideology. The Latin American states after the Great Depression began seeking legitimacy on a different level, utilizing principles of social justice. Within this context, crudely ethnocidal practices were inappropriate, especially for regimes such as the Mexican one that claimed to have emerged from popular movements. Thus, integrationism became a useful focus in that it facilitated the transition from openly ethnocidal practices to a complex strategy that I shall call "ethnophagic." Programs and actions explicitly geared toward the destruction of the indigenous ethnic groups' cultures were abandoned and replaced by a long-term project that relied upon the assimilating effects of the multiple forces put into play by the dominant national culture.

The integration of indigenous peoples was promoted by indirect means as the state and various institutions sought to attract ethnic groups to patterns and values they considered national. What I call ethnophagy is this broad process whereby the culture of domination sought to devour the multiple popular cultures. Their destruction was pursued not by means of any absolute denial of or violent attack on other identities but by means of attraction, seduction and transformation. Indigenist policy was less a series of direct attacks on what was different than a collection of sociocultural magnets deployed by the nation-state and the hegemonic apparatuses to attract, disarticulate, and dissolve groups that were different.[27]

The state can pursue its ethnophagic project while manifesting respect for or indifference to diversity or in the course of exalting indigenous values. To achieve this, it reinforces its domination via hegemony and consensus. Under these circumstances the state may appear to be the guarantor or defender of indigenous values, especially when it is called upon to mitigate the effects of savage capitalism or confront the harsh ethnocidal methods of recalcitrant sectors that do not understand the subtleties of ethnophagy. Indigenist officials often point to their role as defenders of Indians in confrontations with local extremist caciques or governors, but only a few seem to recognize that their own activity leads to the destruction of their object of concern.

The participation of members of ethnic groups is sought for the promotion of the nation-state's policy, all the more effective when it is "of their own will," convinced of the national culture's superiority. This is what is meant by attracting communities "to invest their own efforts to achieve their own betterment and their integration into the nation" (Aguirre Beltrán). It was expected that the Indians themselves, especially their leaders, would abandon and encourage others to abandon their languages, beliefs, customs, particular organizational forms, and so on, noting the advantages that would accrue. Indian leaders were expected to be not indigenous intellectuals but proponents of official indigenism. It was a strategy that operated as a fifth column.

With integrationism, ethnophagy became the fundamental assimilation strategy for many Latin American nation-states, although previous practices persisted as well. Neither genocide nor ethnocide was completely abandoned. Historically, genocidal practices predominated during the colonial period, especially during the phase of conquest and "pacification." But these outbreaks, lasting throughout colonial consolidation (approximately until the end of the sixteenth century in some regions of New Spain), combined with primarily ethnocidal actions as the colonial regime advanced. Similarly, the ethnocide that was prevalent during the liquidationist stage was accompanied by occasional genocide. During the period of hegemonic integrationism, depending on the moment and the locale there were episodes of genocide (for example, against the Amazonian communities and the indigenous peoples of Guatemala, particularly at the beginning of the 1980s), as well as clearly ethnocidal projects and programs (e.g., those promoting the Spanish language). However, the integrationist period can best be characterized by the increasing prominence of ethnophagy as an assimilation strategy, with different rhythms and degrees of development in various regions.

Integrationism performed its theoretical-political role as a preparatory and transitional phase toward more elaborate forms of ethnophagy. By the end of the 1960s the assumptions of integrationism were in crisis, but the strengthening of ethnic cohesion and of indigenous struggles that were at once the cause and the effect of that crisis did not weaken the state's resolve. What made governments begin to question integrationism was the erosion of their discourse for crediting ethnophagy and their way of achieving it. Facing the challenging perspectives within the Indian movement that were quite general by mid–1970s, the state responded with a discourse (ethnicism) and a praxis (ethnopopulism) of renewed indigenist character corresponding to the new threats to the continued use of ethnophagic methods. Thus it can be said that ethnopopulism making use of ethnicist issues is a higher level of ethnophagy.

ETHNICISM: FOUNDATION OF A
NEW INDIGENISM

The absence of counterhegemonic and democratizing political projects adopting a global perspective on the ethnic-national question in Latin America is today's most serious deficiency. Ethnicism or Fourth Worldism has become the most effective of the political-ideological tools used the by dominant classes in Latin America to guarantee hegemony over the indigenous movement. Veiled by statements supposedly oriented toward the defense of indigenous rights, ethnicism was for a time presented as the "progressive" alternative to the old integrationist indigenism. This confused even some sectors of the Latin American left, which declared certain ethnicist intellectuals and spokespersons the most "advanced" in the indigenous movement and uncritically took up some of their projects. Only recently has the true political character of the ethnicist perspective become apparent in its entirety; for example, some of the think tanks utilized by the state and the capitalists in their efforts to manipulate the indigenous movement have begun to codify ethnicist discourse in the context of a Fourth World political theory. These think tanks undertook research and analysis that were supposedly academic and unbiased but had a strongly ideological slant. During the 1980s, in the United States, think tanks were close to the circles of power and sought to influence public opinion and political decisions, coming to be considered "a sixth power in the U.S. political scheme."[28] Disquieting evidence came to light that the activities of certain Fourth Worldist organizations supposedly interested in the defense of ethnic rights in Latin America were part of the political-military strategy known as "low-intensity warfare." Scholars, Indian leaders, and regional indigenous organizations called attention to and denounced their participation.[29]

The elaborations of this indigenist line[30] are not oriented

> toward the definition of the basis of a national project for change—in which the legitimate demands of the sociocultural groups with different identities might find solutions—but toward a unilateral delineation of the elements of an indigenous project 'of their own,' an ethnic project. This is presented as a separate and independent proposal and also as counterposed to any counterhegemonic national or 'Western' initiative.[31]

Whereas integrationism, seeking to foreground national dynamics, ended up underrating plurality and reinstalling a disguised evolutionist ethnocentrism, paradoxically, ethnicism resorts to an extreme culturalism to emphasize plurality and thereby loses touch with the national dimension.

Furthermore, as I have pointed out elsewhere,[32] the indigenous intelligentsia and some anthropologists have attributed the ethnicist position's considerable impact on indigenous communities to its reflection of these communities' values and consciousness. From this perspective, ethnicism is a theoretical formalization of an opaque, naive, and mystified vision raised to the level of "political project," a cunning exploitation of spontaneous Indian consciousness. The ethnicist does not perform the task that Gramsci assigns intellectuals,[33] that is, constructing from social conditions a theoretical-political scheme capable of critically capturing the complexity of a given moment and suggesting a historical utopia that overcomes them. Rather, they convert the most elementary ingredients of ethnopopular perception (a mixture of deaf rancor, inverted ethnocentrism, a tendency toward withdrawal, autistic fantasies, the search for solutions in the past, and so on) into a political theory that results in not only an arbitrary and paralyzing utopia but also all kinds of obstacles to the coordination of the struggles of ethnic communities and other social forces interested against the national arrangement that is the basis for sociocultural discrimination and the promoter of the ethnophagic process.

From the writings of several representatives of this school of thought, the following list of assumptions leading to the proposal of an "ethnic" project can be constructed:

1: An opposition between "Western world" and "indigenous world" is posited, and the former is rejected. This inverted ethnocentrism asserts the cultural superiority of the indigenous world. The Western world is conceptualized as homogeneous and undifferentiated, disregarding its diversity and class composition.

2: A "Western" character is attributed to the nation and to national cultures and repudiated.

3: Contrary to the historical record, an unchanging ethnic essence is articulated as the necessary basis for the continuity of indigenous societies.

4: A "primary contradiction" is identified between Indian civilization and the West. The conclusion is unavoidable: The problem and the solution are outside the nation; a "Western-style revolution" is not the answer.

5: The view that the only solution to this contradiction is outside the Western-national context is translated into the proposal of an independent "Indian project."[34]

This synopsis (varying in detail and emphases) illustrates how ethnicism sidesteps many of the fundamental aspects of the complex ethnic-national question and reduces it to a simplistic Manichaean evaluation of the intricate and contradictory composition, organization, functioning, and dynamics of the total system in which ethnic groups are situated. This ideology imagines that indigenous people inhabit a "world apart" and proposes a Fourth World that can find its own solutions. But it is precisely this extreme simplicity that ensures the strong appeal of ethnicism, at first contact, for many indigenous people. It is therefore not surprising that many indigenous people wake up to the consciousness of their own identity under the influence of ethnicist topics as they put a set of easily manageable oppositions into play. It is equally understandable, however, that many of these indigenous people abandon ethnicist positions once they reach a certain degree of development of the consciousness that ethnicism itself has helped to arouse, that is, once a global perspective and critical discernment have achieved a certain maturity. Ethnicists have made ambiguous declarations about the "ethnic" project but have not specified the conditions, premises, and political resources for accomplishing it. "Politicized" Indians recognize the limitations that ethnicism imposes on analysis and potential action.

At times the state is comfortable with ethnicist discourse, especially its renunciation of "Western-style revolutionary action." The conceptual opposition of indigenous versus Western prevents the concerted action by allies in the two worlds that is required for the development of an alternative to the contemporary expansion of ethnophagy. Latin American governments are not only adopting ethnicist discourse and style but also including outstanding ethnicist ideologues in their makeup. These ethnicists advocate and coordinate the practice of ethnopopulism that supports the new ethnophagic phase of indigenism.

THE ETHNIC-NATIONAL QUESTION
AND SOCIAL CHANGE

Despite the considerable influence of ethnicism on the Latin American indigenous movement, there is a serious lack of consideration of the ethnic-national question within the majority of the continent's progressive organizations. Encouraging new orientations seem to be developing in the context of demands for autonomy, as we shall see in the following chapter, but a significant degree of fragmentation and sectarianism, a disdain for the concerns of indigenous communities, and a lack of knowledge and doctrinairism remain. The ethnic-national question is simply overlooked, subsumed by older integrationist sentiments, or analyzed in an indigenist framework.

Revolutionary marxism in Latin America is still dependent upon a doctrinaire tradition that stems from the elaborations of its founding fathers, especially Marx and Engels. Although they were interested in national and ethnic phenomena and made contributions on the subject that cannot be ignored,[35] they started out with the premise of an imminent proletarian revolution. From this perspective, logically, the problematic of ethnic groups and oppressed nationalities was always considered secondary in theoretical terms in Marx and Engels's work. It was assumed that the ethnic-national question would be resolved more or less quickly in the context of the new socialist society. In brief, the treatment of the "national question" by these intellectuals was more a casuistry (reflecting the Polish, Irish, and other situations) than a formal theoretical-political perspective. Marx and Engels expected a gradual homogenization of societies (begun by capitalism and completed by socialism) that would eliminate borders and ethnic-national identities.[36]

It is quite clear today that the predicted transformations or simultaneous revolutions of the primary European industrial states, dragging the rest with them, did not take place. National and ethnic divisions, in contrast, have not only per-sisted but grown stronger over time. Either by inertia or by tradition, the doctri-naire point of view that national, ethnic, or sociocultural differences are sec-ondary has endured. Thus, an inadequate conception of the modern nation, its nature and dynamics, and the identity issues within it has become one of the most important pitfalls for contemporary marxist theories of change.

The marxist thesis that capitalism has a tendency to universalize and homoge-nize social relations and sociocultural systems often incorrectly supposes the nec-essary expression of this tendency in every case. This encourages disregard for na-tional specificities and ethnic diversity, fundamental aspects of contemporary reality. Capitalism, in its drive toward homogenization, at once provokes unequal development and produces and reproduces social, political, and cultural particu-larities. The "unequal and combined development" formula prevents the achieve-ment of total sociocultural uniformity, even in cases—such as Mexico—in which governing elites set out to achieve homogeneity as a basis for "national unity." In fact, national unity, a prerequisite for the functioning of the capitalist system, does not require the annulment of every sociocultural particularity; the strategy of "national hegemony" adopted by certain classes or fractions thereof was in-tended to absorb the other classes within the context of the nation.[37] The estab-lishment of such hegemony is a central aspect of the process of nation building and of its maintenance.

Dominant groups have never ignored the sociocultural complexity of national societies; instead, they have made use of it to build their domination, spreading their hegemony over the largest number of sectors, including, of course, the so-called ethnic groups. Ethnic groups do not, however, as is assumed by certain cul-turalist conceptions of traditional anthropology, constitute simple compounds of cultural traits rooted in the past (customs, traditions, forms of social organiza-tion, worldviews, and so on.); rather, they are sociocultural realities constantly created and re-created by capitalism. They cannot be adequately understood without considering the history of the sociopolitical hegemony imposed upon them by the dominant groups.

The strategy of national hegemony

> is not only relevant for the bourgeoisie. Just as the bourgeoisie could not base its
> domination only on the dynamics inherent in its economic infrastructure, the prole-
> tariat would not be able to do it either. . . . The differences within the proletariat and
> the middle classes and other particular interests [including the ethnic] are perma-
> nently reproduced as part of the total system; such is the context of the social classes
> that form national majorities. The question of hegemony is, thus, even for the prole-
> tariat, one of the utmost importance.[38]

Therefore, the construction of an alternative democratic hegemony calls for the definition of a new political project of national scope that includes ethnic demands. Such a project requires more than declarations of support: The parties that advocate change must make the legitimate rights and demands of the indigenous peoples and ethnic communities their own and must specify the nature of the new national structure within which these rights will be effective. This is the minimum platform for possible alliances and consensus with regard to the ethnic question.

NOTES

1. Alvin W. Gouldner, "Romanticismo y clasicismo: Estructuras profundas de la ciencia social," in *La sociología actual: Renovación y crítica*, Madrid, Alianza Universidad, 1979.

2. During the twentieth century it became a secondary ingredient of integrationist indigenism and the main inspiration for ethnicism.

3. On Claude-Henri de Saint-Simon, see *Crítica de la política*, Mexico City, Centro de Documentación Política, 1977. On Auguste Comte, see *Primeros ensayos*, Mexico City, Fondo de Cultura Económica, 1977; *The Positive Philosophy*, New York, AMS Press, 1974; and *A Discourse on the Positive Spirit*, London, Reeves, 1903. Some useful complementary readings are Ghita Ionescu (ed.), *The Political Thought of Saint-Simon*, London and New York, Oxford University Press, 1976; Pierre Ansart, *Sociología de Saint-Simon*, Barcelona, Ediciones Península, 1972; and Francis Sidney Marvin, *Comte*, Mexico City, Fondo de Cultura Económica, 1978. The classic work on the evolution of human society is Lewis H. Morgan, *Ancient Society*, New York, Holt, 1877.

4. For a historical survey of the ideas and theories of progress, see John B. Bury, *The idea of progress*, London, Macmillan, 1920.

5. Hector Díaz Polanco, *Las teorías antropológicas: El evolucionismo*, vol. 1, Mexico City, Editorial Línea, 1983, p. 106. On the vigorous influence of positivist philosophy in Mexico, see Leopoldo Zea, *El positivismo en México: Nacimiento, apogeo y decadencia*, Mexico City, Fondo de Cultura Económica, 1978.

6. See Díaz Polanco, *Las teorías antropológicas*, pt. 3.

7. There are some recorded cases of ethnic liquidation via genocide through direct military operations, for example, the Indian massacres organized by General Julio A. Roca in Patagonia.

8. For an analysis of this phase, see Edgar Barillas, "El 'problema del indio' en la época liberal en Centro América: El caso de Guatemala," in *Folklore Americano*, no. 45, January–June 1988; and Antonio Escobar Ohmstede, "Política indigenista en el México del siglo XIX (1800–1857)," *Papeles de la Casa Chata*, 3, no. 4, 1988.

9. Hale notes: "The most consistent liberal policy sought to erase all of society's legal distinctions and theoretically raise the Indians to the universal category of 'citizens.' However, this theory was equivalent to ignoring the indigenous basis of society in saying, in effect, that Indians no longer existed." Charles H. Hale, *El liberalismo mexicano en la época de Mora (1821–1853)*, 8th edition, Mexico City, Siglo XXI, 1987.

10. The first article of this law read, "Every estate, rural and urban, belonging to or being administered as property by civil or ecclesiastical corporations in the republic will be awarded as property to those who hold the lease on it in exchange for the amount of the rent currently paid, estimated at 6 percent annual interest." Jean Meyer, *Problemas*

campesinos y revueltas agrarias (1821–1910), Mexico City, SepSetentas, 1973, pp. 68–70. The legal procedure allowed the lessee to become a proprietor by paying a reasonable amount.

11. Robert J. Knowlton, "La individualización de la propiedad corporativa civil en el siglo XIX: Notas sobre Jalisco," in Various authors, *Los pueblos de indios y las comunidades*, p. 182.

12. "Throughout the republic, during the summer and fall of 1856, indigenous peoples suffered the catastrophe of losing their rented lands." Powell, *El liberalismo y el campesinado*, p. 77.

13. Ibid., pp. 77–78.

14. With regard to the 1856 law, Meyer notes: "It had the double effect of increasing the size of the haciendas and destroying the common-property lands. In this sense, it can be said that the good economic and political intentions of the liberals only accelerated the development of the latifundium and the ruin of the communities' smallholdings." Meyer, *Problemas campesinos*, p. 68.

15. Among the members of the Mexican delegation to this congress were the most outstanding scholars on indigenous issues, several of whom were also political figures: Luis Chávez Orozco (who presided over the conference), Vicente Lombardo Toledano, Manuel Gamio, Moisés Sáenz, Miguel Othón de Mendizabal, and Alfonso Caso. With them there was a group of younger people, many of whom would become distinguished indigenist intellectuals: Julio de la Fuente, Alfonso Villa, Daniel Rubín de la Borbolla, Gilberto Loyo and Mauricio Magdaleno. Some prominent foreigners, such as Paul Kirchhoff and Mauricio Swadesh, were there as well. Gonzalo Aguirre Beltrán, "Introducción," in Vicente Lombardo Toledano, *El problema del indio*, ed. Marcela Lombardo, Mexico City, SepSetentas, 1973, pp. 38–39.

16. Aguirre Beltrán, "Un postulado de política indigenista," in *Obra polémica*, p. 27.

17. Ibid., p. 28.

18. It is no accident that this new integrationist conception arose in Mexico under the auspices of President Lázaro Cárdenas, who was sincerely interested in improving the living conditions of indigenous peoples.

19. Cf. Mechthild Rutsch, *Las teorías antropológicas: El relativismo cultural*, vol. 2, Mexico City, Editorial Línea, 1984, especially chap. 3.

20. G. Aguirre Beltrán, "Etnocidio en México: Una denuncia irresponsable," in *Obra polémica*, p. 226.

21. According to Aguirre Beltrán, for example, "Indigenism is not a policy formulated by Indians to solve their own problems but a policy of non-Indians regarding the heterogeneous ethnic groups designated as indigenous." Aguirre Beltrán, "Un postulado de política indigenista," pp. 24–25.

22. "Gamio, who originally introduced the formula, asserts that there are positive aspects of Indian cultures that should be kept and noxious features that must be eliminated if the native is to be incorporated into civilization on the road to progress." Aguirre Beltrán, "Introducción," p. 28.

23. Aguirre Beltrán, "Etnocidio en México," pp. 225–226.

24. Integrationism can in fact be characterized as a "pragmatic eclecticism" that takes "what it finds appropriate from the most diverse and dissimilar theories without considering their details." Díaz Polanco, *Etnia, nación y política*, p. 145.

25. International Labor Conference, *Partial revision of the Indigenous and Tribal Populations Convention, 1957 (No. 107)*, Geneva, International Labor Organization, 1988. In this document it was accepted (p. 20) that the adoption of the integrationist principle "as

the basic orientation of Convention No. 107 brought some undesirable consequences." Among them the document mentions its "destructive character, due in part to the way in which it has been interpreted by governments; in practice, it has meant extinction for ways of life different from those of the national society." It is noted further that "practically every person who has commented upon the Agreement during the past few years has asserted that its integrationist focus and its implicit presumption of these groups' cultural inferiority make it a totally archaic tool and disqualify it as a basis for national policies." Actually, these critical comments had already become common some twenty years before. The ILO also considered the recommendations in the report prepared by the UN's specialist; see José R. Martínez Cobo, *Estudio del problema de la discriminación contra las poblaciones indígenas*, E/CN.4/Sub.2/1986/7 and Add. 1 to 3.

26. International Labor Conference, *Provisional records, 76th meeting*, Geneva, International Labor Organization, 1989, pp. 25–28.

27. In linguistics we find the use of glottophagy to understand the phenomena that take place within the colonial process. See, for example, Louis-Jean Calvet, *Lingüística y colonialismo: Breve tratado de glotofagia*, Madrid, Ediciones Júcar, 1981, chap. 3. Calvet differentiates three stages in the development of linguistic colonialism: the first two include various situations of bilingualism and monolingualism, while the third stage is "achieved glottophagy, death for the dominated language, definitely digested by the dominant one" (p. 75). Calvet's glottophagic stages express different aspects of the operation of a single digestive logic. In my concept, ethnophagy is a logic of integration and absorption that corresponds to a particular phase of interethnic relations (and, in this case, of indigenism) and assumes a qualitatively different method of assimilating and devouring other ethnic identities.

28. See, for example, Adolfo Aguilar Zinser, "Los fascinantes think tanks: RAND y Heritage, el sexto poder en EU," in *Jueves de Excélsior*, no. 3504, 1989, pp. 9–12. The elaborations and maneuvers of think tanks specializing in indigenous issues seem to have played a key role in the development of an ethnic line in the strategy of the North American power nuclei, particularly after the Sandinista conflict and the intensification of the Guatemalan insurgency at the beginning of the 1980s. Bernard Nietschmann summarizes his Fourth World theory in "Sandinismo y lukanka india," *Vuelta*, 9, no. 107, October 1985.

29. For example, see the denunciation by the Consejo Indio de Sudamérica (South American Indian Council—CISA)—the regional organ of the Consejo Mundial de Pueblos Indígenas (World Council of Indigenous Peoples—CMPI)—with regard to the activities of certain agencies within the framework of the Nicaraguan ethnic conflict. CISA, "Comunicado," *Indigenous World*, 4, no. 1, 1986. See also Hector Díaz Polanco, "*Neoindigenismo* and the ethnic question in Central America," *Latin American Perspectives*, 14, no. 1, 1987, pp. 87–100.

30. For more on the subject, see CLALI, "Declaración de México," in Various authors, *La cuestión étnico-nacional en América Latina*, Mexico City, Instituto Panamericano de Geografía e Historia, 1984; Pablo González Casanova, *Indios y negros en América Latina*, Mexico City, Universidad Nacional Autónoma de México, 1979; Díaz Polanco, *La cuestión étnico-nacional*; Araceli Burguete Cal y Mayor, "¿Quiénes son los 'amigos de los indios'?" *Boletín de Antropología Americana*, no. 5, 1982; Luis F. Bate, *Cultura, clases y cuestión étnico-nacional*, Mexico City, Juan Pablos Editor, 1984; Consuelo Sánchez, "Elementos conceptuales acerca de la cuestión étnico-nacional," *Boletín de Antropología Americana*, nos. 15 and 16, 1987; Gilberto López y Rivas, *Antropología, minorías étnicas y cuestión nacional*, Mexico City, Ediciones Aguirre Beltrán/Editorial Cuicuilco Escuela

Nacional de Antropología e Historia, 1988; Andrés Medina, "La cuestión étnica y el indigenismo," in C. García Mora and M. Villalobos Salgado (eds.), *La antropología en México: Panorama histórico*, vol. 4, Mexico City, Instituto Nacional de Antropología e Historia, 1988.

31. Díaz Polanco, *Etnia, nación y política*, pp. 56–57.

32. Ibid., p. 57.

33. See Antonio Gramsci, *El materialismo histórico y la filosofía de Benedetto Croce*, Mexico City, Juan Pablos Editor, 1975, pp. 22–23.

34. Díaz Polanco, *Etnia, nación y política*, pp. 57–59.

35. In 1869 Marx deduced that it was not that the liberation of Ireland required the emancipation of the English working class but rather that this liberation was the key to the emancipation of the workers: "a condition for the emancipation of the English working class is the transformation of the present forced union—that is, of Ireland's submission—into an egalitarian and free confederation if possible or, if necessary, the demand for complete separation." Far from being in opposition, the social and the national questions were closely intertwined during this stage of marxist thought. See Georges Haupt and Claude Weill, *Marx y Engels frente al problema de las naciones*, Barcelona, Editorial Fontamara, 1978, pp. 85ff.

36. There are several interpretations of the passages in which Marx and Engels developed these central themes. For example, referring to the hypothesis of unavoidable uniformity, Bloom has written: "What the authors foresaw was not the total disappearance of all national distinctions, whatever these were, but specifically the abolition of sharp economic and social differences, economic isolation, invidious distinctions, political rivalries, wars, and the exploitation of one nation by another." Salomon F. Bloom, *El mundo de las naciones: El problema nacional en Marx*, Buenos Aires, Siglo XXI Argentina, 1975, p. 34. In any case, there is no doubt that the homogenizing version gradually imposed itself on the more orthodox and influential marxist tradition.

37. Leopoldo Mármora, *El concepto socialista de nación*, Mexico City, Siglo XXI, 1986, pp. 37ff.

38. Ibid., p. 38.

PART TWO

———— ■ ————

On the Road to Autonomy

■

CHAPTER FIVE

New Ethnic Struggles and Political-Theoretical Transformations

[handwritten margin notes: "There is really no theoretical exploration of the current 1980s strong indigenism here... any r... only development"]

During the 1980s, ethnic politics assumed a higher profile in several countries of Latin America. In Guatemala, Nicaragua, Mexico, Peru, Ecuador, and Brazil, among others, concern about the implications of the region's sociocultural heterogeneity transcended the narrow milieu of scholars and specialists in a new way and became an object of interest for broader social and political sectors. Specialists, particularly anthropologists, began to review and, in some cases, revise their approaches to the ethnic-national question. This was not simply the outcome of scholarly reflections but primarily the consequence of transformations experienced by the indigenous movements in several Latin American national societies.

Indian movements have been transformed in qualitative ways, and, more important, vast ethnic conglomerates, seeking transformations at a national level, have emerged on the political scene. The transformations in question have taken various forms according to the national contexts in which have they arisen, but their common feature is the search for new articulations with political processes that go beyond the communal and regional levels and even beyond the limits traditionally observed by "ethnic" groups.

THE NEW NATIONAL STRUGGLES OF ETHNIC GROUPS

The 1980s witnessed, in Guatemala, a distinct intensification of the popular movement articulated by political-military organizations that explicitly proposed to transform the existing socioeconomic relations and forms of political domination.[1] What is novel about this extension of the decades-long struggle of the Guatemalan people is undoubtedly the massive participation of indigenous ethnic groups in the revolutionary movement. The counterinsurgent activities of the Guatemalan government, especially after 1982, and its particular rage expressed in genocidal action, against indigenous populations, were reactions to this new development. There was panic among the elite over Indian participation in a struggle with national goals.[2] But continuous and systematic repression could not destroy the revolutionary organizations (later united in the Unidad Revolucionaria Nacional Guatemalteca [Guatemalan National Revolutionary Unity—URNG]) or completely eliminate indigenous resistance.[3] Moreover, in the past few years there has been a significant renaissance of ethnic culture, seen, for example, in the practice of Mayan religious rituals and in the emergence of many organizations that celebrate Indian identity.

In Nicaragua, the triumph of the Sandinista Revolution created new, tense, and complex links between the Pacific region, in which Spanish-speaking, Catholic, and mestizo populations predominate, and the Atlantic Coast, inhabited by ethnic communities that speak indigenous languages and creoles, mostly Protestants who also maintain their own cultural traditions. The new political conditions created by the revolution allowed the coastal communities to rethink their distinctive identities, to express their yearning for the resolution of earlier and contemporary issues, and to establish an independent political organization. This was the beginning of a rich and complex ethnic movement shaped in large part by the transformations that the country had experienced. The coastal ethnic groups did not confine their activities to their own region; rather, they burst onto the national scene. The ethnic movement in Nicaragua brought to light the hidden but irrepressible reality of the contradictions spanning the national arena: the historical reality of intense sociocultural tensions and inequities.[4] Encouraged by the political opportunities opened up by the revolution, the ethnic movement sought to extend and deepen the revolution through the achievement of autonomy. In fact, this movement on the Atlantic Coast—a region that remained on the margins of contemporary history—constituted a second phase of the "political revolution" initiated by the Sandinistas.[5]

During the same period in Colombia and Peru, several organized indigenous groups linked to political-military movements were attempting to implement projects of national transformation. In Colombia, three examples of such organizations are the Consejo Regional Indígena del Cauca, (Indigenous Regional Council of the Cauca—CRIC), the Organización Nacional Indígena de Colombia (National Indigenous Organization of Colombia—ONIC),[6] and the Comando Quintín Lame, formed by insurgent Indians as part of the Simón Bolívar organization, which coordinated guerrilla warfare.[7] In Peru there were the myriad communities of indigenous peasants linked in one way or another to the Peruvian Communist party (better known as Sendero Luminoso or Shining Path).

In Mexico, active indigenous groups chose to establish political alliances, more or less formalized, with regional or national organizations within a context of civic struggles for democracy and the restoration of their ethnic dignity, land, and natural resources. Sometimes these alliances took the form of electoral pacts and other political agreements.[8]

In Ecuador, the Confederación de Nacionalidades Indígenas del Ecuador (Confederation of Indigenous Nationalities of Ecuador—CONAIE) has expanded to the national level and developed its own regional and national structure. It has gradually established relationships with other popular sectors and has assumed an increasingly significant role in the national political process.[9] In June 1990, following the agreement of the CONAIE assembly, the Indian nationalities of Ecuador undertook the "First Uprising of the Indigenous Peoples" to protest the government's policy and set forth their own demands. Although the authorities and most political sectors of the country had known about the movement, they had paid little attention to it. The Indian mobilization stunned the country, provoking surprise and alarm in the governing circles and bewilderment in the majority of the political and social organizations. With this campaign the Ecuadorian Indian peoples brought into sharp relief the deep and unresolved ethnic-national conflicts and demonstrated that they constituted a social force that deserved to be taken seriously.[10]

Indian peoples in Chile reached a political compromise with the national government requiring their review of legislation concerning their territories and self-government. Once the military dictatorship was displaced, the Special Commission of Indigenous Peoples was formed, with Indian participation, and given responsibility for developing the bases for new indigenous law. This commission expressed its purpose as creating "better forms of participation of indigenous peoples and communities in the society's social, political, and economic life, acknowledging their specificity and autonomy."[11]

Pressure from indigenous groups and some non-Indian sectors influenced the new Brazilian constitution of 1988, including a complete chapter on fundamental rights of Indian peoples with regard to social organization, traditional practices, languages, land rights, and juridical-political protection for indigenous communities. In spite of the limitations still present in the revised constitution, a new atmosphere was created that opened up new possibilities for Brazil's ethnic groups.[12]

In Paraguay, the National Constituent Convention approved in 1992 the inclusion of a chapter in the new constitution in which "the right of the indigenous peoples to maintain and develop their ethnic identity in their respective habitats" is recognized and guaranteed. There is also recognition of the right of the peoples "to freely implement their systems of political, social, economic, cultural, and religious organization, as well as to abide by their customary norms for the regulation of communal affairs." Guarantees are added regarding the communal ownership of land, cultural specificities, and related issues.

Although the modes of participation in the national political arenas (e.g., armed struggle or legal and constitutional efforts) vary, they share a gradual nationalization of indigenous movements, including stronger links with the sociopolitical forces of the country, a heightened consciousness of global processes, and the broadening and enrichment of their sociocultural, political, and economic objectives. This qualitative change represents extraordinarily important progress because it breaks the ideological bond with an indigenism that seeks to secure the political boundaries of ethnic communities in order to keep them isolated from major national processes. Until now the state has reserved for itself the role of valid interlocutor vis-à-vis indigenous ethnic groups, and governments have declared themselves the exclusive and necessary guarantors of the communities' existence. This view of ethnic groups as political preserves of the state explains the angry reaction of the Latin American indigenist bureaucracies to any form of national organization (excluding the official ones, of course) that undertakes political activity it considers its exclusive patrimony.

Indian peoples are also discovering the advantages of having direct relationships, without the mediation of the indigenist apparatus, with other groups (parties, movements, nongovernmental organizations, and other entities) with which they share purposes on the national level. They insist that these links be predicated on mutual respect. Indigenous peoples are very quickly becoming social subjects and political actors on this level.

This incorporation into the national scene does not imply any weakening of ethnic cohesion or renunciation of the Indians' own demands (a prophecy implicit, as we have seen, in the ethnicist proposal). On the contrary, there is every reason to believe that it will reinforce ethnic consciousness and identity and, simultaneously, strengthen those demands. The indigenous communities' call for better living conditions, democracy, real equality, political participation, acknowledgment of their territories (not only the concession of "plots"), respect for the environment, and so on, bring indigenous ethnic groups closer to other sectors that view such demands as national imperatives. Simultaneously, however, the position of indigenous peoples opens up a broad range of new contradictions between them and the state. The nationalization of the ethnic movement in several countries is strengthening the distinctive identities and emphasizing the historical rights of the various peoples. The lesson is clear: It is not the Indians' specific identities that reinforce their isolation within the hegemonic state but the political marginality that facilitates the domination and manipulation of their communities.

An analysis of the current ideological and political platforms of progressive national organizations shows a significant development regarding ethnic-national issues. Their acceptance of the necessary participation of indigenous ethnic groups in the country's sociocultural, economic, and political life has enhanced their understanding of democracy. This is the context in which autonomy, as a proposal for resolving ethnic-national conflicts and related legal-political controversies has become an issue for debate and analysis in recent years. There have been national and regional gatherings to analyze the question of autonomy, and many ethnic organizations are articulating plans for achieving it.[13] National political organizations have also incorporated regional autonomy into their programs.[14]

Many observers consider these developments an outgrowth of the Nicaraguan autonomy programs, but the essential reason the demand for autonomy is prevalent is probably the nationalization of indigenous struggles. Autonomy as an issue for debate was current in national and regional organizations even before the National Commission for Autonomy was created in Sandinista Nicaragua.

The fact that autonomy is being discussed in international fora such as the United Nations seems to reflect this general change of perspective within the indigenous movement. Certainly there has been an outstanding presence of Latin American indigenous organizations in the annual gatherings of the Task Force on Indigenous Populations created in 1982, where autonomy has been addressed. Indian organizations have also participated in national debates on the topic and developed various proposals.[15] According to the latest version of its Universal Declaration on the Rights of Indigenous Peoples, "The indigenous peoples, in agreement with international law, have the right to self-determination, for which they can freely determine their political status and their institutions, as well as decide the economic, social, and cultural development they aspire to. This includes, as a fundamental part, their right to autonomy and self-government" (article 1).[16] Further, it specifies that "indigenous peoples have the right to be autonomous in issues related to their own internal and local affairs, including: education, information, mass media, culture, religion, health, living facilities, employment, general welfare, activities both economic and administrative, and traditional ones such as the administration of their land and resources, environment, the inclusion of new members in their community, and the payment of taxes that they decide upon to fund these autonomous functions" (article 27). Indigenous peoples also have the right to decide the structure of autonomous institutions, and their membership and election procedures, states being obliged to recognize and respect them (article 28).[17]

A RESTATEMENT OF THE ETHNIC-NATIONAL QUESTION AND AUTONOMY

The development of the indigenous movement is parallel to important changes in the political-theoretical perspective of national organizations. Recently such organizations have advanced proposals beyond the traditional respect for "indigenous people's culture" and presented a new perspective on the nature of the nation (i.e., recognizing its "multiethnic" character) and formulas permitting its members to exercise their historical rights. This new consciousness and response is significant though not yet general; what is important is that the customary indifference to the ethnic-national question has been overcome.

This critical inquiry concerns the marxist paradigm in crisis and other theoretical traditions such as integrationism and ethnicism. I have attempted critiques and positive proposals for overcoming the reductionism that has limited our understanding of the new social movements. I have expanded on the criticism of ethnicism and objectivism in order to elucidate the theoretical and intellectual milieu in which issues such as the ethnic-national question and, particularly, autonomy have been reformulated. These reformulations have some novel characteristics:

1. The indigenist perspective that had been adopted—however hesitantly—by most of the nonindigenous groups and, particularly, by political organizations (even the most radical ones) is being superseded. The use of evolutionist ideas, a product of the nineteenth-century legacy that survived even in marxism, and the disregard for ethnic identity and the national question, which were considered epiphenomena, were outgrowths of a view of social configurations that was limited to classes. This led to positions that were not essentially different from the basic postulates of traditional integrationist indigenism. Ethnic groups were regarded as a passing phenomenon whose fate was necessarily to vanish in the process of national "integration." Prejudices that characterized ethnic groups as an expression of "backwardness" were accepted, and change was inconceivable as long as these groups maintained their own identities. This outlook supposed that it was possible to transform society without questioning the sociocultural foundations of the national formation and, of course, without considering the important role of ethnically differentiated groups in this process.

Indigenism in its most penetrating and resistant form within civil society—as ideology and discourse—has been losing ground as a focus for progressive sectors. It is more widely accepted that ethnic groups have historical rights; that these rights imply the absolute legitimacy of their sociocultural demands; that ethnic groups are not mere relics of the past but contemporary sociocultural configurations strongly articulated within national society; that indigenous peoples have no reason to disappear in the process of formation of a new nation but are worthy and necessary elements in the formulation of a new social synthesis; and that, as such, they may become a political force without renouncing their identities or demands.

2. The relationships between ethnic community and nation and between ethnic communities and class deserve special attention. As a result of the sociopolitical processes and the intense theoretical debates of recent years there have been significant developments with regard to these issues. The persistence and rigidity of doctrinaire positions on these relationships had erected solid obstacles to the development of the idea of autonomy as a solution for ethnic-national conflict. These positions had emerged as defensive reactions to integrationist indigenism. One such position was a reaction to an indigenism that placed national unity, conceived of as sociocultural homogeneity, at the center of its discourse and considered the "proletarianization" of indigenous people inevitable. This position emphasized particular identities, disregarding or ignoring the national structure in which those ethnic configurations existed and had meaning. Within this approach, it was commonplace to oppose the national to the ethnic. The anti-indigenist reaction found its best doctrinal ground in the mere assertion of society's class structure, neglecting or simply denying the relevance or existence of the ethnic question. In fact, the so-called national question was lost in this rigid framework of social classes. Ethnic

groups and social classes were artificially separated, and, fatally, ethnicity was dissolved in favor of class.

Indeed, within the limits of these reductionist perspectives, proposals of autonomy had no opportunity to develop. Any "self-government" scheme for the Indians that emerged from the former perspective had the stigma of approaching the ethnic question independently of the total sociopolitical process and other social classes. Self-government proposals as ethnic projects did not clearly indicate the social conditions under which this goal could be achieved and proved to have, in practice, very little political effectiveness. This resulted in problematic links between the indigenous sectors adopting this ethnicist perspective and the outstanding members of their intellectual circle within state institutions who were attempting to accomplish the Indian project from inside the ethnophagous Leviathan. The outcome was—and continues to be—the co-optation and manipulation favoring the hegemonic state that has so severely damaged the indigenous movement. This, in turn, reinforced the suspicion among the opponents of ethnicism that their proposals were simply a diversionary maneuver by the establishment.

Circumscribed by a theory that allowed no focus but social class, the radical sectors in Latin America generally considered only insubstantial "cultural" rights for Indian peoples that even the most obstinate integrationists could accept. According to this position any solution had to be framed by an exclusive redefinition of class relations in which autonomy was never considered or at best was perceived as leading to confusion in the peoples' political agenda and sowing seeds of division within the popular classes.

During the past few years, the gradual transcendence of such reductionism and one-sidedness has allowed free discussion and consideration of the notion of autonomy. The most recent elaborations make it clear that ethnic group and class are not antithetical categories—that is, that it is impossible to comprehend ethnogenesis, the sociocultural nature and political behavior of ethnic groups, without understanding the socioeconomic matrix and class structure within which they evolve or to assert that the complex configurations of ethnic groups can be described entirely in economic terms. Thus, what is ethnic must not be conceived of as independent of or alien to class structure, nor can classes be approached without considering their sociocultural dimension, especially when it crystallizes as distinct systems of identity.

If this is so, where the national matrix is socioculturally heterogeneous the transformations sought by a more democratic and egalitarian regime must be projected as a reordering of socioeconomic relations among its class components and, at the same time, as a redefinition of the positions and roles of sociocultural groups that have their own identity. This last perspective presupposes some kind of autonomy.

3. There are two kinds of inequalities, clearly differentiated and intertwined, within the context of the national formation—socioeconomic and sociocultural.

This means that

> in those formations that include groups with distinctive identities, the so-called na-
> tional question is not reduced to inequality among social classes; it also involves in-
> equalities among sectors of the population that have remained in different hierar-
> chies because of their languages, their customs, their forms of social reproduction
> and organization, and, above all, their relationships with the state's political struc-
> tures.[18]

Both socioeconomic and sociocultural inequalities were notorious in the recent experience of Nicaragua, and the theoretical-political debate and developments there provoked a new consideration of autonomy. Hence, an awareness
emerged of the urgent need for a project of national democracy to deal with both
kinds of inequality. Democracy, in these cases, must also be conceived as a regime
in which egalitarian relationships exist within a context of mutual respect.

National democracy and autonomy are intimately linked. Autonomy can create
the particular conditions—especially for self-government—that make possible
the exercise of ethnic groups' rights (linguistic, economic, social, etc.), and it can
annul oppressive relationships and resolve issues raised by sociocultural privilege.
In brief, the imperatives of national democracy make autonomy unavoidable.
Thus it is in a democratic project that ethnic groups find a foundation for their
demand for autonomy.

4. Autonomy is required for indigenous ethnic groups precisely because, however necessary, it is not sufficient simply to recognize that they have the same so-
called civil rights as other citizens. These rights, while generally essential, do not
contain or reflect the whole range of these groups' collective necessities. In some
cases, the way in which the civil law is formulated makes it restrictive of the sociocultural practices of Indian peoples. This means that on occasion ethnic groups
are temporarily or permanently "outlaws."

Abandonment of the "class" reductionism presupposes acceptance of other social entities besides classes. These configurations—ethnic groups among them—
have their own nature and demands. Acceptance of this idea constitutes a first
fundamental theoretical advance. A second important achievement is the recognition of indigenous ethnic groups as social subjects and of their ability to act as
mobilizing forces for change.

However, these achievements cannot be considered definitive. The strength
of deeply rooted ideas and mental habits must not be underestimated. Hegel
cautioned that under certain circumstances "it is far more difficult to make
fixed thought fluid than to make sensible existence fluid."[19] Only as ethnic
groups maintain their activism and broaden their organized presence as social
subjects, accumulating political strength, will prejudices come to an end. Autonomy may then overcome its condition of contingency and become an organic and strategic reality.

The autonomous utopia needs a subject to be its historical architect. The regime of regional autonomy would be no longer a concession but a political victory. It is under these conditions that autonomy has become a reality in many countries of the world. But in Latin America autonomy is still a historical utopia even though integrationist and ethnicist indigenisms no longer prevail politically or ideologically. The main difference is that ethnic subjects capable of making autonomy a political and social reality are now developing.

NOTES

1. The Ejército Guerrillero de los Pobres (Guerrilla Army of the Poor—EGP), the Fuerzas Armadas Rebeldes (Rebel Armed Forces—FAR) and the Organización del Pueblo en Armas (Organization of the People up in Arms—ORPA) guided this popular insurgency that began in 1979 and reached a climax during the early 1980s. Some sectors of the Partido Guatemalteco del Trabajo (Guatemalan Labor Party) participated in these efforts.

2. Cf. Miguel Angel Reyes Illescas, "Guatemala: en el camino del indio nuevo," *Boletín de Antropología Americana*, no. 11, 1985; Centro de Estudios e Investigaciones para Guatemala, *Contrainsurgencia y desarrollo rural en Guatemala (1965–1985)*, Mexico City, 1986; Arturo Arias, "Cultura popular, culturas indígenas, genocidio y etnocidio en Guatemala," *Boletín de Antropología Americana*, no. 7, 1983; Centro de Estudios Integrados de Desarrollo Comunal, *Etnocidio o etnodesarrollo en Guatemala: La desestructuración de las comunidades indígenas y los llamados "polos de desarrollo,"* Mexico City, 1987, chaps. 2 and 3.

3. Thousands of members of various ethnic groups, organized in the so-called Communities of the Population in Resistance, remain in the Guatemalan mountains, not to mention the combatant Indians that make up the bulk of the guerrilla forces. Federico Gómez, "Testimonio sobre las poblaciones indígenas en resistencia," MS, Mexico City, 1988; Comunidades de Población en Resistencia, "Declaración," *Servicio Mensual de Información y Documentación*, no. 134, January 1991.

4. There is also, of course, the reality of the socioeconomic inequalities accumulated in the course of centuries of imperialist plundering, exploitation of Nicaraguan workers, and harsh dictatorships. After the triumph of the revolution, the Sandinistas immediately looked for ways to modify these lacerating conditions, setting aside ethnic-national conflicts and tensions.

5. Orlando Núñez Soto, *Transición y lucha de clases en Nicaragua (1979–1986)*, Mexico City, Siglo XXI Coordinadora Regional de Investigaciones Económicas y Sociales, 1987, p. 18. For analyses of the revolutionary process on the Atlantic Coast, see Jorge Jenkins Molieri, *El desafío indígena en Nicaragua: El caso de los miskitos*, Managua, Editorial Vanguardia, 1986; Roxanne Dunbar O., *La cuestión miskita en la revolución nicaragüense*, Mexico City, Editorial Línea, 1986; Hector Díaz Polanco and Gilberto López y Rivas, *Nicaragua: Autonomía y revolución*, Mexico City, Juan Pablos Editor, 1986; Carlos M. Vilas, *Del colonialismo a la autonomía: Modernización capitalista y revolución social en la Costa Atlántica*, Managua, Editorial Nueva Nicaragua, 1990.

6. The CRIC, founded in 1971, is basically oriented toward defending the right to autonomy of the indigenous refuges (*resgualdos*) in the region. See, for example, the 1985 "Resolución de Vitoncó," in *Cartilla de legislación indígena (para las comunidades indígenas*

del Cauca), Cali, CRIC, 1986, pp. 163–167; see also *Ponencias y conclusiones, Séptimo Congreso del CRIC, Caldono, 14–19 de noviembre, 1983*. In contrast, the ONIC has as the first point of its program the "defense of indigenous autonomy" (*Cartilla de legislación indígena*, p. 54).

7. This indigenous organization is named for Manuel Quintín Lame (1883–1967), who fought for the interests of his Indian brothers and sisters. In 1915 he organized an uprising of Indian communities against large landowners that failed and was persecuted and more than once incarcerated. To the end of his days he promoted education for his people and raised consciousness among them concerning their rights. He is considered a hero by many Colombian indigenous communities.

8. This is the case, for example, of the Coalición Obrero Campesino Estudiantil del Istmo (Worker-Peasant-Student Coalition of the Isthmus—COCEI) in Oaxaca. For a view of the recent indigenous struggles in Mexico, see María Consuelo Mejía Piñeros and Sergio Sarmiento Silva, *La lucha indígena: Un reto a la ortodoxia*, Mexico City, Siglo XXI/Instituto de Investigaciones–Universidad Nacional Autónoma de México, 1987.

9. CONAIE, *Las nacionalidades indígenas en el Ecuador: Nuestro proceso organizativo*, Quito, Ediciones Tinkui, 1989; Natalia Wray, "La constitución del movimiento étnico-nacional indio en Ecuador," in *América Indígena*, 49, no. 1 (3), January-March 1989; Agustín Cueva, "Los movimientos sociales en el Ecuador contemporáneo: El caso del movimiento indígena," in Marcos Roitman R. and Carlos Castro-Gil (eds.), *América Latina: Entre los mitos y la utopía*, Madrid, Editorial Universidad Complutense, 1990.

10. *El levantamiento indígena en la prensa ecuatoriana (mayo-junio 1990)*, Quito, CONAIE, 1990; Luis Macas, *El levantamiento indígena visto por sus protagonistas*, Quito, Instituto Científico de Culturas Indígenos, 1991; José Almeida et al., *Sismo étnico en el Ecuador: Varias perspectivas*, Quito, Ediciones Abya-Yala/CEDIME, 1993.

11. Comisión Especial de Pueblos Indígenas, *Nueva ley indígena (borrador de discusión)*, Santiago, 1990, p. 6.

12. *Constituisão da República Federativa do Brasil, October 5, 1988*, São Paulo, Editora Atlas, 1988, especially title 8, chap. 8. See also Sílvio Coelho dos Santos, *Povos indígenas e a Constituinte*, Florianópolis, Editora da Universidad de Florianópolis Santa Catarina/Movimiento, 1989, chap. 3.

13. Besides the cases already examined (Colombia's CRIC and ONIC, Ecuador's CONAIE, and the Nicaraguan and Chilean organizations), the Mexican Frente Independiente de Pueblos Indios (Independent Front of Indian Peoples—FIPI) should be mentioned. Point 1.B of its founding document establishes "the right to autonomy . . . to select and organize our social life with our own forms of government and self-defense. To exercise authority and jurisdiction over our ethnic territories. To arrange our societies on the basis of our traditions or internal laws. . . . It is the Mexican state's duty to recognize the status of autonomy . . . and legality for the people's customary law." FIPI, "Un proyecto alternativo para la liberación de los pueblos indios de México," MS, Mexico City, 1988, p. 4. Several regional and local Mexican organizations are making similar demands. Regarding Guatemala, several organizations have demanded the right "to local and regional autonomy for ethnic-national groups." See "Derechos indígenas en Guatemala," *Otra Guatemala*, no. 3, February 1988, p. 57; Consejo de Organizaciones Mayas de Guatemala, *Derechos específicos del pueblo maya*, Guatemala, 1991; and Mario Payeras, *Autonomía maya en Guatemala: Argumentos y desbroces preliminares*, Temas, 2nd series, 4, no. 12, 1992.

14. See for example, the program proposed by the Partido Mexicano Socialista (Mexican Socialist party—PMS) to contend in 1988's national elections; see also PMS, "México: Nación multiétnica y plurilíngüe," Mexico City, Departamento de Grupos Étnicos, 1988; Heberto Castillo, "Es necesario un nuevo pacto nacional (Primer Encuentro de Pueblos Indios, Juchitán, Oaxaca)," *La Unidad*, no. 30, suppl. 6, March 1988. More recently, the Mexican Partido de la Revolution Democrática has raised the issue in "Plenos derechos a los pueblos indios," *Expediente*, no. 7, 1990. In Guatemala, the FAR stated that it favored autonomy ("La cuestión étnico-nacional y la revolución en Guatemala," MS, Mexico City, 1987); Octubre Revolucionaria (Revolutionary October—OR) made a similar statement (see "Tesis sobre la cuestión étnico-nacional," *Opinión Política*, no. 11, September 1987, p. 6) acknowledging "the right to local and regional autonomy of indigenous Peoples."

15. See, for example, the discussion jointly organized in 1989 by the Asamblea de Autoridades Mixes (Mixe Authorities' Assembly—ASAM), SER and the Escuela Nacional de Antropología e Historia, "Derechos indígenas en Naciones Unidas: Reflexiones y propuestas," *Boletín de Antropología Americana*, no. 19, 1989, pp. 173ff.; and ASAM, "Propuesta de declaración universal sobre los derechos indígenas," *Boletín de Antropología Americana*, no. 19, pp. 187ff.

16. This version is more advanced than previous ones (e.g., the one of 1988) in that it recognizes the Indians as "peoples" and links their right to self-determination to the right to autonomy.

17. Grupo de Trabajo sobre Poblaciones Indígenas (Task Force on Indigenous Populations—GTPI), "Declaración universal sobre los derechos de los pueblos indígenas," *Foro*, 1, no. 4, 1993, pp. 30ff; ASAM (ed.), *Documentos de trabajo sobre los derechos indígenas y Naciones Unidas*, SER, MS, Mexico City, 1989.

18. Díaz Polanco, *Etnia, nación y política*, pp. 15 and 19.

19. G.W.F. Hegel, *Fenomenología del espíritu*, Mexico City, Fondo de Cultura Económica, 1985, p. 24.

CHAPTER SIX

———————— ■ ————————

Foundations of a Regime of Regional Autonomy

Regional autonomy is being discussed in Latin America as one of several proposals for resolving the indigenous issue. Many Indian organizations are already insisting on autonomy as a central demand. However, in spite of the more or less conscious support for it, the concept of autonomy has been little examined, and its implications have begun to seem promising to some and threatening to others. There is a risk of its becoming a catch all for the most disordered set of ideas, perspectives, and illusions. The diversity of outlooks and even of conclusions is not in itself negative. What can be damaging is the abundance of myths and nonsense associated with the notion, such as autarchy, separatism, sovereignty, and reversion to "natural" life.

Not all Indian movements appropriate the autonomous utopia in the same way. Autonomy is sometimes conceived of as a regime designed to give the nation a new dimension stemming from new relationships among Indian peoples and other sociocultural groups. Here autonomy would outline the links between ethnic groups and the state as a foundation for changing basic aspects of politics, economics, and culture on a global, national level.

Alternatively, it is common for proposals of autonomy to become an elaboration of specific demands, that, in their own way, reflect the peoples' aspirations but lack any alternative proposal for the organization of the national society, or the multiethnic state or of the new political links that would be necessary to accomplish practical fulfillment of the demands. The political-administrative apparatuses in charge of implementing ethnic groups' demands and defining their authority, jurisdictional milieus, and ability to modify the national society are as yet unformulated. Autonomy is not an articulating axis for other demands but a petition vaguely associated with the importance of freedom to tend to each group's own affairs. It is not yet a comprehensive political program that would allow for the organization of a multiethnic state. This idea of autonomy as a list of demands is still predominant.[1]

Autonomy is in fact no panacea; it is merely one resource that society can use at a given point in its development to resolve ethnic-national conflict.

Autonomy has at least two meanings. The first, found in certain documents produced by intellectual circles that sympathize with the Indian movement or in the declarations of some indigenous organizations, implies a situation of laissez-faire. That is, autonomy is conceived of as more or less broad permission for ethnic groups to tend to their own affairs or to retain their customs (or at least some of them). The greatest disadvantage of this representation of autonomy lies in its ambiguity and indeterminacy. How far will the permission extend, and how long will it last? Under what conditions are the prerogatives established? How are they guaranteed? These and other crucial questions remain unanswered, except in terms of some undefined "tradition," the generosity of those who hold power, or their whims. Many Indian peoples have enjoyed some kind of autonomy of this nature at different historical moments. However, since this "autonomy" depends on the permission of the powerful or on their inability to impose their will entirely at a given time, these prerogatives, grants, or favors are sooner or later withdrawn by the same whim that bestowed them.

There is a second meaning of autonomy, and it is more than laissez-faire. It is a political-juridical regime, agreed upon and not merely granted, that implies the creation of a true political collectivity within the national society. Broadly speaking, autonomy can refer to a special regime that is a form of self-government for certain integrated communities that choose their authorities from among themselves, exercise legally attributed responsibilities, and have some minimal faculty for legislating their internal life and administering their affairs. A more specific definition may be impossible because of the variety of situations covered by the concept of autonomy.

To attempt to identify specific characteristics common to all regimes of autonomy independent of the sociocultural, economic, and political conditions under which they exist would be futile. The specific features of autonomy will be determined, on the one hand, by the historical nature of the collectivity that exercises it—the social subject that ultimately turns it into a historical reality and gives it life—and on the other, by the political orientation and degree of democracy of the state in which it acquires institutional and practical existence.

Acknowledgment of certain broad capacities (e.g., legislative ones) may be considered essential and nonnegotiable in establishing autonomy for certain ethnic groups, but it may be secondary or irrelevant for others. Therefore it is impossible to identify a priori any collection of elements or a way of functioning that constitutes the necessary content of the regime of autonomy. This quality can only be established to the extent to which the system satisfies the historical aspirations of the group and permits the full development of its sociocultural life. Thus, each autonomous system must be evaluated in terms of the historical conditions it stems from and for which it tries to provide responses.

Yet, not everything that is called self-government is autonomy. Theodor Adorno observed that "the relativism of all knowledge can only be asserted from outside, while it has not yet been known conclusively."[2] I will briefly examine the foundational elements that constitute the most relevant framework for autonomy.

AUTONOMY AND THE NATION-STATE

Autonomous regimes are established within the context of given nation-states; their construction takes place as part of the political-juridical life of a state. The regime of autonomy aims at finding means for the political integration of the nation-state based on coordination rather than subordination of its partial collectivities. Therefore, as a political collectivity, an autonomous community or region is established as a component of the corresponding nation-state.

Autonomy seeks not only to satisfy the interests and aspirations of partial communities but to ensure a more adequate integration of the national society. What makes autonomy worthwhile today is the common recognition, in a given society, that optimal solidarity and integration of the nation can be achieved by satisfying the regional or local aspirations of particular communities. Autonomy is therefore a search for the maximum "congruity between plurality and the unity of political integration."[3]

The purpose of autonomy, in such a scheme, is not to express the contradiction between regional or local interests and those of the society as a whole but to provide a set of formulas for keeping these interests from creating conflict within the life of the state. Hence, the capacities and competences associated with autonomy cannot be exercised in opposition to the interests of other constituent communities and individuals. Eduardo Llorens has written that autonomy attempts

> to institute or retain a distribution of competences through which constituent political collectivities are charged with specific measures. The distribution of the competences is realized, like all collective activity, with a view to satisfying at once the interests of the collectivity as a whole, of its constituent collectivities, and of individuals. Thus, the satisfaction of local interests can be justified if they are at least compatible with general ones.[4]

Because autonomous entities originate in the nation-state, they cannot be constructed in terms of their own interests alone. But because it is intended that these partial interests be satisfied, special faculties are conferred upon the constituent political collectivities and autonomous decentralization is attempted.

The political and juridical foundation that gives life to and regulates the operation of a regime of autonomy derives from a source that is, so to speak, external to the community it affects; it issues from the substantive law that is the basis for the life of the nation-state, the social pact. Although in some cases they may have legislative faculties, autonomous communities do not have constituent power which is reserved for the central state. Therefore, instead of constitutions autonomous communities have statutes that acquire meaning precisely within the context of constitutional law. At the same time, the regime of autonomy is an institution that influences the nature of the state itself since, for example, it limits or modifies the state's territorial powers.

AUTONOMY AND ETHNIC RIGHTS

A regime of autonomy is instituted so that certain groups with common historical traditions and sociocultural characteristics (customs, beliefs, language, and so on) may freely develop their lifestyles, exercise the rights they have as ethnic or national communities, and conduct their own affairs. Thus, it also has an internal basis: recognition of the plural makeup of the nation, that is, of the existence of the constituent ethnic communities and of their right to laws effective within the framework of the state.

The harmonization of national life requires not only compatibility between the interests of certain sociocultural collectivities and other interests—including the majority's—but also adjustment of the overarching principles that guide the life of the nation to make room for the rights of the constituent communities. There cannot be a regime of autonomy if the interests and vision of the majority with regard to either its size or its political power are imposed as a limitation that suffocates plurality, especially when matching those interests and perspectives to those of the state. The interests of the majority, says Llorens, "are also partial if they do not consider those of the other elements of the union."[5] In societies that are socioculturally heterogeneous, the internal foundation for autonomy derives from the need to do away with the rigid structure of majority and minority based upon ethnic characteristics wherein the majority tends to identify its interests as those of the state. Autonomy stresses, politically and juridically, the character of the state as arbiter of common and plural interests.

To dismantle the majority/minority arrangement in which indigenous ethnic groups are placed in a subordinate, disadvantaged position and a permanent situation of inequality, it is not enough to seek sociopolitical symmetry. This was the formula the liberals adopted, and we have reviewed the unsatisfactory outcome. To decree equality among the unequal without establishing the conditions that effectively compensate for the de facto disadvantages only deepens the inequality. In present-day societies, the inequality suffered by ethnic groups is expressed as negative asymmetry. Rather than any fictional symmetry or purely formal equality, autonomy involves the establishment of a positive asymmetry whose compensating effects lay the foundations for real equality. To achieve equality it is necessary that, at least for a time, the traditionally disadvantaged receive not the same but more recognition of special rights, guarantees, support, and resources. In brief, the spirit of autonomy assumes the implementation of national solidarity and fraternity in the form of positive asymmetry. It is in this sense that the system of autonomy is a special regime.

But the aforementioned internal foundation derives not from the mere existence of sociocultural difference but from the fact that identity becomes the substance of or "pretext" for political demands in the corresponding collectivities. The imperative of autonomy stems internally from a collectivity's manifest will to effect a difference politically.[6] As the demand is embodied in politically active communities, autonomy may be the outcome of a commitment (a complex arrangement around social, cultural, economic, and political issues) that seeks to harmonize the diverse interests at play. If the regime of autonomy is to last and be effective, it must stem from negotiation, and the statute that is its organic law is a tool for achieving consensus that reflects a manifest agreement among national forces (including, of course, the ethnic collectivities). Naturally, because the national society is dynamic, there is no definitive consensus in historical perspective.

The political-juridical frameworks and the institutional forms that guarantee the achievement of the integrating goals are a consequence of such commitments. In real terms, this supposes the definition of the constitutional status of autonomy and the adoption through some participatory method by the subject groups of its statutes. These statutes, which may vary in form (constitutional, organic, or customary), specify the rights of the groups, the territories of the autonomous communities, their competences with regard to those of the central state, the political-administrative organs with which they will operate as public entities, and so on.

AUTONOMY AND SELF-DETERMINATION

Being a regime grounded in the demands of the communities themselves, autonomy is a system through which sociocultural groups exercise their right to self-determination. Autonomy synthesizes and politically articulates the array of demands advanced by ethnic groups. Therefore it can be said that autonomy is the fundamental demand.

Self-determination and autonomy are often thought of as dissimilar options available to peoples for exercising control over their affairs and directing their sociopolitical life. This is probably incorrect; instead, autonomy should be viewed as one way of exercising self-determination. The general or abstract principle of a right to self-determination must be distinguished from the very diverse concrete meanings of it that emerge from its exercise in particular situations.

The distinction between self-determination and autonomy is usually based on an identification of the former with the right to political independence and the establishment of a nation-state while the latter is reserved for the assumption of certain special faculties (such as self-government) without statehood or political independence. This perspective arbitrarily limits self-determination to one of its possible concrete forms, independent statehood. Such a restrictive point of view has contributed to considerable confusion by identifying ethnic groups' self-determination exclusively with the search for political independence.[7]

In the international milieu, the implicit identification of self-determination with state independence has had important consequences for the indigenous cause. For example, the ILO's Convention on Indigenous and Tribal Peoples in Independent Countries[8] severely restricts the rights of Indians as peoples because of the fear aroused by their association with self-determination. Actually the convention quotes, in its introduction, the terms of the International Pact of Economic, Social, and Cultural Rights and of the International Pact of Civil and Political Rights. Article 1 of both pacts clearly indicates that "all peoples have the right to self-determination. In virtue of this right they freely establish their political condition and provide for their economic, social, and cultural development."[9]

Several members, representatives of both government and, especially, business, were fearful of the political effects that the use of the term "peoples" in Convention No. 169 might provoke and expressed misgivings about it. Indeed, the terms "peoples" and "territories" were heatedly debated during the sessions of the commission in question. Some governmental members (e.g., Argentina, Venezuela, and Peru) expressed serious reservations about the term "peoples," preferring "populations"; others were prepared to accept its inclusion provided that it was adequately "qualified." Representatives of business interests concurred that the term "presented problems as to its political interpretation and because of its connotations of national self-determination" and also favored a limiting qualification. In contrast, representatives of labor not only expressed "their belief in the importance of self-determination for indigenous and tribal peoples" but "unconditionally supported the use of the term 'peoples' throughout the agreement." Nongovernmental organizations (with no voting rights) unanimously and "vigorously supported the use of the term 'peoples' without further qualifications, comment, or condition that might damage it." However, the restrictive proposal was forced upon the others. Thus, a point 3 was added to article 1 of Convention No. 169: "The use of the term 'peoples' in this Convention should not be interpreted in the sense that it has any implication with regard to the rights that might be conferred on said term in international law."[10]

Instead of restricting ethnic groups' character as peoples, there was another option: to define self-determination—a right recognized for all peoples—in this case as the right to autonomy within national contexts. Nevertheless, the idea of emptying the term "peoples" of its juridical-political content when referring to indigenous peoples won out, according to the one-sided formula people/self-determination/independence. Members of several indigenous nongovernmental organizations present while the debate took place rightly considered this restriction "discriminatory." The principle of self-determination clearly implies that a great variety of roads may be traveled, from the construction of a nation-state of their own to the creation of autonomous entities within the framework of a given state.[11]

Those who adopt a narrower concept of self-determination often represent themselves as the only defenders of indigenous freedom. They argue that rejecting self-determination in the sense of state independence amounts to opposing any self-determination. Nothing could be farther from the truth. A crucial element thus obscured is worth repeating: The general or abstract principle of self-determination "freely determining its political condition and freely providing for its economic, social, religious, and cultural development,"[12] is one thing, and the various concrete meanings that may derive from this principle as peoples exercise this right is another. Using this principle peoples may, for example, decide between (a) independence and the establishment of a nation-state of their own and (b) some form of autonomy within the context of a preexisting or emerging nation-state.

Self-determination as a right of Indian peoples is not being questioned. However, political and ideological organizations seemingly in the service of national and/or international interests identify this general principle with independence when the subject is indigenous ethnic groups that might ally themselves with progressive popular movements (the aim being to undermine popular unity and weaken an opposing political project). These same forces systematically oppose any national aspiration on the part of autochthonous groups in their own environment (e.g., North American Indian peoples) or of nationalities or ethnic groups struggling for freedom and independence against governments allied with the powers they represent; the double standard is obvious. One cannot help but notice the apparent influence of such political maneuvers in the effort to impose upon Latin American indigenous people the notion of self-determination as separation and independence, that is, of creating nation-states of their own as the only politically significant objective. Indigenous peoples' right to self-determination is meaningless if they do not have the capacity to decide what kind of political organization is in their own best interest; how they want to be reintegrated (assuming that they do want to) into the broader society in which they have been immersed for historical reasons, and what kind of political, economic, social, and cultural relations they wish to establish with the other groups of the national formation.

Critics of indigenous peoples' demands for autonomy obviously do not believe in their right to free self-determination but insist on the ability of metropolitan power centers to decide for them. This is a persistent form of colonialist arrogance: the Indians do not know what is best for them and must be taken by the hand by those who do. For example, in the mid-1980s, metropolitan advisers imposed on Miskitos, Sumos, Ramos y Sandinistas Unidos the requirement to negotiate with the Sandinista government, in effect to separate the Atlantic Coast from the Nicaraguan national unity. This interpretation of self-determination was a response not to the demands of Nicaraguan ethnic groups but to the particular obsession of the U.S. administration: separating the indigenous people from the Sandinista popular project and, in general, undermining the national unity and the liberation program created by the Sandinista Revolution.

This strategy ruled out any possibility of reaching a fair and reasonable agreement between the parties, which was exactly what the coreligionists of then-President Ronald Reagan wanted. Separation was not the indigenous ethnic communities' demand, nor is it what they want today. They have chosen a political space within the context of the new nation to exercise their historical, social, economic, and cultural rights. This has been demonstrated by the coastal people's obstinate defense of the regime of regional autonomy agreed upon first with the recalcitrant groups among the Sandinistas and, after their electoral defeat, with the centralist UNO. The North American think tanks display the same kind of one-sided and imposing attitude toward indigenous peoples' self-determination. In fact, most indigenous organizations lean toward the exercise of self-determination within the context of the nation-states of which they are part—that is, they favor the system of self-government conventionally called autonomy or some similar regime. Considering the highly democratic procedure of most indigenous organizations, it appears that pro-independence intentions are not based on popular opinion in the Indian communities.

In Latin America, no representative indigenous organization is seeking to de- clare political sovereignty, to create its own nation-state, or to pursue independence. What indigenous people want is to retain and develop their own forms of sociocultural life within the framework of their respective national structures, simultaneously with the transformation of current relations of oppression and exploitation. Indigenous ethnic communities and organizations have chosen to struggle within the context of the nation-states to which they belong. Indian peoples are concerned not with separation but with guarantees in the exercise of their rights.

To realize this it is sufficient to examine the various documents and pronouncements of Latin American and other indigenous movements with an unprejudiced eye. In the declaration of the World Council of Indigenous Peoples, Indian peoples are not necessarily conceived of separately from nation-states; rather, they talk about recognition by "the states in which indigenous peoples live" (principle 2) and mention that the "indigenous peoples and their members are authorized to participate in the state's political life" (principle 7). The Declaration of Principles issued by several nongovernmental organizations on July 26, 1985, in Geneva speaks of the right of indigenous people (item 10) "to participate in the life of the state just as the nation, community, or indigenous people desire."[13] In a document of the Four Winds Council, the same open, respectful attitude is adopted. This text mentions protection against "political discrimination . . . inasmuch as an indigenous community would rather remain as part of a state"; it also refers to "indigenous rights within the national juridical system in the cases in which autonomy is chosen over total independence."[14] On the continental level, in 1990 American indigenous organizations chose autonomy within national contexts.[15]

When popular movements demand independence, sovereignty, and the creation of a nation-state of their own, whether they are "indigenous" or not, they deserve the support of democratic forces and of the international community. It is possible that these kinds of national movements will someday emerge among the Indian peoples of Latin America, but this is not the current trend. Instead, there are politically motivated organizations inciting indigenous ethnic communities to separate not as a response to real indigenous demands but with the purpose of undermining and destroying popular movements such as the Sandinistas or the Guatemalan opposition.

THE TERRITORIAL BASIS OF AUTONOMY

Historically, autonomous communities have been established as territorial entities. Based on the territorial principle, the constitutional or, more often, statutory instrument specifies the place in which the ethnic-national groups in question will exercise their rights and in which the autonomous organs will have jurisdiction. However, this has been the object of serious disputes either because, out of fear of separatism, the territorial aspect of the regime of autonomy is often consciously avoided and not clearly defined or because another principle is more or less explicitly opposed to the territorial: the so-called personality principle.

The controversy between the advocates of territorial autonomy and the advocates of "personal" autonomy was the focus of theoretical-political debate on the ethnic-national question during the early twentieth century. The more systematic defenders of personal autonomy were the Austrian socialists Otto Bauer, Karl Renner, and Rudolf Springer, proponents of an interesting political tendency known as Austromarxism. These intellectuals advocated a national-cultural autonomy that had numerous followers in several countries, including sectors of Russian revolutionary Social Democracy.

The Austromarxists proposed, in brief, that autonomy should be recognized for the members of a nationality independently of territory. The population would be divided according to individuals' cultural self-ascriptions, which would correspond to nationalities freely chosen by the citizens. Therefore, autonomy was established not as a "territorial embodiment" but as an "association of people."[16] Such an autonomous entity would then fulfill the functions of "overseeing the nation's cultural needs" (schools, theaters, libraries, and so on). "Thus national autonomy would be based on the pure principle of personality. Each nation would possess the power to administer and foster cultural development; no nation would then have to struggle for power within the state. The personality principle would be the most perfect means for national defense." In Springer's more developed version, autonomous communities would also control public administration to "provide security" for the nations in the face of possible abuses by the state without forfeiting the "advantages" of the personality principle.[17]

The advocates of the territorial principle firmly opposed the formula, calling it culturalist. Lenin's and the Bolsheviks' repudiation of this position had a strong impact. They argued that national-cultural autonomy provoked the artificial separation of nationalities, ignored class struggle and class structure within them, and left aside the very important question of power.[18] After 1913, Lenin and his organization supported the idea of "regional autonomy," the proposal that an regime of autonomy should be established for certain territories in which there were ethnic or national groups that had integrally (not only in the "cultural" area) achieved the capacity for self-government.

Although the national-cultural position persists in the political perspective and ideology of certain intellectuals, as a rule regimes of regional autonomy (for example, in the former USSR, in the Spanish state, and in Nicaragua) have been based on the territorial principle. This is not accidental, since such a regime not only identifies rights for a given category of persons but creates true political-administrative entities within a state, and it is difficult to conceive of such collectivities without territory.

In the Latin American case we may expect the territorial principle to continue to be indispensable to the design of projects of autonomy, since territory, linked to natural and productive resources, to the environment, and even to sacred spaces, is a central demand among indigenous peoples. Nevertheless, the need to adopt elements of the personality principle in particular cases or situations must not be overlooked. It is possible that cultural autonomy, at least as a complementary formula, will prove more important for resolving complex ethnic-national issues than we can now imagine.

THE LEGAL AND CONSTITUTIONAL CHARACTER OF AUTONOMY

An additional criterion for recognizing the regime of regional autonomy is its legal and in particular its constitutional character. The capacities of an autonomous regime derive not from an administrative organ but from the law. Because of this legal character, the life of an autonomous entity is not subject to simple administrative measures or decisions made by a higher authority. It is in this sense that autonomy is more than mere decentralization. Llorens wrote, "Autonomy can be corrected only in the legislative and judiciary arenas; decentralization allows for correction in the administrative arena too. The decisions of the decentralized organs may be replaced by the state; the decisions of autonomous organs may be annulled but not definitively replaced." In other words, what distinguishes autonomy is what Llorens defines as "freedom within the law."[19] Regimes of autonomy introduce the territorial separation of powers.[20]

Several scholars distinguish between the constitutional relevance of autonomous communities or regions and their constitutional nature. Enrique Álvarez Conde explains, "That the autonomous communities have constitutional relevance means . . . that the constitution includes dispositions relative to the existence, organization, and functions of autonomous communities, and that autonomous communities have a constitutional character refers to their juridical position in relation to the state and to the functions they perform."[21] Not everyone agrees about the constitutional character of the regimes of autonomy existing in European countries such as Italy, Portugal, and Spain. Some analysts maintain that autonomous regions are fully constitutional entities even though their faculties are limited by the constitution, since they hold powers of their own and organs to exercise them; others deny this, saying that inasmuch as autonomous entities do not directly participate in the supreme direction of the state, they are under the central authority's control and have a relationship of dependence with regard to the powers of the latter.[22]

There is, however, practically unanimous agreement about the constitutional relevance of autonomous regions, including in this case both the European examples and the regions of the former USSR. This seems to confer higher juridical-political status on autonomous regions compared with other administrative entities, such as municipalities, because often the latter's powers and functions are limited not only by the constitution but also by ordinary law. In some countries (e.g., the autonomous regions of the Nicaraguan Atlantic Coast and Spain's autonomous communities) municipalities are subdivisions of autonomous entities and subject to higher organs with regard to their boundaries and other issues. In that sense, the "autonomy" of municipalities is limited in comparison with that of the regions. Besides, in many cases, the responsibilities of municipalities do not extend beyond very limited administrative ones.

THE DISTRIBUTION OF COMPETENCIES

The regime of regional autonomy is a response to the need to ensure democratic representation of the country's sociocultural regions within the state's political and administrative organization in a way compatible with the plural ethnic-national makeup of the society. In these terms, regional autonomy implies a certain political and administrative decentralization of the state. Decentralization involves the assignment of certain powers or competences, mainly legislative and regulatory in character to the autonomous entity, either exclusively or shared with the central state. Specific competences correspond to vertical powers, and their distribution among the different levels is the basic guarantee of autonomy.[23]

The decentralization brought about by autonomy is juridical-political rather than simply administrative. It depends on the law rather than on the assignment or transfer of functions by a higher administrative organ that can also revoke them. This administrative transfer of functions to a preexisting autonomous entity of course occurs on a regular basis, but this is not the foundation of autonomy. It is typical for a regime of autonomy to provoke decentralization, but not all forms of decentralization involve autonomy.

Some writers see the essence of autonomy in the possession of legislative powers (constitutionally limited, of course). They generally have in mind broad powers that tend to erase the distinctions between the federal and the regionally autonomous. In fact, some believe that there is no actual difference between the two regimes; in some countries the distinction between the federal and the regional system is minimal.[24] In my opinion what is critical for autonomy is that the political collectivity may satisfactorily regulate its internal life within definite constitutional and legal limits, whatever the number and quality of its assigned powers. The latter will depend on the historical milieu and the conditions under which the national commitment to autonomy is attained. According to the development achieved by an ethnic group in the socioeconomic area and in relation to its demands, self-government to administer its own affairs (legally regulated) might be considered an adequate formula for autonomy. Under other circumstances (e.g., those of the European nationalities), autonomy with an administrative emphasis would be considered insufficient for the satisfaction of their demands.

We can distinguish between "minimal" and "maximal" forms of autonomy and envision a complex spectrum of gradations that must be evaluated in terms of their historical circumstances. Thus, what may be seen as maximal autonomy in one situation may be considered minimal in another and vice versa. Also, the degree of autonomy that would be considered minimal for one group might simply be unacceptable for another. Besides, every regime of autonomy is, by definition, dynamic: no arrangement is considered definitive. Therefore, under certain circumstances the acquisition of administrative or regulatory capacities and executive functions may be considered a stage in a process that gradually incorporates other powers as the group's political and economic development requires them and as the democratic process proceeds.

The issue of competences and their distribution is thus resolved in terms of the nature and degree of the autonomy of the regime in question. Maximal autonomy with broad legislative and executive faculties will commonly require a distribution of competences that is constitutionally regulated and supported by status.[25] For regimes based on administrative foundations, it is generally enough to note, in their statutes, which elements constitute the competence of regional self-governing institutions and their regulatory means, indicating in the constitution only the principles supporting such competences.

NOTES

1. For example, the proposal of the so-called Consejo de Organizaciones Mayas de Guatemala (Council of Guatemalan Maya Organizations—COMG)—which in other respects is advanced compared with previous propositions—shows this limitation. See *Derechos específicos del pueblo maya*, Guatemala City, COMG, 1991.

2. Theodor W. Adorno, *Dialéctica negativa*, Madrid, Taurus Ediciones, 1975, p. 44.

3. Eduardo L. Llorens, *La autonomía en la integración política*, Madrid, Editorial Revista de Derecho Privado, 1932, p. 24.

4. Ibid., p. 68.

5. Ibid., p. 69.

6. Ibid., pp. 95–96.

7. This is the case with certain organizations concerned with dividing the Latin American indigenous movement. During the 1980s, several North American think tanks tried to foster separatist tendencies within the Indian movement, seeking influence especially over the ethnic-national conflicts in Nicaragua and Guatemala. See Díaz Polanco, "*Neoindigenismo* and the ethnic question in Central America"; see also "El movimiento indio y la ética política," MS, Mexico City, 1988.

8. Convention No. 169 was adopted by the ILO's General Conference on June 7, 1989; it revisited and updated the prior Convention No.107, passed in 1957. International Labor Organization, *Convention No. 169: Convention on Indigenous and Tribal Peoples in Independent Countries*, Geneva, 1990.

9. These pacts include some rather specific rights pertinent to the Indian peoples, since they indicate that "all peoples may freely make use of their wealth and natural resources" within the framework of international law and that in no case "can a people be deprived of its means of subsistence". Academia Mexicana de Derechos Humanos, *Manual de documentos para la defensa de los derechos indígenas*, Mexico City, 1989, pp. 22 and 44.

10. International Labor Conference, *Provisional records, 76th Meeting*, Geneva, International Labor Organizaion, 1989, pp. 1–6. It is fair to note that this restriction does not diminish the value of the other contributions of Convention No. 169.

11. For an opinion on the subject, see Gurutz Jáuregui Bereciartu, *Contra el Estado-nación: En torno al hecho y la cuestión nacional*, Madrid, Siglo XXI de España Editores, 1986, pp. 213–214: "The right of peoples to self-determination is structured . . . as generic in character, and therefore has no univocal content, presupposing a series of widely diverse options including such formulas as aggregation to a preexisting state, integration into a higher entity through autonomy, federation, or confederation, or separation from a preexisting state and the establishment of a national state of their own."

12. This definition was proposed by the World Council of Indigenous Peoples. CMPI, "Declaración sobre los derechos de los pueblos indígenas," in *Guchachi'Reza (Iguana Rajada)*, 2d series, no. 25, December 1985, p. 10.

13. "Declaración de principios," in ibid., p. 13.

14. Consejo de los Cuatro Vientos, "Propuestas para una declaración de principios sobre los derechos de los pueblos indígenas," in ibid., pp. 15–16.

15. Primer Encuentro Continental de Pueblos Indios, "Declaración de Quito," *Servicio de Información y Documentación*, reprint no. 130, August 1990.

16. Otto Bauer, *La cuestión de las nacionalidades y la socialdemocracia*, Mexico City, Siglo XXI, 1979, p. 344.

17. Ibid., pp. 346 and 348.

18. V. I. Lenin, "Notas críticas sobre la cuestión nacional," in *Problemas de política nacional e internacionalismo proletario*, Moscow, Editorial Progreso, n.d., pp. 26–33; "La clase obrera y la cuestión nacional," in *La lucha de los pueblos de las colonias y países independientes contra el imperialismo*, Moscow, Editorial Progreso, n.d., pp. 88–89.

19. Llorens, *La autonomía en la integración política*, p. 81.

20. "These decentralized forms, among them the federal state and the state with regional autonomies, lead, in time, to a 'separation of powers' on a territorial basis. . . . To the 'horizontal' separation between legislative, executive, and judicial powers, is added the territorial or 'vertical' separation of powers. These powers are separated or divided, in turn, among the central state organs and the organs of the territorial entities that participate in its formation." J. J. González Encinar, "La descentralización como proceso: España," in J. J.

González E. (ed.), *Autonomía y partidos políticos: Italia, Alemania Occidental, Gran Bretaña y España*, Madrid, Editorial Tecnos, 1984, p. 120.

21. Enrique Álvarez Conde, *Las comunidades autónomas*, Madrid, Editora Nacional, 1980, p. 57.

22. Ibid., pp. 58–67. As we shall see, the situation was quite different in the case of the former USSR, especially with regard to the autonomous republics; their constitutional nature did not seem to be in doubt.

23. "It is well known that the way competences are distributed is the central problem of autonomy, and in every modern decentralized state . . . this has a meaning that is definitely analogous to the separation of powers: if the separation of powers is a guarantee for the individual, the distribution of competences is the guarantee for territorial autonomy." Antonio la Pérgola, "La técnica constitucional de la autonomía: Aspectos de derecho comparado," in González E., *Autonomía y partidos políticos*, p. 34.

24. Ibid., p. 35.

25. On the various forms of distribution of competences (both horizontal and vertical) and the kinds of competences (exclusive, complementary, and integrating) found in practice, see E. Álvarez Conde, *Las comunidades autónomas*, pp. 154–156; and La Pérgola, "*La técnica constitucional de la autonomía*," pp. 36ff.

CHAPTER SEVEN

———————— ■ ————————

Examples of Regional Autonomy: The USSR, Spain, and Nicaragua

It is common for powerful metropolitan countries seeking to establish hegemony and political, economic, or military control of given areas they consider critical to foster separatist movements in dependent or relatively weak countries under the pretext of supporting struggles for "freedom" and encouraging "self-determination" of ethnic-national groups. These efforts have nothing to do with regional autonomy. The cases of the Congo, Vietnam, Afghanistan, Angola, and Nicaragua's Atlantic Coast illustrate the instigation of ethnic-national conflicts as a weapon of blackmail against peoples who are "rebellious" vis-à-vis the metropolitan states. The intertwining of this intervention with the authentic struggles of peoples seeking self-determination makes the national scene all the more intricate. Amid the confusion and disorder created by foreign forces, it is often difficult to distinguish between the peoples' demands and the intrigues of outsiders.

These maneuvers, which distort and disfigure peoples' rights to self-determination, have not gone unnoticed by the international community. During the Twenty-fifth Session of the United Nations General Assembly it was established that "any attempt directed at partially or totally undermining national unity and the territorial integrity of a state is incompatible with the objectives and principles of the UN's Constitution."[1] Similar concerns and forthright rejection of such manipulation have been expressed in other contemporary fora.[2]

The autonomous settlements I refer to are included in what have been called "constructive agreements" between states and ethnic or national groups. Active and decisive participation of the peoples as independent parties is crucial in these cases.[3] Although autonomy is thought to be an oddity, it has been part of the juridical-political structure of a large number of nation-states around the globe, including (1) the autonomous republics, regions, and provinces set up during the establishment of the Union of Soviet Socialist Republics; (2) Catalunya and Euskadi during the Second Spanish Republic (1931–1936) and, after the Franco interregnum, the many autonomous communities created by the 1978 Spanish constitution; (3) the autonomous entities that have played a key role in the Balkans,

108

Are those *autonomous* or *regions* "stable"?

particularly in the former Yugoslavia; (4) the autonomous regions of the Aosta Valley, Sicily, and Sardinia instituted in Italy under the 1947 constitution; (5) the autonomies of Madeira and the Azores Islands in Portugal as of the constitution of 1976; (6) the autonomous regions of Tibet and Inner Mongolia in the People's Republic of China; (7) the Finnish Oland Islands; (8) the Faeroe Islands and Greenland, which belong to Denmark,[4] and, (9) the two autonomous regions of the Nicaraguan Atlantic Coast legally established in 1987. The elements of the system of regional autonomy analyzed from a broad perspective in the previous chapter will be observed in practice through the examination of the historical examples of the former USSR, Spain, and Nicaragua.

THE REGIME OF REGIONAL AUTONOMY IN THE USSR

After the revolution of October 1917, the huge and baffling "prison of the peoples" of the czarist empire disintegrated. Many of the 146 nations, nationalities and ethnic groups that made up the empire (of which almost 60 percent were non-Russian) gave free rein to their aspirations to independence and autonomy.[5] During 1918 the situation of the revolutionary vanguard became desperate because of the invasive intervention of foreign powers (British, French, Japanese, and North American) and the activities of internal counterrevolutionary forces. The Bolsheviks seemed incapable of stopping the centrifugal forces originating in such conflicts and in the empire's heterogeneity. The area over which the revolutionaries exercised complete political control was reduced to a territory equivalent to medieval Muscovy, while the various peoples and nationalities seemed to be following their own paths on the margins of the Bolshevik project.[6] However, new centripetal forces gradually began to have a contrary effect, in time achieving the almost complete reintegration of the peoples that had been part of the vast czarist empire. This was accomplished with the establishment of the Union of Soviet Socialist Republics (USSR) at the end of 1922.

In that critical moment, given the obvious nationalism unleashed by the revolution itself, the Bolsheviks had to consider a federation as the form for the new socialist state even though they had previously rejected it. This was a positive change of perspective more compatible with the new reality and with the various peoples' aspirations (as the ensuing practice would demonstrate) that was partly due to Lenin's having elaborated a complex and detailed theory on the national question in which he openly endorsed the right of nations to self-determination:

> If we want to understand what self-determination of nations means without fashioning juridical or abstract definitions but examining the historical-economic conditions of the national movements, we will inevitably arrive at the following conclusion: self-determination means separation of the state from the collectivities of an alien nationality and the formation of an independent national state.[7]

Thus, the Bolsheviks did not have to improvise with regard to a theory of the relations between nations or their rights. Russian revolutionaries were well-informed of the elaborations and polemics that their European colleagues (German, Polish, Dutch, and so on) were engaged in, and some of them, such as Lenin, had actively participated in their debates.[8] These theoretical developments allowed the Bolsheviks to accomplish what few regimes have been able to achieve: reuniting nearly all of the constituents of the old empire in a single state, the first multinational state of the twentieth century.

This nation-state federation was not merely a territorial grouping in which the component parts lacked or had already lost their own ethnic-national character (as was the case, for example, with the North American and Swiss federations). The Soviet federation, in effect, was organized as a union of "nation-states"[9] that simultaneously included sovereign federated republics and political collectivities conceived to allow the exercise of autonomy by numerous ethnic-national groups organized in autonomous republics, regions, and provinces.

Let us take a look at their organizational process and their formal structure, keeping in mind that these do not perfectly reflect the process that took place. The Russian Soviet Federal Socialist Republic (RSFSR), constituted on November 7, 1917, was the first component, a grouping of nationalities organized as states or as autonomous entities. In time, the RSFSR became part of the USSR as a federated republic. The Russian nationalities and peoples, as an organized group, played a crucial role in the association process of the then dispersed parts of the old regime: They constituted the powerful initial nucleus that was afterwards capable of attracting other peoples (though not the Slavs) into a confederated structure.[10] Carr concludes that the challenge

> faced by the Bolsheviks of reuniting the scattered fragments of the czarist empire, could have been insurmountable had it not been for the huge preponderance of the Great Russians, who acted as a magnet for the people as a whole. . . . The Great Russians exercised the same centralizing pressure over the Ukrainians and White Russians as was exercised by Prussia in the Germanic Confederation.[11]

The Transcaucasian Soviet Federal Socialist Republic (TSFSR) was founded in May 1922, grouping within it the independent republics of Azerbaijan (which was born in April 1920), Armenia (November 1920), and Georgia (February 1921).[12] The federal Soviet state (USSR) was established at the Soviets' Constituent Congress on December 30, 1922, with the union of four republics as federated (the RSFSR, the TSFSR, the Ukrainian Soviet Socialist Republic, and the Byelorussian Soviet Socialist Republic), to which others were later added. After World War II, the Soviet Union was made up of fifteen federated republics, with the incorporation or annexation of the three Baltic republics and Moldavia.

According to the USSR's 1977 Constitution, a federated republic had every attribute of a sovereign state: It could approve its own constitution without any ratification by a higher body; its territory could not be modified without its consent; it held the same power rank among the Union's institutions regardless of the size of its population and territory; it was represented in the Soviet of the Union and in the Soviet of Nationalities, which consisted of thirty-two deputies per federated republic; it retained the right to offer legislative initiatives and administered its own socioeconomic, political, and cultural affairs. The Supreme Soviet's Presidium included fifteen vice presidents, one for each federated republic. Article 70 of the federal constitution established that the federated republics possessed equivalent rights and their association was voluntary; article 72 indicated, on the Leninist principle, that each federated republic retained "the right to separate freely from the USSR."[13]

On the next level in the Soviet state organization were the autonomous collectivities. Their foundations lay in the Union's constitution, and the constitutions of the federated republics defined their juridical statutes. All of them, therefore, were at least constitutionally relevant entities.

The Soviet socialist autonomous republic was part of the federated republic and not a sovereign state; its constitution had to be authorized by the federated republic of which it was part. However, autonomous republics participated in the full exercise of power within the Union and within their corresponding federal republics. Each autonomous republic sent eleven deputies to the USSR's Soviet of Nationalities, and the president of its own supreme soviet's presidium was vice president of the corresponding higher organ of the federal republic. The territory of an autonomous republic could not be modified without the federal republic's approval. It legally possessed broad socioeconomic, political, and cultural competences. Thus it could be considered an entity of constitutional character that gave shape to the typical form of political autonomy. There were twenty autonomous republics in the USSR as late as 1990, sixteen of which belonged to the RSFSR; two more were part of the Georgian, one of the Azeri, and another of the Uzbek Soviet Socialist Republic.

In contrast, the autonomous region was characterized as a "national-state formation" with political-administrative powers that allowed national and ethnic groups to exercise their rights within the context of a given territory, whereas the autonomous republic was considered, by Soviet specialists, a nation-state (though without sovereignty). The statutes proposal presented by the deputies of the soviet of peoples of the autonomous region had to be promulgated by the supreme soviet of the federated republic to which it belonged. The autonomous region had its own government and administrative organs and relatively broad powers to manage its own affairs. Although it was classified, according to the terminology of Soviet jurists, as possessing "administrative autonomy," it enjoyed high juridical-political status in that it was represented by five deputies in the USSR's Soviet of Nationalities. Until the USSR was reformulated, there were eight autonomous regions in the USSR. Five were part of the RSFSR and one each of the Georgian, Azeri, and Tadzhik soviet socialist republics.

There was no necessary correspondence between the size of the autonomous entities' territory and their juridical-political rank within the USSR. There were autonomous republics with more territory than certain federated republics, as well as autonomous regions with more territory than some autonomous republics. As a rule, what characterized Soviet autonomous entities was their territorial vastness: Many of them had larger territories than some Latin American countries and, of course, European countries as well. For example, the Yakutsk ASSR was 3,103,000 square kilometers, the autonomous region of Gorni Altai was more than 90,000 square kilometers, and there were several regions larger than 700,000 square kilometers.

Finally, the autonomous province was characterized as a "national-territorial formation" and an autonomous form with an administrative emphasis. The provinces were established through a law promulgated by the supreme soviet of the federated republic that acknowledged the sociocultural particularities of the peoples that lived in them. These provinces included territories (in the majority of cases even larger than those of autonomous regions) of the extreme northern and eastern part of the country, occupied at the time of the Bolshevik Revolution by numerous nonliterate ethnic groups, some in the process of dissolution, which a tribal or semitribal form of organization. These were territories in which intense interethnic interaction took place and several ethnic-national groups coexisted. The autonomous province had its own governmental organs (council of deputies of the people) and administration, and by order of the 1977 constitution it was represented by a deputy in one of the chambers of the Soviet of Nationalities. There were ten autonomous provinces in the USSR, all of them part of the RSFSR.

How did this juridical-political scheme operate in practice? It is tempting, considering the present situation, to maintain that ethnic-national policy in the USSR was totally disastrous from the beginning. However, the many achievements (economic, social, cultural) of the peoples and nations within the federal and autonomous organization of the Soviet system cannot be denied. That such a variety of peoples and ethnic groups could live and flourish together for decades, overcoming the profound economic backwardness, cultural oppression, and obscurantism inherited from the czarist period, was an extraordinary achievement; the fact that it happened with relatively little friction and conflict is even more remarkable.

Any system of relations generates new disagreements and contradictions, however, these new problems were added to the difficulties with which the regime of autonomy was born, framed by a centralist tradition to which the new socialist leadership was already strongly inclined, and the challenges arising from a constantly changing outside world. The Soviet process illustrates the degree to which the system of regional autonomy is conditioned by the sociopolitical development of the nation-state, in this case a political system that soon lost any flexibility, inhibited the development of opportunities for democracy, discouraged or blocked popular participation, and reduced to a minimum regional and local participation in national affairs while giving free rein to centralism, bureaucratism, and in general, all the authoritarian controls that prevent the exercise of democracy. The federal-autonomous order was suffocated by a lack of national democracy. If the system of regional autonomy lost its dynamism and substance it was mainly because the sociopolitical regime in which it was embedded did so. It is possible, however, that a political structure of this kind would have collapsed much earlier, because of uncontrollable friction among its constituent parts if it had not had a regime of autonomy to vent its contradictions.

The spirit and meaning of the 1922 agreement, which established the premises for an ethnic-national arrangement and, for a while, perhaps, guaranteed an authentic unity, was diluted over time, and the right to self-determination of nations and peoples lost its original meaning. Within the framework of a multinational union the concept of self-determination is meaningless if the union is no longer voluntary and therefore voluntary separation from or revision of the terms of the union is no longer possible.

It is true that fundamental Soviet law officially conformed to the Leninist principle of voluntary union and separation until the 1977 constitution, but it was very early understood and never discussed or doubted that no one would wish to exercise the right to separation. Thus the conditions under which a federated republic could legally leave the union or redefine its relation to it were never specified in detail. Why should mechanisms be articulated for a separation that no one would need? This assumption was the reflection of an untenable presumption of unanimity, of absence of conflict or disagreement, that, ironically, was anti-Marxist. In reality, the expression of conflict or discord was concealed and/or suppressed, but avoiding the articulation of a legal procedure for separation, which was, in principle, constitutionally valid, amounted in fact to forbidding separation. In an already overheated political environment, the highest legislative organ of the country concerned itself with the establishment of these rules (support for the secession of two-thirds of the population of the corresponding republic, through a plebiscite, and a transition period of several years) only in 1990.

By then national and ethnic conflicts that threatened to tear the USSR apart had gained strength in the context of the changes brought about by perestroika. In 1987, in his masterpiece on the renovation of the Soviet system, Gorbachev's discourse regarding the national question still reflected complacency typical of official ideology, warning that "this does not mean that national processes are free of problems" and lamenting the habit of "accentuating our achievements" and evaluating "the situation in pompous terms."[14] At the beginning of 1988 the Soviet leader emphasized the damaging effects of nationalism and chauvinism, but he also admitted that "in the present stage we must seriously consider the issues of national politics. We must do it in every aspect: theoretically and practically. It is a vital question, essentially important for our society. I believe that we must devote the plenary sessions of the Central Committee to the problems of national politics."[15] But the ponderous bureaucratic system moved quite slowly, and the country's new leadership, hesitant and erratic, was not up to the task.

A serious ethnic confrontation between Armenians and Azeris over the national character of the autonomous region of Nagorno-Karabakh began in February 1988, and restlessness and conflict erupted in other republics. The Baltic republics began to express their desire for independence openly, and diverse and aggressive nationalisms appeared in Moldavia, Ukraine, Georgia, and elsewhere.

Nagorno-Karabakh is merely one example of the innumerable ethnic conflicts that had accumulated in the USSR and were only waiting for the right moment to explode. Nagorno-Karabakh is an autonomous region within a federated republic (Azerbaijan) with close to 80 percent of its population originally Armenian and claimed by the Federated Republic of Armenia. Besides the ethnic-national identities, religious ones are at play, since most Armenians are Christian and the Azeris are Muslims. In 1989 the clash took on the character of a virtual civil war between Armenians and Azeris, with many casualties, forcing Soviet authorities to send troops to take control of the situation. In the midst of the crisis, in early 1990, the religious dimension caused unexpected international complications when ultranationalist Azeri groups (Muslim fundamentalists) attempted to erase the border with Iran and expressed their intention of forming a new political organization with their Iranian coreligionists. The bewilderment and ineffective response of the Soviet authorities indicated the degree to which they were unprepared for this kind of conflict, having assumed that these differences were a thing of the past.[16]

There was little familiarity with the country's ethnic-national conflicts, and there were no independent scholars or policymakers capable of offering timely guidance and useful suggestions. Ethnic conflicts exposed the bankruptcy of the Soviet social sciences, which had routinized the exaltation of the founding fathers of marxism and the Soviet leadership. Propaganda had been substituted for scientific reflection, and when propaganda was ineffective no objective knowledge was available.[17] The enmity between the groups battling over Nagorno-Karabakh and other conflicts indicated the absurdity of the fantasy of "Homo sovieticus." There was no new overarching identity immune to ethnic chauvinism, although its achievement had been proclaimed by anthropologists and sociologists over and over again.[18] The development of a culture of tolerance ("indifference") with regard to national or ethnic difference, a primary political goal of Lenin, had not taken place.[19]

The most serious challenge lay in the Baltic states. There the independence project launched by the nationalists was the essence of the conflict between the federated republics and the state. In other regions interethnic conflicts surfaced in which the central power was indirectly involved (for example, Ukraine and Uzbekistan, in addition to the aforementioned Azerbaijan and Armenia). The movements that emerged with national political demands in these areas were not well organized. In the Baltic republics, not only was the demand for independence fundamental to the movement but also there were well-coordinated organic structures, the so-called popular fronts. The interethnic conflict here (as in Moldavia) stemmed from the national movement itself, since the Slavic population (the so-called ethnic Russians) and other groups asserted their rights as minorities in the context of the changes advocated by the nationalists. In Estonia, Russians, Byelorussians, and Ukrainians staged demonstrations and strikes in July 1989 against the measures (electoral, linguistic, and other) undertaken by the supreme soviet (dominated by Estonians). Similar measures were taken in Moldavia in August of the same year, provoking protests by Russian-speakers that contributed to the emergence of ethnic demands among other peoples. Stimulated by Moldavian nationalism, a desire for autonomy was expressed in Gagauz. These conflicts not between the central power and the republics but within the latter helped complicate the situation.

The Baltic republics achieved their independence within the USSR through procedures that resolved the main controversies and guaranteed a more or less orderly separation. This should not have been perceived as a tragedy; the legal structure of the USSR allowed for such a contingency. The independentist initiatives of the Baltic republics (particularly those of Lithuania) may have been somehow precipitated by outside influences, but they did not lack historical legitimacy. The Baltic areas were incorporated into the Union late and problematically; their language and other cultural attributes, geographical location, and socioeconomic characteristics all contributed to their desire for autonomy.[20] The impatience shown by the tiny republics found its justification in the denial of their right to self-determination within the context of the Union.

The separation of the Baltic republics was not a great setback for the USSR. The solid core of the Soviet multinational state continued to be the Russian population and, in some measure, other Slavic peoples that, as groups, had expanded throughout a considerable part of the planet. The loss of the Baltic territories (among the smallest of the Union in terms of territory and population) had a primarily symbolic meaning: the political shattering of a fossilized structure that could have served to reawaken the awareness of its complex composition and the diverse national interests it had to satisfy if it hoped to survive intact. In this sense, it could be regarded as positive. It might have suggested the need for reorganization of the USSR's federal and autonomous system—for the establishment of an authentic democracy and real political, economic, and social decentralization.

Considering that ethnic antagonisms would not disappear but would become greatly accentuated, these radical changes might have arrested the centrifugal forces that had begun to increase in strength after seven decades of relative state stability. With a renovated federal and autonomous system based on new democratic relations and some political and territorial modifications that the conflicts had revealed were necessary, the core of the Union could have survived. Steps toward political, economic, and social reform were outlined in the midst of an acute crisis. For example, by mid-March 1990 the project of strengthening self-government for the autonomous republics and entities in the management of economic and financial matters was announced, and, at the same time the excessive interference of state institutions was reduced.[21]

If changes like these, complemented by daring transformations of the political and sociocultural foundations of the Union, could have been effected, the USSR might well have overcome the situation without enormous disruption. However, policymakers were swimming against the tide. Various interests and inertias opposed the renovating initiatives. The immediate alternative for the USSR was clear: national renovation or disintegration.

The attempted coup d'état against Gorbachev by a powerful faction within the Soviet apparatus accelerated the process that destroyed the Union. The coup failed, but it terminated Gorbachev's political leadership and canceled the search for solutions within the framework of a new multinational state. The political promotion of Boris Yeltsin, the leader of a group that put the interests of the Russian Republic ahead, favored the dissolution of the Soviet state. The republics were freed to face their individual fates. With the dissolution of the USSR, the independence of the Baltic republics was also sealed.

Obviously, the ethnic-national problem did not disappear after the events just described; it was simply transferred to the domain of the independent republics. Ethnic conflicts will probably become more acute both within the republics and as a consequence of the links between them. It is impossible to predict the future course of these republics, but it is certain that autonomy will continue to be a pressing issue in the context of most of the new states, especially in the large and heterogeneous Russian federation. Autonomy will be a continuing theme in their national and, in some cases, international arrangements.

AUTONOMOUS COMMUNITIES WITHIN THE SPANISH STATE

In Spain regimes of autonomy have historically been linked to the country's efforts at democratization. The first of three attempts to reflect the diversity of Spanish sociocultural configuration took place with the First Republic of 1873, whose constitution established a federal system of seventeen "states," each with its own constitution and economic-administrative and political autonomy limited by the fundamental law of the federation.[22] In the context of this constitution (article 40), "state" really corresponds to region and "federation" to nation. This ephemeral experiment was thwarted by the Restoration.

The second attempt came with the Second Republic, whose 1931 constitution said that "the Republic constitutes an integral State, compatible with the autonomy of municipalities and regions" and recognized the right of "one or several adjacent provinces with common historical, cultural, and economic characteristics" to present "their Statute" to "be organized as an autonomous region and form a political-administrative nucleus within the Spanish state," according to proce-dures established in the constitution. Catalonia became an autonomous region in accordance with the statute of September 21, 1932. It included the provinces of Barcelona, Gerona, Lerida, and Tarragona. The autonomy statute for the Basque Country was approved in 1937 in the midst of the civil war.[23] All these measures were rendered obsolete by the reestablishment of centralism under Francisco Franco.

The third phase resulted from the rebirth of liberal democracy in the country. The 1978 constitution, obviously inspired by the Spanish constitution of 1931 and the Italian constitution of 1947, "acknowledges and guarantees the right to autonomy of the nationalities and regions" that make up the country. Further, it establishes that "in the exercise of the right to autonomy . . . adjacent provinces with common historical, cultural, and economic characteristics and insular terri-tories and provinces with historical regional unity will be able to attain self-government and become autonomous communities."[24]

Thus the present Spanish constitution describes a state whose uniqueness lies in its inclusion of autonomous communities. Some writers call this kind of state "au-tonomic," something equivalent to the integral state of the Second Spanish Repub-lic and the regional state of the Italian republic.[25] Others use designations such as "federal-regional state," "state with constitutionally guaranteed autonomies," or "autonomic state with federal undertones."[26]

The Spanish constitution is organized around three fundamental axes: unity of the nation, autonomy, and solidarity among its constituent parts. It is more specific with regard to the solidarity principle, indicating that the state guaran-tees its effective application, "overseeing the establishment of an adequate and fair economic balance among the different parts of the Spanish territory" and, further, prohibiting the different statutes of autonomous communities from im-plying "economic and social privileges." With the object of resolving interterrito-rial economic imbalances, a "compensation fund for investment expenses" was established, to be distributed by the general courts. In addition, the constitution contains a principle of "equal treatment" to which the statutes of the au-tonomous entities must adjust, according to which "all Spanish have the same rights and obligations in any part of the State's territory" and neither the circula-tion and settlement of people nor the free circulation of goods will be hindered in any part of the territory.

With this set of principles and a formative stage of "preautonomous" regimes begun in 1977, autonomous communities took shape until there were seventeen in all. They included traditional nationalities with a strong nationalistic spirit such as Catalonia and the Basque Country, insular territories such as the Canary Islands, and various other regions. Autonomous communities are public entities with constitutional relevance based upon their own statutes as institutional norms. They have limited territories with constitutionally limited regulatory and legislative capacities and their own organs of self-government to handle their affairs. There is a constitutional distribution of competences in accordance with a bilateral arrangement indicating the matters in which the central state has exclusive power and those that may be under the jurisdiction of autonomous communities. According to the "residual or remnant clause," all matters not constitutionally assigned to the central state may be statutorily assumed by the autonomous communities, returning to the central state's jurisdiction in the event that the communities do not do so.[27]

The organization and regulation of self-governing institutions are the exclusive responsibility and right of the autonomous communities and therefore subject to their particular statutes. However, the constitution establishes basic guidelines for the institutional organization of communities with total autonomy, foreseeing the existence of (a) a legislative assembly, elected by universal vote, in which all the zones of the autonomous territories are proportionally represented; (b) a government council "with executive and administrative functions"; (c) a president elected by the assembly from among its members and politically responsible to it, "who is in charge of the course of the government council, the supreme representation of the community, and the ordinary representation of the state in it," and (d) a higher justice court "without detriment to the jurisdiction of the Supreme Court."

After more than a decade it seems clear that the various nationalist and regionalist perspectives of the country have found a peaceful avenue for satisfying their aspirations in the new form of organization. Sharing among the nationalities and more or less cooperative relationships between the collectivities and the central state would have been inconceivable without the autonomous regimes. Without autonomy it is quite possible that the tensions now constitutionally channeled would have become unsettling disagreements.

Social dynamics often hinder permanent solutions. In recent years, especially since 1989, there have been indications of a strengthening of nationalist demands, especially in Catalonia, the Basque Country, and Galicia, no doubt influenced by events in Eastern Europe and the USSR and, particularly, by the prospect of European union. Although some groups want to maintain the status quo, traditional nationalist groups—in the Basque Country, for example—are pressing for an intermediate solution that would provide more independence for the regions (a kind of shared sovereignty) without abandoning the established constitutional framework. There are also some radical forces (e.g., the Basque organization ETA and its political organ, the Herri Batasuna party) that seek to define self-determination as independence.

It may soon be necessary to explore new formulas for revitalizing or revising the political arrangements of the late 1970s, conferring more responsibilities and freedoms on some collectivities that are actively demanding them (perhaps as much as a fourth of the population, according to a public opinion poll). The latent aspirations of even larger nuclei may spring up again and prove uncontrollable.

AUTONOMOUS REGIONS IN NICARAGUA

The historical development of Nicaragua has shaped two large sociocultural and economic regions: on the Pacific Coast a population with mestizo cultural patterns and on the Atlantic indigenous peoples (Miskitos, Sumos, and Ramas) and other ethnic communities (creoles and Black Caribs).[28] In the Atlantic region, coastal peoples and communities interacted with the mestizo population which in time also formed a vast group gradually augmented, especially during the 1960s by immigrants from the west, advancing the agrarian frontier.

The ethnogenesis of these coastal groups must be understood from the perspective of over four centuries of colonial and neocolonial history. First there was the dispute between England and Spain for control over this territory during the colonial period.[29] Then there was Nicaragua's lack of real sovereignty over this part of its territory for nearly the whole of the nineteenth century, despite its formal political independence, because of the expansion of British rule under the Mosquitia Protectorate (1824–1860) and the Mosquitia Reserve (1860–1894). Finally, the constant concession of coastal territory to foreign interests, particularly to North American enterprises interested in the exploitation of its natural resources and native labor force, by conservative and liberal governments (especially during the dictatorship of the Somoza family),[30] determined the specific sociocultural characteristics that differentiate the Atlantic Coast people from the people of the Pacific region with regard to historical tradition, customs, language, religion, forms of social organization, and economic conditions.

The ethnic identity of the peoples and communities of the Atlantic was shaped in part as a response to the repressive policies of the prerevolutionary governments, whose intent was the dissolution and disintegration of these groups. It provided the cohesion that arises from contrast: Anything that sharply exposes the "other" strengthens the sense of self-identity. In effect, the episode known in Nicaraguan history as the "reincorporation" of the Atlantic Coast, central to which were the political and military actions of General Rigoberto Cabezas in 1894, in practice meant not an acknowledgment of plurality but an intensification of cultural repression. In 1899 the post of indigenous mayor was eliminated, and in 1900 the teaching of the Spanish language was imposed, the use of the languages of these peoples and their communities forbidden.[31] The same homogenizing integrationist policy, disrespectful of coastal ethnic characteristics, was applied up to the Sandinista triumph in 1979 and, in a different way, even thereafter.

These communities recovered their ethnic identity and openly presented their demands during the first years of the revolutionary government. In Nicaragua, as in the cases previously examined, the process of political transformation and the social change it brought about led to the creation of opportunities for open discussion of the ethnic-national question and the search for a formula that might allow ethnic groups to exercise their historical rights. This formula was regional autonomy.

Indeed, after an initial period of vacillation, confusion, and errors of omission and commission,[32] the Sandinistas initiated the formal establishment of regional autonomy in 1984. This process took place in the face of U.S. aggression against Nicaragua (destruction of ports, sabotage, economic blockade, and so on) and, in particular, a sharp dispute over control of the coast. The U.S. administration, taking advantage of the historical struggle between the coast and the rest of the country, placed special emphasis on creating unrest in the region during this period. Official spokespersons of the U.S. government undertook a broad public opinion campaign (for example, denouncing general human rights' violations—later proved false—in the zone), in various fora. Forces under U.S. control conducted various maneuvers, denounced by independent organizations, to foster massive mobilization and armed actions of coastal people against Honduras. In brief, a strategy that came to be known as "low-intensity warfare" was employed throughout the coastal area.[33] The fact that even under such adverse circumstances the autonomy process produced a widely accepted agreement and political model was one of the major achievements of the Sandinista Revolution, one that required great tact and political skill.

By September 1987, regional autonomy was a juridical-political reality in Nicaragua. This was not merely an improvised scenario; the Nicaraguan autonomy plan was the culmination of a painstaking process that had begun three years before with the indigenous ethnic groups' active participation. During this period important meetings were organized that allowed them to discuss their problems and aspirations and to express their points of view. At least six fundamental steps can be distinguished:

1. Theoretical-political consideration and discussion of the bases for a possible regime of regional autonomy. Intense debate on the Nicaraguan ethnic-national question began in mid-1984. Sandinista intellectuals, researchers from the country's study centers the Centro de Investigación y Documentación de la Costa Atlántica [Center for Documentation and Research of the Atlantic Coast—CIDCA], the Instituto Nicaragüense de Investigaciones Económicas y Sociales [Nicaraguan Institute of Economic and Social Research—INIES], and the Centro de Investigaciones y Estudio de la Reforma Agraria [Center for Agrarian Reform Research and Studies—CIERA] and invited specialists from Mexico participated. These discussions and deliberations, which lasted several months, examined the historical implications of the coastal question, including an appraisal of the sociocultural policies applied up to that time, and considered the strategic importance of a comprehensive solution to the problem in the context of the broader changes undertaken by the Sandinistas. In the end the initial bases were established for a project of autonomy with democratic foundations.

2. Establishment of the Comisión Nacional de Autonomía (National Commission for Autonomy—CNA). Immediately after these initial discussions, a National Commission for Autonomy with two regional commissions in the two tra-

ditional zones of the coast was created. For four months after its founding on December 5, 1984, the NAC compiled the opinions of the representative sectors, especially in the two coastal capitals, Bluefields and Puerto Cabezas. On May 1985 a preliminary document was circulated for further discussion.[34] The document was discussed in June by eighty coastal delegates. This forum resulted in the first consensus text produced by coastal representatives.[35] Both documents included the three basic elements of the regime of regional autonomy: the historical rights of the peoples and communities, national unity, and the principles of the Sandinista Revolution.

3. Popular consultation on autonomy. To survey the opinion of local people about the preliminary document, representatives chosen by the coastal people traveled throughout the region (visiting every town, village, and house) collecting the views of every sector. This consultation not only determined what the members of the different ethnic groups thought but also established the popular legitimacy of the project. In November 1985 the representatives from Special Zone 2 (Department of South Zelaya) presented the report to their regional commission; the representatives for Zone 1 (North Zelaya) presented it in December.[36] Approval was practically unanimous. Thus, this autonomy project was based upon respect for the opinion of ethnic groups and attention to democratic procedure, a rarity in the history of Latin America.

4. Constitutional consultation and incorporation. The autonomy project was submitted to a still broader public for new nationwide discussions (called "open town councils" in memory of an old tradition) to determine the content of the new constitution in June 1986. It was also put to an international test.[37] The rights of indigenous ethnic groups compiled in the project were then incorporated into the new political constitution approved by the National Constituent Assembly on November 19, 1986. This third step marked another unusual event in the continent: For the first time both the sociocultural rights and the mandate to create a regime of autonomy were explicitly included in a constitutional text.

5. The Multiethnic assembly. Once the fundamental rights of the coastal people had acquired constitutional status, it was necessary to determine the content of the statute of autonomy. The democratic character of this fundamental step in the process was guaranteed by proceeding, once again, from the bottom up. Each of the communities selected representatives to debate the content of the draft statute developed by the National Commission for Autonomy. A Multiethnic Assembly was held April 22–24, 1987, at Puerto Cabezas, and 220 delegates from the various ethnic groups participated, along with numerous journalists, international observers, and special guests. The representatives publicly discussed each article of the draft, accepting some in their original form, modifying others, and including new elements.[38] At midnight on April 23 the assembly approved a text that in fact became a proposal for the statute.

6. The Autonomy Statute. Finally, the proposal backed by the communities was submitted by Daniel Ortega, Nicaragua's president, for the congress's consideration. The congress approved it with few modifications. Thus, the will of the in-

digenous peoples and communities of the Atlantic Coast became national consensus and a law of the republic.[39]

Although the law of autonomy lacks constitutional status,[40] the Nicaraguan
regime of autonomy has undoubted constitutional relevance. In several titles of
the constitution there are references to the rights of the coastal ethnic communities and an explicit mandate to organize a regime of autonomy. However, the constitution does not define the characteristics, functions, and institutional bodies of
the autonomous region, leaving all these issues for the statute. Legislative powers
and forms of participation in the state's supreme powers are also left unspecified.
In the autonomy project's preparatory documents, competences were specified
for the autonomous entities alongside those of the central state,[41] but this distribution did not appear in the substantive law; statutory and legislative competences
remained under the central state. This is, therefore, a typical "administrative"
form of autonomy.

The Nicaraguan political constitution establishes a basic foundation in Title 2
(on the state), namely, that "the Nicaraguan people is multiethnic in nature" (article 8). In addition, while Spanish is declared the state's official language, it is also
established that coastal languages are official according to the law.[42]

The constitution includes two chapters specifically addressing the Atlantic
Coast. In Title 4 (relating to the rights and guarantees of the Nicaraguan people),
chapter 6 deals with "rights of the Atlantic Coast communities." Basically, it establishes (a) that the coastal communities "are an indissoluble part of the
Nicaraguan people and, as such, enjoy the same rights and have the same obligations"; (b) that they have the right to "preserve and develop their cultural identity" within the national unity and to "provide themselves with their own forms of
social organization and to administer their local affairs according to their traditions"; (c) that the state recognizes "communal forms of landownership" and the
"enjoyment, use, and benefit of the water and forests of their communal land;"
and (d) that the state is obliged to see that "no Nicaraguan be an object of discrimination due to her/his language, culture, and origin."

The other chapter on the Atlantic Coast is in Title 9, on the political-administrative division. Here (chapter 2, articles 180 and 181) the particular rights that
correspond to the communities are reiterated, adding the guarantee that these
may freely elect "their authorities and representatives." Equally, the constitutional
mandate of organizing "the autonomous regime in the regions the Atlantic Coast
communities inhabit so that they can exercise their rights" is established.

The statute sets forth three principles considered basic to the revolution and to
autonomy: "unity, fraternity, and solidarity among the inhabitants of the Atlantic
Coast communities and all the nation" (article 3), equal treatment for all
Nicaraguans in the territory of autonomous regions (article 10), and equality of
all ethnic communities among themselves "without regard for the size of their
population and level of development" (article 11.1).

The solidarity principle, inseparable from national unity and fraternity in
keeping with the aforementioned positive asymmetry, is concretely expressed in

the creation of a "special development and social promotion fund" for the pursuit of balanced social development and socioeconomic prosperity for the country's autonomous regions.

The principle of equal treatment seeks to avoid any violation or disregard, anywhere in the national territory, of the basic social or individual rights validated in the constitution. In other words, the autonomy regime was established to achieve sociocultural equality, not to create new inequalities or privileges.

Finally, the principle of equality among all communities is obviously directed at discouraging any ethnic group's attempt to dominate others, a historical tendency endemic to the region. In particular, this principle is crystallized in the composition of the highest regional political body (the regional council), in which "all ethnic communities of every autonomous region must be represented."

Nicaraguan autonomy therefore favors the administrative tendency toward decentralization that allows coastal people to manage their affairs through institutional organs created to meet this need. The autonomy statute establishes two autonomous regions: the North Atlantic Autonomous Region, whose jurisdiction covers the territory of Special Zone 1, the Department of North Zelaya, and the South Atlantic Autonomous Region covering the territory of Special Zone 2, the Department of South Zelaya, with administrative seats at Puerto Cabezas and Bluefields respectively.

The autonomous regions are juridical embodiments of public rights and have among their main attributes the following: participating in the elaboration and enactment of the region's national development projects, managing health, education, culture, and other programs in coordination with the central state, launching their own socioeconomic and cultural projects, protecting and conserving the local ecology, and establishing regional taxes according to the law. The statute also defines the particular constitutional rights of coastal people.

Each autonomous region has the following administrative organs: a regional council, a regional coordinator, municipal and communal authorities, and other authorities corresponding to the administrative subdivision of the municipalities.

The regional council, the highest community organ, is a forty-five-member assembly including representatives of all ethnic groups, elected "by universal, equal, direct, free, and secret vote" for a four-year term; the region's deputies to the National Assembly are also members of the council. This council has broad powers in the administration of regional affairs (article 23), including the regulation "through resolutions and ordinances" of all the affairs that article 8 of the statute, identifies as "general attributions" of the autonomous regions. The council elects a board of directors from among its members in which "every ethnic community" of the region must be represented and whose functions are, basically, coordination of the council itself and of this council with other regional and national authorities.

The regional coordinator, elected by the council from among its members, is in charge of executive functions and representation of the region. Municipal administration in the region is governed by the statute and the law in question. In particular, the council prepares the preliminary plan for the establishment of bound-aries and municipal organization in its jurisdiction and resolves boundary dis-putes in the communities. Other local authorities follow the resolutions of their regional councils.

 At present in Nicaragua the realization of the regime outlined in the statute of autonomy has been slow and difficult because of the complicated conditions gen-erated by intense internal conflict and outside interference, as well as by the per-sistent economic crisis and other calamities that have fallen upon Nicaraguan na-tional society. For example, the destruction caused by Hurricane Juana in 1988, which practically razed the Atlantic Coast (especially in the south), aggravated the region's critical situation. In spite of these problems, pilot programs were imple-mented in some zones, and drafts for projects were prepared under the Sandinista government.

Elections in both regions to choose members of the regional councils took place together with the national elections on February 25, 1990. These elections constituted a great step forward in the consolidation of the system of autonomy. The political-administrative bodies of the autonomous entities were formally es-tablished. In theory, from that moment on the regions began the exercise of self-government. However, the outcome of those elections led to new challenges for the people of the Atlantic Coast.

Even in the aftermath of the national and regional elections, in which the oppo-sition (UNO) won a majority of the votes, the results did not seem to affect the im-mediate future of autonomy as a legal system, but they did provide an opening, once again, for the most rancid centralist tradition. The new government does not seem inclined to give full recognition to regional self-government; on the contrary, a central governmental body, the Instituto de Desarrollo de la Costa Atlántica (In-stitute for the Development of the Atlantic Coast—INDERA), paradoxically led by one of the leaders whose clamor for autonomy in relation to the Sandinista gov-ernment was among the most strident, was created. It intends to operate without regard to local bodies on which the constitution and laws confer very precise func-tions. This development indicates that the new rulers, favoring the former central-ized state, do not wish to recognize any authority other than their own on the coast.

This opens a new stage in the historical struggle between the centralism of the Pacific region and the autonomy of the Atlantic Coast, but since support for the regime of autonomy by the indigenous peoples and communities has grown, this regime does not seem to be at risk. Autonomy will most likely be retained as one of the triumphs of the coastal people in the context of the Sandinista Revolution, de-spite the fact that the Sandinistas are now the opposition. Progressive Latin Ameri-can sectors will be able to glean valuable lessons from the results of the 1990 elec-tions in the conflict-ridden coastal area.[43]

It is clear that the development of the regime of regional autonomy on the At-lantic Coast will depend on developments in the larger society, particularly in re-gard to internal peace, political stability, economic growth, and, above all, democracy. The people of the coast now have a clearly defined project that will remain a guide, an objective, and a program worth fighting for.

NOTES

1. United Nations Organization, *Declaración sobre la concesión de la independencia a los países y pueblos coloniales*, Resolution no. 1514, New York, December 14, 1960.

2. In the same spirit as the UN's resolution, the Universal Declaration of the Rights of Peoples, signed at Algiers in 1988, establishes (article 21) that the rights of peoples "cannot be a pretext for assaulting the territorial integrity and political unity of the state when the latter acts within the limits established by the principles stated in this Declaration." ASAM, *Documentos de trabajo sobre los derechos indígenas y Naciones Unidas*, Servicios del Pueblo Mixe, MS, Mexico City, 1989, p. 52.

3. The special official appointed in 1989 by the UN's Economic and Social Council to study these topics included, within constructive agreements, the "specific legislative dispositions that regulate more general aspects of the lives of indigenous peoples, such as the establishment of institutions with self- or autonomous government under the condition of significant participation by the indigenous party in the legislative process and an explicit acceptance both of the process leading to the arrangement and of its outcome." Cf. Miguel Alfonso Martínez, *Discriminación contra las problaciones indígenas: Estudios sobre los tratados, convenios y otros acuerdos constructivos entre los Estados y las poblaciones indígenas*, First Report, Economic and Social Council, E/CN.4/Sub.2/1992/32, UNO, August 25, 1992, paragraph no. 340.

4. Greenland, considered the largest island in the world (with 2,175,000 square kilometers, of which 341,000 are not covered by ice) has one of the most recent regimes of regional autonomy. Instituted in 1980, autonomy was negotiated between the people of Greenland and the Danish authorities beginning in 1975. The law of autonomy issued by the Danish parliament (No. 577, November 29, 1978) was approved by the population of Greenland in January 1979. The statute confers broad faculties on the autonomous organs for the "negotiation and administration of the affairs of Greenland." These organs are an autonomous parliament elected by the Greenlanders for a four-year term and an autonomous government whose members, including a president, are chosen by the parliament. Chapter 2 of the law regulates the transfer of competences to the autonomous organs, and Chapter 3 regulates relations between these and the kingdom's authorities (including external affairs affecting Greenlander interests).

5. Albert Nenarokov and Aleksandr Proskurin, *La solución del problema nacional en la URSS*, Moscow, Editorial de la Agencia de Prensa Nóvosti, 1983, p. 8.

6. The British historian E. H. Carr wrote: "By the end of 1918 the Russian Soviet Federal Socialist Republic was approximately circumscribed within the same limits as medieval Muscovy before the conquests of Ivan the Terrible, and very few people, perhaps even among the Bolsheviks themselves, believed that the regime could survive." *La revolución bolchevique (1917–1923)*, *1, La conquista y organización del poder*, Madrid, Alianza Editorial, 1979, pp. 271–272.

7. V. I. Lenin, "Sobre el derecho de las naciones a la autodeterminación" (1914), in *Obras escogidas*, vol. 1, Moscow, Editorial Progreso, n.d., p. 618. See also H. Díaz-Polanco, "La cuestión nacional en la obra de Lenin y Stalin," in *La cuestión étnico-nacional*, Mexico City,

Fontamara, 1988, chap. 5. Applying this self-determination principle, the Soviet government recognized Finland's and Poland's independence, as well as the right of the other nationalities to constitute their own nation-states within the framework of the USSR.

8. See, for example, Richard Calwer et al., *La Segunda Internacional y el problema nacional y colonial*, pt. 2, Cuadernos de Pasado y Presente 74, 1978; See also Rosa Luxembourg, *La cuestión nacional y la autonomía*, Cuadernos de Pasado y Presente 81, 1979.

9. L. Grigorian and Y. Dolgopolov, *Fundamentos del derecho estatal soviético*, Moscow, Editorial Progreso, 1979, p. 330.

10. The Slavs played the important role of cohesive force and "leading" sector that Gramsci attributes to the Piamonte during the Italian Risorgimento. Antonio Gramsci, *El risorgimento*, Mexico City, Juan Pablos Editor, 1986, p. 142.

11. Carr, *La Revolución bolchevique* pp. 273–274.

12. The SFSRT was dissolved in 1936; each of its constituent republics became a federated republic in its own right, part of the Union.

13. *Constitution (Fundamental Law) of the Union of Socialist Soviet Republics*, October 7, 1977, Editorial de la Agencia de Prensa Nóvosti, Moscow, 1987.

14. Mikhail Gorbachev, *Perestroika*, Mexico City, Editorial Diana, 1987, pp. 135 ff.

15. Mikhail Gorbachev, *Reformas revolucionarias requieren una ideología renovadora*, Speech given by the Secretary General of the CPSU's Central Committee (plenary session of February 18, 1988), Editorial de la Agencia de Prensa Nóvosti, Moscow, 1988.

16. An indication of the confusion and disorientation of the central authorities was shown in the press conference held by the Supreme Soviet's vice president and high state officials after the session of the Presidium that discussed the "unprecedented situation" around Nagorno-Karabakh, on July 19, 1988. See *En defensa de los intereses comunes: Acerca de la solución del problema nacional en Nagorno-Karabakh*, Moscow, Editorial de la Agencia de Prensa Nóvosti, 1988.

17. In his evaluation of Soviet society, Gorbachev mentioned this aspect as a constraint for the country: "In the social sciences scholastic theorization was fostered and developed. Creative thought was expelled from the social sciences, and superficial gratuitous judgments were declared uncontestable truths. The scientific and theoretical discussions indispensable to the development of thought and creative effort were castrated." Gorbachev, *Perestroika*, p. 21.

18. Without a doubt, the system's practices had ended up causing the majority of ethnographers, linguists, historians, and other academics to neglect the critical function inherent in intellectual and scientific work, turning them into state ideologues. Their work was disseminated only by official organs. Many examples may be found in the compilations of the series *Problems of the Contemporary World*, published in Moscow by the Academy of Sciences of the USSR.

19. V. I. Lenin, "Balance de la discusión sobre autodeterminación," in *La lucha de los pueblos de las colonias y países dependientes contra el imperialismo*, Moscow, Editorial Progreso, n.d., p. 250.

20. The Baltic republics showed the most extensive economic development within the USSR, with per capita production 40 percent higher than the average for the country as a whole.

21. According to the plan, the republics would control basic production for consumption, assume the protection of the environment, and administer services, commerce, tourism, construction, and so on. On the average, it was estimated that the enterprises of the republics (including their autonomous collectivities) would provide 36 percent of na-

tional production given the planned changes. This would have meant an important step forward, because the republics' enterprises at the time provided only 5 percent, an impressive sign of economic centralism. Besides, the project contemplated even greater decentralization in the tiny non-Russian republics. While Russian decentralized enterprises would provide 27 percent of national production, the Caucasian republics (with an index of 7–9 percent) were to reach 72 percent.

22. See the text of the federal constitution of 1873 in Francisco Pi y Magall, *Las nacionalidades*, Madrid, Cuadernos para el Diálogo, 1973, pp. 401ff.

23. "Constitución de la República" and "Estatuto de Cataluña," in Llorens, *La autonomía en la integración política*, pp. 317ff.

24. *Constitución Española*, Madrid, 1978, title 8, article 143.1.

25. Juan-Ferrando Badía, "Prólogo," in Álvarez Conde, *Las comunidades autónomas*, p. 10. Álvarez Conde (p. 60) wrote that "the prefigured juridical form of the state is that of an autonomous state that implies the existence of a single constituting power—the central state—and the existence of multiple centers—that of the central state and those of the autonomous communities—with legislative power."

26. Pedro Arrieta, "Nacionalidades, autonomías y minorías étnicas en España," *Papeles de la Casa Chata*, 1, no. 2, 1986, pp. 82–83.

27. For an analysis of the competences, their distribution and types, see Álvarez Conde, *Las comunidades autónomas*, pp. 145ff.

28. Consuelo Sánchez, *Identidades ardientes: La conformación étnico-nacional en Nicaragua*, Mexico City, Instituto Nacional de Antropología e Historia, 1993.

29. Partly for reasons of colonial history (i.e., their support for British domination), the Miskitos became the hegemonic ethnic group in relation to other autochthonous groups.

30. More on the historical development of the Atlantic Coast can be found in Eduardo Pérez-Valle, *Expediente de campos azules: Historia de Bluefields en sus documentos*, Managua, n.p., 1978; see also CIERA, *La Mosquitia en la revolución*, Managua, Colección Blas Real Espinales, 1981; Jenkins Molieri, *El desafío indígena en Nicaragua*; Héctor Díaz Polanco and Consuelo Sánchez, "Cronología de los hechos históricos de la Costa Atlántica de Nicaragua," *Boletín de Antropología Americana*, nos. 23–24, July and December 1991.

31. Armando Rojas, Galio Gurdián, Amalia Chamorro, and Vilma Núñez, "Estado, derecho y autonomía: Perspectiva revolucionaria de un nuevo ordenamiento jurídico-político en Nicaragua libre," *Revista Nicaragüense de Ciencias Sociales*, 1, no. 1, 1986, p. 6.

32. On this period and the Sandinista mistakes, see the testimonies of Tomás Borge, "Autonomía, nación y revolución," and Luis Carrión, "Nicaragua: La autonomía en la revolución," in Díaz Polanco and López y Rivas, *Nicaragua: Autonomía y revolución*, pp. 57–75.

33. More detailed information can be found in Díaz Polanco, *Etnia, nación y política*, chap. 4.

34. The text's title is "El derecho de autonomía para los pueblos indígenas y comunidades de la Costa Atlántica de Nicaragua," MS, Managua, 1986.

35. CNA, *Principios y políticas para el ejercicio de los derechos de autonomía de los pueblos indígenas y comunidades de la Costa Atlántica de Nicaragua*, Managua, Casa de Autonomía, 1985.

36. Hazel Law, "1987: Aquí no se rinde nadie," *Anuario Indigenista*, 47, no.3, 1987, p. 122.

37. From July 13 to 15, 1986, the International Symposium on State, Autonomy, and Indigenous Rights was held in Managua with the participation of over one hundred indigenous representatives, social scientists, and international law specialists from Latin America, the United States of America, and Europe. There was a positive evaluation of the

Nicaraguan autonomy project. For a record of the proceedings of the symposium, see *Cerca de la vigilia: Memoria de un sueño, autonomía de la Costa Atlántica*, Managua, Ediciones Centinela, 1986.

38. See "Anteproyecto de ley sobre las Regiones Autónomas de la Costa Atlántica," for the draft; for the version approved, see *Autonomía: Rescate de la unidad nacional*, Managua, Comisión Nacional de Autonomía, April 1987.

39. Law no. 28 (September 7, 1987); "Estatuto de autonomía de las regiones de la Costa Atlántica de Nicaragua," in *Boletín de Antropología Americana*, no. 17, July 1988, pp. 157–167.

40. According to the 1986 constitution, the only constitutional laws are the electoral, the emergency, and the protection laws (Political Constitution, article 184). For reforming these laws the constitution itself establishes very strict procedures.

41. See the NCA documents cited earlier. (Notes 34 and 35).

42. Linguistic equality as an individual right is expressed as the right of any person detained to be informed "in a language s/he understands" and to be "helped by an interpreter, free of charge, if s/he does not understand or speak the language used by the court" (articles 33.2.1 and 34.6); regarding education, the people of the coast must have access to it in their "mother tongue" at the levels determined by national plans and programs (article 121).

43. A group from the Universidad Centroamericana and the Instituto Histórico Centroamericano noted: "The only places where, paradoxically, their [the Sandinistas'] electoral results were not bad, despite their serious mistakes during the first years of revolutionary process, were the two Autonomous Regional Councils of the Atlantic Coast. . . . The vote in Region VII (Autonomous Region of the North Atlantic) had peculiar characteristics. The FSLN had quite important victories in the mining zones, basically inhabited by mestizos and Sumos, while the UNO defeated the FSLN in the Miskito areas." "Cómo votó Nicaragua: Los resultados electorales," *Envío*, 9, no. 102, April 1990, pp. 6 and 15.

CHAPTER EIGHT

■

Prospects for Regional Autonomy

A specter is haunting Indian America: the specter of autonomy. Up until a few years ago only a few indigenous organizations were demanding autonomy, and this only in an extremely unclear way. By the end of the 1980s, however, the goal of autonomy had emerged as the primary demand of Indian peoples. Isolated and narrow petitions had given way to a more general demand for the right to self-determination defined as achieving a regime of complete autonomy. The demand for land had been transformed into a demand for control over indigenous territory without abandoning agrarian struggles, and the pursuit of political democracy had become a proposal for profound modifications in the organization of states to allow for Indian self-government within national contexts.

These aspirations to autonomy were clearly confirmed at the First Continental Meeting of Indian Peoples held July 17–21, 1990, in Quito, Ecuador, in which the majority of the continent's Indian organizations participated. In the concluding document, the Declaration of Quito, the indigenous peoples declared: "Now we are fully conscious that our definitive liberation can only be expressed as the full exercise of self-determination." Self-determination acquires a specific form: autonomy. Another resolution reads: "In exercising our right to self-determination, Indians or indigenous people struggle to achieve our complete autonomy within national contexts." Autonomy means "the right Indian peoples have to control our respective territories, including control and management of all the natural resources of the soil, the subsoil, and aerial space, the defense and conservation of nature . . . , the ecosystem's balance and the conservation of life . . . [and] the democratic constitution of our own governments (self-governments)."[1]

Some Latin American governments have expressed concern about this politicization of Indian peoples. In several cases there have been attempts at eliminating or at least defusing this new threat to the strategy of ethnophagous neoindigenism. Ironically, the same state action that once hindered indigenous independent coordination has created new conditions that made stronger organization possible. Now coordination takes place around a common program with deeper political implications: the demand for self-government. Indian peoples aspire not to indigenist revisions but to participation in the process of national change. The Declaration of Quito reads: "Partial integrationist ethnodevelopmental policies applied by governmental entities are not enough. Our problems will not be solved that way. What is needed is a comprehensive and profound transformation of the state and national society, the creation of a new nation."

It is not coincidental that some governments proposed certain legal amendments just as the Indian movement raised these exigencies. The governments' hastily crafted initiatives were intended to soften the impact of the Indian's demands and to relieve the pressure arising from the official celebration—unanimously rejected by the Indians—of the quincentenary of "America's discovery" or the "encounter of two worlds." The governments did not want to arrive at the quincentenary without showing some "renovation" with regard to the pressing recommendations of the commissions created for the commemoration.[2]

A CASE OF LEGAL REFORM

In Mexico, a constitutional reform proposal developed by the National Commission on Justice for the Indian Peoples of Mexico sought to recognize the "plural ethnic" composition of the Mexican nation and the "cultural rights" of the Indian peoples,[3] but it represented only a few of the state's growing concerns. The Mexican executive had established this commission in April 1989, appointing to it academics (anthropologists and jurists), and indigenist intellectuals and bureaucrats, but no indigenous representatives. By August the commission had prepared a proposal that reached the president by mid–1990 after superficial consultation with Indian groups.[4]

In brief, after considering the Indian peoples' situation the commission suggested the following addition to article 4 of the political constitution (part of chapter 1, "On Civil Rights"):

> The Mexican nation has a plural ethnic composition, fundamentally sustained by the presence of the indigenous peoples of Mexico. The states' constitutions and the laws and ordinances of the Federation and of the states and municipalities will establish the norms, measures, and procedures to protect, preserve, and promote the development of languages, practices, customs and specific forms of social organization of the indigenous communities that do not infringe this Constitution. These dispositions will be public policy and will be of interest to the whole of society.
>
> The law will establish procedures to ensure effective access to state jurisdiction for the indigenous people. In federal and local trials involving an indigenous person, his/her practices and juridical customs will be considered during the whole process and final resolution.

The proposal provoked numerous critiques from intellectuals and even more from indigenous organizations,[5] including the following:

1. The proposal's character and scope are so limited that the economic, social and political rights of the Indian peoples are not delineated, although the com-

mission mentions inequalities on economic, social, and political grounds. Throughout the text there is a curious dissociation between the analysis of the situation of the Indian peoples and the commission's proposals.

2. The appropriate constitutional article in which to place the addition, given its wording, is indeed the fourth. It is the failure to recognize indigenous people's administrative capabilities as collective entities that is responsible for the reform's narrow focus on "cultural" issues and its inclusion in the chapter on civil rights. From a different perspective, considering the ethnic-national problem as an economic and sociopolitical question as well as a cultural one, the proposal would mean the addition of a whole new chapter—in this case to the second title of the constitution—as occurred in countries in which a comprehensive solution was sought. Modifications of other constitutional sections, such as the fifth title, especially article 115, would foster a political-administrative reordering that takes Indian peoples into account.

3. Considering the reform in its own terms, that is, limited to "cultural rights," its present formulation is extremely vague. For example, what are the "cultures," "practices and customs," and "specific social organizational forms" of indigenous ethnic groups? These concepts are far too ambiguous and imprecise and allow for regulations via procedural laws that would likely violate indigenous rights (including "cultural" ones). These reforms should identify fundamental rights and prerogatives deriving from the ethnic groups' cultural characteristics. It is not being suggested here that highly detailed regulatory law be incorporated into the constitution, but it is necessary to know what is to be regulated.

4. If the reforms do not explicitly include the specific rights (in economic, social, political and cultural matters) of Indian peoples, any regulation, however daring and broad, will be ineffective. This must be considered because official indigenism has exaggerated the "broad possibilities" supposedly opening up in the legislative arena. False expectations are created because the promised regulatory laws (even for limited cultural rights) will have to be reduced to tangential questions or they will be unconstitutional. This proposal seems to imply that "everything that the logic of substantive law precisely forbids can be protected, preserved and promoted."[6]

5. If the proposal represents "a national political resolve to confront the inequality and injustice affecting indigenous peoples," as the official commission states, it is important to recognize that the commission's formulation does not express the historical aspirations of the country's indigenous peoples or the democratic goals that the nation has defined for itself. Whereas the present international disposition is to recognize the *right to autonomy* of Indian peoples, the proposal, instead, seems to move in the opposite direction in that it places emphasis only on the "cultural" issues, eroding more basic rights.

On December 7, 1990, the Mexican president sent his own initiative to Congress, and it was approved unmodified.[7] It made several formal alterations to the commission's proposal and introduced certain subtle changes in its formulations, in no case extending indigenous rights, and to the list of cultural features it added "resources."

The fact that for the first time in its history as an independent country there was constitutional recognition of the existence of Indian peoples and of the plural composition of the nation must be evaluated in a broader context. The government's gesture is offered in the midst of a serious crisis of legitimacy and the increased political relevance of the indigenous movement. However, it reflects a most interesting shift. In the present national and international contexts, these superficial reforms seem to be merely a prelude to the introduction of new mechanisms of control of indigenous peoples.[8]

A lasting solution for the ethnic-national conflict in Mexican society has yet to be formulated. It was an illusion to expect that the recognition of the pluricultural composition of the nation would lead to a new multiethnic foundation for the state. The obstacles to this were aggravated by the additions and unexpected changes in constitutional article 27 in early 1992 and by the contents of the corresponding regulatory law that was approved shortly thereafter.[9] These modifications substantially reduced the Indians' collective and internal control of their resources, especially land. Equally, they diminished the possibilities for indigenous communities to protect themselves from the persistent outside pressure with regard to their resources and means of subsistence. The resulting agrarian legislation liberalized group controls and created juridical mechanisms by which *ejidatarios* (and *comuneros*) could cede the usufruct rights to their resources, as a group or individually, divide their lands into lots, bestow them upon third parties for purposes of exploitation, and even sell them. Thus the reforms in agrarian legislation narrowed the possible contents of article 4, and set back the changes in sociocultural matters even more.

THE POSTPONEMENT OF TERRITORIAL REORGANIZATION

Continual reorganization without fundamental structural change has taken the place of the elementary creation of a special sphere within the sociopolitical organization of the nation-state in which the historical aspirations of the Indians, socioculturally subordinated and on the margins of essential public issues, acquire an institutional character.

After independence, particularly in those countries with a majority or a significant amount of indigenous population, there have been territorial divisions—with further revisions or modifications—that fail to take the regional identities upon which socioethnic cohesion is founded into account. The various territorial divisions have expressed the interests of local groups (criollos, mestizos, or ladinos), leading to federative entities, provinces, departments, and cantons, none of which displays the sociocultural plurality of the national cluster. For the political-territorial organization of the Latin American nation-states, indigenous ethnic groups have been an *invisible population* because of the economic subordination, social dispersion, and consequent political weakness of the Indian peoples and the habitual ethnocentrism of non-Indians.

The result is a deformed and undemocratic territorial organization. Consequently, there is an ongoing tension within many countries between a centralist scheme that ignores the ethnic composition of the country and one that strives (often in an erratic and obscure way) to make that composition explicit and have it included in the sociopolitical organization of the nation. In the majority of Latin American countries there are two historical disputes: that between centralists and federalists,[10] the focus of traditional historiography, and a more concealed one between those who champion a mode of organization capable of reflecting sociocultural plurality and both centralists and federalists.

Mexico's territorial division is telling. Several studies of the history of the territorial divisions of the country clearly describe the difficulty of finding a formula to suit the nation's needs. O'Gorman has written that a "defect of origin" in political-territorial organization was adopted by the new independent state, reproducing with few substantial changes the "old division" that existed during the colonial period. This was the result of the "recognition and acceptance of certain geographical entities from the period before the conquest" and "the creation of territorial portions that emerged as a result of European penetration." The defect stems from the fact that such "cartographic" continuity contradicts the new sociopolitical reality it should express, since "it is not backed by any ideological continuity."[11]

The "original sin" with which Mexico began its existence as an independent country has not been remedied. It is not that the problem has been ignored but that its solution has been consistently postponed. In fact, when the Constitutional Laws were reformed in 1840, during the constitutional debates in 1856–1857, and again in 1916–1917, these issues were put forward without having been fully discussed—this despite the acceptance in the sessions of 1916–17, that "the present territorial division . . . is a geographical, economic, social, and political aberration that must be rectified, because it entails a germ of dissolution that sooner or later will have obvious manifestations."[12] It is symptomatic that the question of political-territorial organization was avoided even though its defects and difficulties were clearly acknowledged. However, with the idea of solving particular problems, new entities have been created that only reproduce the same basic structure.

Neither the Constitutional Convention nor those who study the issue—some of them truly concerned with the need to "develop a scientific division"—seriously consider the ethnic dimension as a relevant variable in territorial organization. The Constitutional Convention, presented with petitions to establish political entities on the basis of ethnic identity (within the context of the nation-state), has ignored or rejected them. This was the response to the petition for regional autonomy and recognition as a political entity presented by the inhabitants of the Isthmus of Tehuantepec in 1917. This example not only illustrates the attitude of the members of the Constituent Congress toward such petitions but also reveals the historical background of such efforts.

A STRUGGLE FOR AUTONOMY IN THE ISTHMUS OF TEHUANTEPEC

The Isthmus of Tehuantepec was the backdrop for intense disputes even before European penetration. Because it is strategic for transit between central and southern Mesoamerica, it became a key area for commercial activity and the political control of the populations of southern Mexico and part of present-day Central America. It is not surprising, therefore, that Mexicas and Zapotecs found themselves constantly fighting for control over the region.

Immediately before the conquest, King Cosijoeza[13] ruled the Zapotec region of the valley (with its seat in Zaachila) and his son, Cosijopi, controlled Tehuantepec. Zapotec domination over the isthmus was still being consolidated by the beginning of the sixteenth century. The Zapotecs had forced several groups to retreat toward the mountains or toward the coastal strip of the Gulf of Tehuantepec; at the same time, they controlled the route of the Mexicas toward their dominions in Central America. They had a pact with the latter, secured by marriage, but they closely watched the Aztec emperor's forces' march to the south. When the Europeans arrived, Zapotecs ruled over many peoples who paid them tribute. After Tenochtitlan fell, the Zapotecs of the valley and of the isthmus allied themselves with the Spanish. The Zapotecs of the highlands (Netzichus) and other groups (Cuicatecs, Mixtecs, and others) resisted. The Mixes stood out in this respect.[14]

After the Spanish triumph, some important parts of the isthmus became the Marquesado del Valle.[15] The alcaldía mayor of the isthmus originally included Tehuantepec, Tapanatepec, Chimalapa, Tequizistlán, Guichicovi, Jalapa (del Marqués), San Mateo del Mar, and San Francisco del Mar, a vast territory that included Zapotec, Zoque, Mixe, Huave and Chontal towns.[16] In 1560 Tehuantepec became the property of the crown because it was a port and according to royal decree could not belong to individuals.

During the first decades of colonial domination, the sociocultural system of the isthmian Zapotecs enjoyed relative autonomy compared with the stricter control exercised over the natives elsewhere. This was due to the remote location of the zone at the southernmost extreme of New Spain, the paternalistic protection of Cosijopi, and the shield provided by the Marquesado del Valle (which until well into the sixteenth century prevented any further Spanish settlement in the area). Among the measures that the royal authorities employed to limit the marquisate's power there was one that established that, in the territory of the "state" of the marquis, the Spanish could not be considered his vassals. As Chevalier recalls, "this rule had very important consequences, since the marquises took care not to found Spanish villages within their possessions, for these would have limited the scope of their jurisdiction."[17] The people of Tehuantepec escaped the voracious *encomenderos* as well, because when the territory became the crown's once again the moment of liberal concessions in the form of *encomiendas* had already passed and the Spanish state wished to retain as many tributaries as possible.

Rivalry between the royal authorities and the marquises for jurisdiction over the region was beneficial for the communities. For example, by the mid-sixteenth century, after the *alcalde mayor* named by the second marquis decided to grant estates and stables to individuals in the isthmus, the reaction of the monarch's representative was to prohibit such transactions, which he maintained, "greatly harmed and damaged" the natives. It is clear that what worried the viceroy was less the welfare of the indigenous people than the interference of the marquis's employee in a territory considered to be the state's. On April 4, 1555, Don Luis de Velasco issued an order forbidding the practice.[18]

Given its strategic location on the route south, "the Isthmus of Tehuantepec was the object of particular attention for the king's representatives because of its importance for communications with Peru."[19] All of these elements indirectly favored the isthmian communities. Under these conditions the Zapotec community was consolidating its way of life and redefining elements of ethnic cohesion in the new situation. Although its autonomy (in the sense of laissez-faire) was affected by various events,[20] this period was crucial for the groups later development.

The isthmian peoples had developed an intense regional and interregional commerce in foodstuffs. The coast was rich in marine products, and control over the mining of salt, useful in the processing of foodstuffs, gave them a valuable advantage over traders from other regions in that their goods (e.g., fish or meat) kept longer and could therefore travel longer distances. For centuries keeping these resources within the community was the central focus of these peoples' struggles for autonomy. The first fifty years of colonial domination over the isthmian Zapotecs involved severe tribute exactions and political control by the new masters but also productive and commercial alternatives that allowed them to adapt to the new conditions without acute confrontations with the colonizers. The Europeans achieved control over marine commerce and some terrestrial trade routes, but the isthmian Zapotecs had enough room for their market activities. At the same time, they maintained control over their basic resources and their regional preeminence.

In the last quarter of the sixteenth century and into the seventeenth, the indigenous population and its agricultural production declined, while the non-Indian population (Spanish, criollos, and mestizos) experienced notable growth. Although there were fewer people to feed in the communities, there was also less of a labor force to produce a surplus, and the demand for it did not decline proportionally. In fact, there is every indication that the demand for products and services among the Spanish population, particularly the royal bureaucracy, and the indigenous nobility remained constant, and therefore pressure increased.[21]

In the early seventeenth century the demands on Indian labor in Tehuantepec, and probably elsewhere in Oaxaca as well, increased because of the voracity of the *corregidores* and *alcaldes mayores*. This was the crisis, according to Borah's controversial thesis, that New Spain's society suffered from the end of the sixteenth century to the end of the seventeenth (what Borah has called the "century of the depression"). It brought about practices such as the commercial *repartimientos*, that exacerbated the tension in the social environment.

Pressure on the Indian peoples in the isthmus eventually produced an uprising called the Tehuantepec rebellion, after its initial nucleus. The peoples' rage was mainly directed at Juan de Avellán, the *alcalde mayor* of Tehuantepec, who had increased exactions and *repartimientos* to unbearable extremes and imposed cruel punishment when his demands were not met, even on native governors and mayors.[22] On March 22, 1660, thousands of indigenous people who were in Villa de Guadalcázar (the previous name of Tehuantepec) for religious festivities, attacked the houses of the royal authorities, setting them on fire. "They took to the streets, occupied the plazas, surrounded their houses and took the hills; there were more Indian women and men than needed; in each place they took over, the women were the worse and the more stubborn, daring and courageous rock slingers."[23]

The enraged mob killed the *alcalde mayor*, several of his servants, and the cacique of Quiechapa (considered a "traitor to the Indians"). The rest of the Spanish took refuge in the convent. The clerics could not appease the Indians and had a hard time dissuading them from entering the church to capture the refugees. The rebels seized the muskets laid out in the armory and adopted precise and daring measures: they formed a "guard" and established a watch in key places; they disavowed the indigenous officers and chose their own authorities, and they sent messengers to the nearby towns to extend and consolidate the movement. In a few hours they had control of the situation.

The Zapotecs and their allies from other ethnic groups retained control over the region for over a year. Their success had regional repercussions; the uprising spread to other provinces. The Indians from Nejapa rebelled on May 27; in August the Indians from Ixtepeji rebelled against "the vexations, aggravations, and *repartimientos*" of the *alcalde mayor*;[24] in San Pablo Nisiche, the indigenous governor was removed from office and humiliated; the peoples of Villa Alta also joined the movement, as did the Mixes from Ayacaxtepec and Ocotepec.[25] Some two hundred towns joined in the uprising.

This rebellion was the struggle of these peoples for a modicum of autonomy; they were defending their traditions as well as control over their resources and production. The terrible repression that followed a year later was the response of a group of *corregidores, alcaldes mayores,* and their associates in Antequera and Mexico City that was unprepared to accept any kind of autonomy that might affect their large businesses and despotic power.[26] Even the paternalistic mediation of Oaxaca's bishop, Alonso de Cuevas Dávalos, who had a more lenient attitude in that situation, was considered unwelcome by the official and merchant elite.[27]

Despite its limitations (it was, above all, a revolt against the officials and ex-cesses of the colonial regime rather than against the system) and its stifling by fire and sword, the Tehuantepec rebellion was the most important political move-ment of the seventeenth century in New Spain.[28] Though it did not end the abuses, this uprising was a challenge that shook the colonial government and left the germ of a lasting libertarianism in isthmians' historical memory.

In 1715 the indigenous people of Tehuantepec rebelled again, developing a movement similar to the last one, including the participation of Indian women and rejection of indigenous authorities who were loyal to the Spanish. Subse-quently, throughout the eighteenth century the struggle followed legal avenues. In 1736 the Zapotecs of Juchitán initiated a suit "for the restitution of their commu-nal lands" against a Dominican friar who had appropriated them. In 1762 the Zo-ques of three towns in the region went to Tehuantepec to help recover land in the hands of the church. Late in the century, in the context of the Bourbonic reforms, the isthmians fought the crown's measures to appropriate the salt mines.[29]

During the nineteenth century the Juchitecos organized in defense of their communal property and political autonomy. The central character in the events of the first half of the century was José Gregorio Meléndez (called Che Gorio Me-lendre), who headed several armed rebellions. Up until his death in 1853, "this leader directed every struggle not only of the Zapotecs but also of the Huaves, Chontales, and Zoques who lived throughout the southern coast of the isthmus, from Guelavichi, west of Salina Cruz, to Tonalá and Chiapas in the east."[30] The most notable struggles between the peoples and the authorities were related to the salt mines, the rights to which the latter were seeking to assign to private entrepre-neurs. In 1870 the Juchitecos rebelled against the government of Felix Díaz, and, during the Porfiriato (in 1881) another indigenous rebellion exploded, this time involving Zapotecs and Zoques under the leadership of the Juchiteco Ignacio Nicolás.

The examples just offered are enough to indicate the existence in the area of an idea of a sustained regional identity and a tradition of fighting for autonomy. The dissenters seldom recorded their motivations, and when they did "the rebel chiefs did not express the underlying reasons—such as communal property and exploita-tion of the land and salt mines, taxes, etc.—at the roots of the rebellions, which were subsumed by the defense of *regional autonomy*."[31] They did, however, articulate their aspiration to autonomy in one exceptional document.

On January 11, 1917, the deputies to the Constitutional Convention for Tehuan-tepec and Juchitán, Crisóforo Rivera Cabrera and José F. Gómez, presented an ini-tiative to establish the "state of the isthmus of Tehuantepec." Citing the historic aspi-ration to "regional autonomy" of the isthmian people, the representatives presented their arguments classified by "element": constitutional, geographic, historical, eth-nic, psychic, or political (domestic and international). First, they showed that the territorial fractions that would make up the new entity (i.e., the districts of Tehuantepec and Juchitán in the state of Oaxaca and the cantons of Acayucán and

Minatitlán in the state of Veracruz) contained twice the number of inhabitants required by the constitution and had the necessary economic means (showing a better situation in every respect than the state of Querétaro, for example). As for the geographic element, the isthmus more than satisfied the requirements, since "it would have a territory larger than that of [the states of] Aguascalientes, Colima, Morelos, Tlaxcala and others of the Republic's central area."[32]

The deputies' argumentation included historical considerations that began with the struggles of king Cosijoeza to defend the "Zapotec kingdom," continued with the period of "autonomous life" that the territory had enjoyed during the colony, and proceeded to the struggles of these peoples during the nineteenth century and those stemming from the revolution of the twentieth. They summarize: "These three armed movements, although apparently originating from separate causes, acknowledge only one profoundly central objective: the regional autonomy in question."[33]

Referring to "ethnic elements," as was the norm in those days, the deputies stressed features of race, here biological and cultural factors were mixed, since they were supposedly derived from the "essential characteristics" of the isthmians. They asserted a Zapotec reality expressed in language, usages, and customs damaged by rules from Oaxaca and determined that they had created "a soul of their own."[34]

The internal political reasons that justified the creation of the new entity, were summarized by the authors of the motion in terms of the obvious inability of "the provincial governments of Veracruz and Oaxaca" to ensure the isthmians' welfare. In particular, the deputies stressed the governments' incapacity to help "maintain the community of interests and of similar sentiments and ideas" that was the "essential basis of any political collectivity."[35] Regarding the international factor, the deputies concentrated on a refutation of the "childish, groundless argument that, once the isthmus became a State, it would easily fall in the hands of the Yankees or some other foreign power." To counter this thesis and support autonomy they presented political arguments[36] of a historical character, including regional sentiment,[37] patriotism,[38] and authority.[39]

The Constitutional Convention's commission in charge of "territorial problems" rendered its judgment on January 26, 1917. In it the commission reported receiving several petitions for territorial reforms, including the initiative of Rivera Cabrera and Gómez, supported by the inhabitants and the authorities of the isthmus. According to the commission the initiative had "the sympathy of the president." In each case the commission also noted the protests received. Against the isthmian initiative, for example, it had received a protest from the "Oaxacan constitutionalist party." As justification for its decision the Commission suggested that it lacked the necessary information to take a position, saying that such

> written requests are the only existing data available on which to base a resolution of
> the territorial issue. The Commission was unable to secure a satisfactory map in

order to examine the various territorial petitions in detail. They also lacked other statistical data on which to base a judgment on the appropriateness or inappropriateness of altering the present division of the various entities.

But instead of indicating a need for a formal study and more careful consideration of the issue, it proposed to reaffirm "its original decision," ignoring all the petitions.[40] Thus the political division approved on February 5, 1917, by the Constituent Congress, sanctioned the constituent parts of the federation from then on (except for the conversion into states in 1974 of the territories of Baja California and Quintana Roo). In the end, the demand for autonomy of the isthmians remained unsatisfied.

The isthmus was not unique in its appeal for autonomy. The frustrated aspirations of several municipalities of the mountainous region of Puebla (Tepetzintla, Anizatlán, Olintla and Xopala), which sought to create a new political entity called "Zempoala," are a matter of public record.

The restrictions confronted by regions seeking legal recognition of their sociohistorical unity arise in the fact that, since they already are part of municipal entities, they have only one option for achieving their goal—statehood within the federation. Tensions arise because a new entity can emerge only at the expense of the integrity, territory, and jurisdiction of another. Separation from the nation was undesirable and foreign to the logic of autonomy, and this limited the possibilities for political-territorial organization. The isthmus of Tehuantepec went through various political-administrative stages: in 1823 it was a province; by a decree of May 29, 1853, it became a territory, and in accordance with the territorial organization of Maximilian's empire, on March 3, 1865, it was declared a department. Later, it was dismembered, and once the federal system had been established it could only regain its regional unity by becoming a state. This explains its 1917 search for "regional autonomy" in the only available form, that of a federative entity.

AUTONOMY: MYTH AND REALITY

The lack of opportunity within the political and administrative organization of nations for regional aspirations founded upon ethnic identity is common to many Latin American countries. Article 43 of the Mexican political constitution, for example, enumerates the states (together with the Federal District) that are the constituents of the federation, and article 115 refers to the basis of the states' territorial division as a "free municipality." In this scheme there is no room for other public entities or vertical powers. The first section of article 115 states that "there shall not be any intermediate authority between this [the municipal city hall] and the State Government."

Municipalities are, however, inadequate to the task of developing an authentic autonomous life. Their legal powers are very limited; they cannot "coordinate and associate" among themselves, except to "render the corresponding public services," and their political self-determination is restricted by the power of the state to which they belong. Local legislatures (that is, those of federal entities) may "suspend local governments, declare that they have been dismantled, and suspend or revoke the term of any of their member, for any of the reasons foreseen by local law." Once a local government is declared nonexistent, a municipal council may be designated to complete its term.

Thus, there is a need to create a new *level* of political-territorial organization with the dual purpose of being able to establish regional entities (which might include several municipalities) and to achieve autonomy, especially in regions with a majority of indigenous peoples. The juridical structure constituted by the municipalities might be broadened and enriched so as to transform them into true autonomous entities, but then they would no longer be municipalities as we know them in Latin America. The juridical-political form in which a possible association of municipalities (or parts of them) would form virtual regional units remains to be designed. In principle, what is necessary is not to annul existing levels of territorial division but to *create a new one* that might solve the countless problems that have accumulated over time. It is unnecessary to modify the present federal organization (or any other) or to dissolve the municipalities. Historical experience illustrates the potential compatibility between the federal regime and both autonomous and municipal organizations.[41]

In Latin America the potential for regimes of regional autonomy has been thwarted by the socioeconomic and political structures that would be affected by any just and democratic social transformation. On ideological grounds, the project of autonomy has been hindered by a collection of myths, fears, and prejudices that have been nourished for almost two centuries by those in power and their apparatuses. An examination of some of these ideas and sentiments will help delineate an accurate profile of the autonomous entity:[42]

1. Technical issues take precedence over political principles in debates over autonomy, concealing a conservative political logic. Autonomy is an essentially political issue, and it must be discussed primarily in political terms.

2. That centralism is the guarantor of unity is the most common mythical argument against autonomy. The formal identification of centralism with a unitarian regime and decentralization with a federal system is mistaken. The unitarian regime can accept ample decentralization, and federalism often embodies the harshest type of centralism. To posit such a relationship is a *petitio principii*; it has yet to be theoretically and historically demonstrated that the two are correlated or that one is the basis for the other. Considering only the historical perspective, the experience of many countries seems to demonstrate that if there is any relationship at all between national unity and centralism it is and inverted one: The more centralized the nation, the weaker its social and political fabric, and the firmer national decentralization, the greater the internal cohesion and the more vital its development. Hence, because an autonomous regime supposes political, economic, and sociocultural decentralization, advocating it can be simultaneously an argument in favor of national unity.

3. That unity requires sociocultural homogeneity is another prevalent myth. If unity is directly linked with decentralization, it is linked with diversity as well. The firmest unity is the one founded upon respect for diversity. A society with unrecognized sociocultural diversity is rife with tensions. The denial of diversity encourages intolerance, which is definitely not the best medium for democracy.

4. Regimes of regional autonomy are often associated with supposed dangers to national sovereignty. This fear arises from their territorial character. It is argued that granting self-government and powers of their own to portions of the nation's territory would weaken sovereignty and even endanger it. But autonomy does not question the territorial unity of the nation-state; it simply defines a new political entity and opens up competences, among other things, favoring better coordination of the nation's components. If autonomy increases national unity, then it should favor sovereignty. The experience of some countries that have created regimes of autonomy strengthens this argument. In some cases, the danger of external aggression or intervention has been suggested, but the questions raised in 1917 by the people of the isthmus of Tehuantepec still stand: Would the intentions of an external aggressor be altered by a change in the nature of the region? And, once the change had been accomplished, would the national society defend the region any the less because of its autonomy?

5. The recognition of sociocultural rights through autonomy raises uncertainties regarding their compatibility with constitutional civil rights and guarantees. Indeed, it is imperative to face what seems to be a *cultural* contradiction between specific ethnic rights and "universal" individual rights. Often, the content of the so-called ethnic rights (with their emphasis on communal values, control over individuality, and strict collective norms) seems in conflict both with the ethics of late-twentieth-century Western society and with internationally sanctioned principles and guarantees identified with notions of liberty, equality, justice, and human rights. It is a question of what Geertz has characterized as the tension between essentialist ("the indigenous way of life") and epochalist ("the spirit of the times") impulses, the former emphasizing the inheritance of the past and the latter the "wave of the present." The goals of essentialism—commended by certain tendencies of Latin American anthropology— may be "psychologically apt, but socially isolating," while the epochalist proposals so cherished by a social science that considers itself "postmodern" tend to be "socially unparochializing, but psychologically forced."[43]

Cornelius Castoriadis has observed the paradox of asserting equal rights for all cultures, including those cultures that do not admit that all cultures have equal rights.[44] How are we to resolve this paradox? Can the limitations of particularism and universalism be overcome? Can the foundations or basic premises of a creative and democratic synthesis of these tendencies be discovered? The effort to avoid a confrontation of "values," based on a poorly understood relativism, only fosters suspicions of a profound incompatibility attributable to the anachronistic or pernicious norms of Indian communities. An open debate might demonstrate that any possible shortcomings could be resolved through dialogue and tolerance.

Since autonomy implies a meaningful dialogue among "cultures," fear that recognizing sociocultural rights would create distinctions that threaten individual rights is groundless. The *social pact* would be renewed without disturbing the individual guarantees and rights that are obvious historical achievements of our nations. New ethnic-national bases for democracy would be created, invalidating the ethnocentric project that causes centralization, exclusion, and inequality. This sociocultural inequality is expressed as discrimination against Indian peoples, disdain for their culture, social oppression, and denial of their rights to be distinctive and manifest a unique identity.

In order to attempt to transcend deeply rooted ethnic inequalities, at the same time ensuring individual rights and the unity of the nation, autonomy must be founded upon four basic principles: *the unity of the nation, solidarity and fraternity* among the diverse ethnic groups and regions of the country; *equal treatment* for every citizen, regardless of social position or ethnic group, and *equality among ethnic communities.*

The principle of national unity is self-explanatory. That of solidarity and fraternity recognizes the need to confer certain prerogatives (what I have called positive asymmetry) on groups that have been denied the full exercise of their rights relative to the majority of the population.[45] This solidarity must not generate new forms of inequality, hence the compensatory effect of the principle of equal treatment for every citizen (including those in autonomous regions) with regard to both human and social rights and the responsibilities of citizenship. The principle of equality among ethnic communities discourages any tendency toward domination by any one group (indigenous or mestizo) over the others. This principle must be considered in the composition of the political or administrative organs of the regions or communities, in which all ethnic collectivities must be represented according to existing norms and legal mechanisms.

The constitution must be amended to indicate the fundamental and specific rights of ethnic groups. The articles of such an additional chapter must indicate the constitutional *mandate* to establish, through statute, regional autonomy and the democratic self-government of ethnic groups. The necessary modifications or additions to the various constitutional sections would follow.

6. One of the most frequent arguments against autonomy is the consequent separation of the country's sociocultural groups, creating serious problems for the non-Indian populations that might be forced to leave territories under the new system. This mistaken scenario stems from the illusory segregationist scheme of Indian towns, of the colonial period. Autonomy assumes that, normally, *various sociocultural groups will have to live together in these regions*, in Latin America including mestizos and other non-Indian groups. It is obvious that, in some instances, the Indian population might be nearly the totality of the population of an autonomous entity, but in general Latin American ethno-regions include a diverse mix of sociocultural sectors. The regime of autonomy does not presume to expel non-Indians from territories where they have lived for generations. Rather,

the purpose is to mandate a new kind of sharing. In brief, autonomous regions should be conceived of as *pluriethnic regions.*

7. The greatest threat to the viability of a regime of autonomy lies in the identification of the territories that would adopt such system. The complexity of indigenous settlement in several Latin American countries makes it almost impossible to identify clearly demarcated territories for all parties. The importance of this issue should certainly not be underestimated, but there are ways to facilitate a solution. In countries where this demarcation has taken place it has been achieved by consulting the subjects of autonomy themselves through democratic means rather than by bureaucratic, vertical decisionmaking. Preconceived criteria must not be employed; consultation must involve participation by the interested communities throughout all phases of the process leading to the regime of autonomy. In Nicaragua this was called "popular consultation" and in Spain the "preautonomy" process.

PROSPECTS

There is no universal pattern for autonomy. It assumes various forms according to the historical milieu in which it emerges. There are, however, some prerequisites, The first of these is that, as a rule, autonomy requires a context of major *sociopolitical transformation* on a national scale. The attempt to create marginal "self-governing" systems in the framework of a centralist, homogenizing status quo would be a fiasco. The temptation (quite real in several Latin American countries) to use autonomy or analogous "amendments" to silence ethnic-group demands and dismember popular movements must be avoided. Pseudo-autonomous formulas in themselves change nothing; they must reflect fundamental transformations in society.

The second is authentic *participation of the groups involved*, since without it, their true aspirations and desires cannot be expressed. Without popular participation, autonomy becomes a mere concession and not what it should be, *a seizure and expression of rights.* This means that autonomy implies the democratization of the society; it feeds the democratic impulse and, at the same time, deepens it.

The achievement of self-government and other rights requires that ethnic communities become social subjects, a *political force* working toward national change. Because autonomy is the outcome of sociopolitical negotiation, the ethnic-national party must have political strength derived from its organization and mobilization. Autonomous rights do not arise from their juridical formalization; rather, the juridical form and the degree of autonomy achieved depend on the effectiveness of the political force embodied by the ethnic collectivity.

There is nothing inevitable about regimes of regional autonomy in Latin American countries. The aforementioned national conditions of transformation and democratization are necessary. At the same time, ethnic movements must persist in and intensify their nationalization in alliance with political projects that seek change at a national level and the consolidation of their ethnic consciousness as *political* consciousness. Understanding their particular situation as pertinent to the global society as a whole will lend strength to their demands. This will involve distancing themselves both from the traditional indigenist perspective (which ties them to the established regime) and from ethnicist neoindigenism (which attempts to place them on the margins of the nation). The national progressive organizations must continue to develop and enrich their perspectives in the direction of a better understanding of the ethnic-national question.

If some of the tendencies currently present in Latin America persist, then wherever there are regional groups with distinct identities it is very possible that there will soon be regimes of autonomy.

NOTES

1. Primer Encuentro Continental de Pueblo Indios, "Declaración de Quito." These positions were corroborated in subsequent meetings in Guatemala (Quetzaltenango, 1991) and Nicaragua (Managua, 1992). See II Encuentro Continental: Campaña de 500 años de Resistencia Indígena, Negra y Popular, "Declaración de Xelajú," ALAI Special Service, October 1991, and III Encuentro Continental de la Resistencia Indígena, Negra y Popular, "Declaración de Managua," *Boletín de Antropología Americana*, no. 24, December 1992.

2. The Seventh Ibero-American Conference of National Commissions for the Commemoration of America's Discovery: Encounter of Two Worlds, held in Guatemala City in July 1989, recommended that "the national commissions urge their governments to work toward the revision of constitutional and legal ordinances to guarantee the acknowledgment and application of indigenous rights with indigenous participation." Conferencia Iberoamericana de Comisiones Nacionales, *Presencia y significación de los pueblos indígenas de América*, Madrid, VII Reunión, Secretaría Permanente, 1989.

3. Comisión Nacional de Justicia para los Pueblos Indígenas de México, *Propuesta de reforma constitucional para reconocer los derechos culturales de los pueblos indígenas de México*, Mexico City, Instituto Nacional Indigenista, August 1989.

4. More than a posteriori "consultation," such reform would have required the participation of Indian peoples from the beginning. But leaving aside the defects of the "consultation" for the moment, what is most striking is that the opinions, criticisms, and suggestions aired in some of the meetings that the commission or other civic groups arranged were ignored. The original proposal did not undergo any substantial change. Thus, the meager consultation was, if anything, a propagandistic device and a bureaucratic formality.

5. See, for example, Frente Independiente de Pueblos Indios (FIPI), *Reforma constitucional: Un nuevo cambio de piel del indigenismo, Boletín de Antropología Americana* no. 21, July 1990. For critical approaches by academics, see various authors, *Foro de discusión de la propuesta de reforma constitucional para reconocer los derechos culturales de los pueblos indígenas de México*, Mexico City, Colegio de Etnólogos y Antropólogos Sociales/Colegio Mexicano de Antropólogos/y Escuela Nacional de Antropología e Historia, 1990.

6. FIPI, *Reforma constitucional,* p. 17. Regarding the "forms of social organization," for example, any interpretation that acknowledges the legality of a given indigenous authority (council of elders, communal assembly) will violate article 115.

7. The addition, published in the *Diario Oficial de la Federación* on January 28, 1992, reads: "Article 4. The Mexican Nation has a pluricultural composition originally founded in its indigenous peoples. The Law shall protect and promote the development of their languages, cultures, practices, customs, resources, and specific forms of social organization and shall guarantee effective access to the State's jurisdiction. In the trials and agrarian procedures in which they may take part, their juridical practices and customs shall be considered in the terms established by law."

8. Some indigenous sectors have considered the reform a simple "change of skin for indigenism," leading "to the creation of new instruments for the State to extend control over our societies, establishing new bases for the continued usurpation of our rights." FIPI, *Reforma constitucional*, p. 160.

9. See *Diario Oficial de la Federación*, Mexico City, January 6, 1992; cf. "Agrarian Law," *Diario Oficial de la Federación*, Mexico City, February 26, 1992.

10. Cf. José Mario García Laguardia, "Federalismo y centralismo en América Latina: Siglo XIX," in *El pensamiento latinoamericano en el siglo XIX*, Mexico City, Instituto Panamericano de Geografía e Historia, 1986.

11. Edmundo O'Gorman, *Historia de las divisiones territoriales de México*, 6th edition, Mexico City, Editorial Porrúa, 1985, p. 170.

12. These considerations were presented to the Constituent Congress of 1916–1917 by Francisco Ramírez Villarreal. O'Gorman, *Historia de las divisiones territoriales*, pp. 172–173.

13. I use terms like this out of convention. They are quite common in the colonial and contemporary literature, despite their ambiguity and imprecision.

14. In fact, the Spanish never had a military victory over the Mixes. Every military party the Spanish sent to the rugged mountains and northern cliffs to reduce them, was met with ferocious resistance and strategic skill. These natives were conquered, instead, by the slow ideological work of the clergy. José Antonio Gay, *Historia de Oaxaca*, Mexico City, Editorial Porrúa, 1982, pp. 149ff., 243.

15. Cortés's original dominion included land and vassals in seven provinces: four estates in Oaxaca and the demarcations of Coyoacán, Cuernavaca, Charo, Tehuantepec, Toluca, and Tuxtla (Veracruz). Even after the reduction of his property by the Second Tribunal, the marquisate was still about 75,000 square kilometers. José Luis Martínez (ed.), "Cédula de Carlos y la reina Juana en que hacen merced a Hernán Cortés de veinte y tres mil vasallos," in *Documentos cortesianos*, vol. 3, 1528–1532 (sections 5 to 6, pt. 1), Fondo de Cultura Económica/Universidad Nacional Autónoma de México, Mexico City, 1991, pp. 49–52; Borah, *El juzgado general de indios*, pp. 331–332; Lesley Byrd Simpson, *Muchos Méxicos*, Mexico City, Fondo de Cultura Económica, 1986, p. 42.

16. José María Luis Mora, *Mexico y sus revoluciones*, vol. 2, Mexico City, Editorial Porrúa, 1977, p. 183.

17. François Chevalier, *La formación de los latifundios en México*, Mexico City, Fondo de Cultura Económica, 1976, p. 168.

18. Luis de Velasco, "Para que los alcaldes mayores de Teguantepeque no den nyngunas estancias ni caballerías de tierras en Teguantepeque syn lycencia de Su Magestad," Archivo General de la Nación, Mexico City, Mercedes vol. 4, l. 140, 1555.

19. Chevalier, *La formación de los latifundios*, p. 171.

20. The dominion of the marquis over Tehuantepec was canceled in 1560, and Cosijopi died in 1564. Besides, the viceregal authorities began to grant concessions (land) to Span-

ish people within the boundaries of the marquisate after the conspiracy in which the Second Marquis was involved was stopped: "Precisely in 1567 those concessions appear in Tehuantepec, and, afterward, there are several there and in other places." Ibid., p. 171. In the sixteenth century, 166 concessions were granted to Spanish people in the form of land for cattle, 28 for raising sheep, 26 for agriculture, and 16 for horses and mules; the indigenous people got only 14, for sheep. Cf. Borah, *El siglo de la depresión en Nueva España*, table 13, pp. 76–77.

21. Borah has maintained that "the demands on indigenous villages for the support of local officials, communal activities, and the large class of indigenous nobles perhaps did not diminish at the same rate as the population. . . . As a consequence, the indigenous inhabitants could not contribute support to the European sector of the population, not only because of the abrupt abatement in their production but also because of the extreme pressure within indigenous society itself for the remaining food and services." Borah, *El siglo de la depresión en Nueva España*, p. 19.

22. This is how the Indians described it in their letter to the viceroy, the duke of Alburquerque, following the uprising. They denounced the *alcalde mayor's* "exorbitant *repartimientos*," the "whipping, stocks, prison and other ordeals with which he mistreated everyone," and the tributes "that increased every day or every month." Cristóbal Manso de Contreras, *La rebelión de Tehuantepec*, 2nd edition, Mexico City, Ediciones Toledo, 1987, pp. 22–23.

23. Ibid., p. 16.

24. Luis González Obregón, *Rebeliones indígenas y precursores de la independencia mexicana en los siglos XVI, XVII y XVIII*, 2nd edition, Mexico City, Ediciones Fuente Cultural, 1952, pp. 387 and 391.

25. See the chronicle of Juan de Torres Castillo, "Relación de lo sucedido en las Provincias de Nejapa, Ixtepeji y la Villa Alta . . . ," in García, *Documentos inéditos o muy raros para la historia de México*, pp. 273–305.

26. Punitive political action was directed by the judge Juan Francisco de Montemayor y Cuenca at the beginning of the term of the new viceroy, the Count of Baños. This official had succeeded in entering the territory through lies and false promises of amnesty, and with the aid of the indigenous authorities who had been deposed by the rebels he imprisoned the nonconformist leaders. In July 1661 he pronounced severe sentences: death for the outstanding leaders and mutilations, lashings, exile, and so on, for the others. Manso de Contreras, *La rebelión de Tehuantepec*, pp. 45–46; Díaz Polanco and Manzo, *Documentos sobre las rebeliones indias*, pp. 183–184.

27. Díaz Polanco, *El fuego de la inobediencia*, pp. 183–184.

28. Enrique Semo, *México: Un pueblo en la historia*, vol. 1, Mexico City, Universidad Autónoma de Puebla/Editorial Nueva Imagen, 1981, p. 286.

29. A survey of these episodes of indigenous resistance can be found in Víctor de la Cruz, "Rebeliones indígenas en el istmo de Tehuantepec," *Cuadernos Políticos*, no. 38, October-December 1983, pp. 62–63.

30. V. de la Cruz, *La rebelión de Che Gorio Melendre*, Juchitán, Oaxaca, Publicaciones del H. Ayuntamiento Popular, 1983, p. 9.

31. De la Cruz, "Rebeliones indígenas," p. 70.

32. "Del diario de los debates del Congreso Constituyente de 1917," in *Guchachi'Reza (Iguana Rajada)*, Juchitán, Oaxaca, Publicaciones del H. Ayuntamiento Popular, 1983, p. 15.

33. Ibid., p. 17.

34. Ibid., p. 3. It is interesting to note the Zapotec slant of the linguistic reference, excluding the other languages of the region.

35. Ibid., p. 4.

36. In the event of an attack, they asked, "would either the empire of the Rising Sun or the Yankee one subject their actions to the consideration of whether the isthmus was part of the districts of Oaxaca and Veracruz or a federal territory or a state?" Ibid., p. 6.

37. Isthmians throughout history have shown their capacity to fight in defense of the nation's integrity, and "once our aspiration was satisfied, the idea of the region's invulnerability would take even stronger root in our souls, and therefore, we would protect it with more love and passion." Ibid.

38. "We want regional autonomy because we firmly believe that it would bring about the enhancement of the region and the country: hence, the sentiment that inspires us is a highly patriotic one." Ibid.

39. The consitutionalist leader Don Venustiano Carranza had told them a few days earlier, "Besides, the satisfaction of this longing of yours . . . would make the idea of the region's invulnerability stronger in your hearts, which, hence, you would defend with greater zeal in case of foreign violations." Ibid., p. 5.

40. The exception to the rule was the incorporation in article 48 of some observations in relation to the islands of the national territory. This rendering can be found in O'Gorman, *Historia de las divisiones,* document no. 37, pp. 270–274.

41. See chap. 7.

42. The name given to this entity in each of the cases ("autonomous region," "pluriethnic region," "autonomous community," "autonomous territory," etc.) is irrelevant here.

43. Clifford Geertz, *La interpretación de las culturas,* Barcelona, Editorial Gedisa, 1990, pp. 208–209.

44. Cornelius Castoriadis, *Los dominios del hombre: Las encrucijadas del laberinto,* Barcelona, Editorial Gedisa, 1988, p. 144.

45. This could be done through the creation of special programs and funds for development and sociocultural promotion that would seek balance and ethnic equality between indigenous and nonindigenous regions.

Epilogue

What is often most stimulating about forecasting is not the accuracy of the predictions, but the uncertainties that surround them. I ended this book, at the beginning of the 1990's, speculating about the prospects for autonomy in Latin America. It was impossible to specify places, moments, and outcomes, but there seemed to be considerable likelihood of it in some countries, particularly given the new national dimension of indigenous struggles and demands. Since then we have already seen advances with regard to the constitutional recognition of communities' rights in several countries, among them Paraguay and Peru.

Now, after the establishment of autonomous regions in Nicaragua in 1987, it is in Colombia that a regime of autonomy for Indian peoples is most clearly apparent. In the country's 1991 constitution, "indigenous territories" are identified as part of the organization of the state, and these "territorial entities possess autonomy in the negotiation of their interests" (article 287). Accordingly, they have the right to (1) be ruled by their own authorities, (2) exercise the corresponding competences, (3) administer the resources and establish the taxes necessary for the fulfillment of their functions, and (4) share in the national income."

The Colombian constitution also establishes that competences will be distributed between the nation and the territorial entities and that "indigenous territories will be governed by councils and regulated according to the habits and customs of their communities." These councils have broad functions detailed in the constitution itself (article 330). With regard to national representation, article 171 prescribes that two senators be elected by the indigenous communities.[1] The judicial bases for a regime of regional autonomy, including territory, self-government, and competences, have been established. After a reasonable interval it will be possible to evaluate their practical effects.

INDIGENOUS REBELLION IN CHIAPAS AND AUTONOMY

Undoubtedly, the most outstanding fact with regard to advances toward autonomy for the Indian peoples of Latin America is the armed rebellion of Tojolabal,

Tzeltal, Tzotzil and Chol communities that began on January 1, 1994, in the Mexican state of Chiapas. Although the Mexican government spokespeople at first tried to portray this as just one more uprising led by outsiders and based on the well-worn proposals of time past,[2] it was soon evident that the movement embodied by the Ejército Zapatista de Liberación Nacional (Zapatista National Liberation Army—EZLN) had surprising novel elements; the people in arms did belong to indigenous regional groups, they were empowered by moral courage and by a distinctive discourse that fascinated both locals and foreigners, and their demands were a happy combination of national claims and deeply felt aspirations of native peoples.[3] The movement quickly attracted support both in Mexico and abroad, and the government was therefore forced to halt all military action against the rebels and open itself to dialogue by January 12.

The EZLN made an extraordinary contribution to making the ethnic-national question for the first time a central issue on the public agenda. Autonomy became a topic of national debate. The Chiapas rebellion did not invent the idea of autonomy in Mexico, but it did give it a political aspect and a programmatic profile never before seen. Until the uprising, many people had considered autonomy a joke or a passing fad. Since then public sentiment on autonomy had changed significantly. Political parties, social organizations, religious dignitaries, and intellectuals and analysts of the most diverse orientations have all expressed themselves in favor of autonomy.[4]

A few weeks after the beginning of the rebellion, both the indigenous leadership of the EZLN, the Comité Clandestino Revolucionario Indígena (Clandestine Revolutionary Indigenous Committee—CCRI), and its spokesperson or "interpreter," Subcommander Marcos, openly expressed the peoples' aspiration to autonomy. By the first days of February, for example, the CCRI members were saying, "As indigenous peoples we need our autonomy, we need that identity, that dignity, dignity to live, and respect." Subcommander Marcos was more explicit: "The kind of autonomy the comrades mean is the autonomy of the Basque people or of the Catalans, which is a relative autonomy."[5] Several days later, when a *New York Times* special correspondent asked him what was the most important element in the negotiations with the government, Marcos answered, "Political and administrative autonomy for indigenous regions." The journalist asked, "At the level of communities?" Marcos clarified: "For whole regions." He went on to say that for this to happen it would be necessary to reform article 4 of the constitution "to recognize the existence of regions with various ethnic groups that have their own structure."[6]

At the end of February 1994, the dialogue between the EZLN and the Peace Commissioner designated by the government began in the cathedral of San Cristóbal de las Casas. One of the central ideas of the Zapatistas was autonomy. The fourth item on their list of demands was "a new pact among the members of the federation that does away with centralism and allows regions, indigenous communities, and municipalities to practice self-government with political, economic, and cultural autonomy."[7] The EZLN spoke of autonomy at three levels: communal, municipal, and regional, the latter being considered "pluriethnic."[8] This implied profound constitutional changes. The government commissioner offered recognition at the *communal* level through the regulations of article 4; that is, the government rejected reform of the constitution.[9] This first attempt at resolving the conflict through dialogue ended without any agreement when the Zapatista rank-and-file rejected the official proposals. Among the reasons for the rejection was the government's limitation of autonomy.[10]

Dialogue between the parties was suspended for the rest of the year, although linkages were maintained. On February 8, 1995, the government launched a surprise attack on Zapatista territory, and the EZLN fell back. Once more, the pressure of public opinion was able to halt the military action. By September the parties had agreed to resume negotiations.[11] It was decided to have six sessions of dialogue and negotiation, each dealing with a particular topic in four phases. The participants in these sessions were to be permitted to designate guests and advisers. The topic of the first session was "Rights and Indigenous Culture," and it was broken up into six more specific topics to be addressed in working groups. The sessions began in October.

The first working group discussed "Community and Autonomy: Indigenous Rights." Autonomy was discussed in great detail by this group, but it was also a subject of debate in all the other groups, at all times, from the beginning. In the first jointly produced document, autonomy was identified as the route to find a solution. During the second phase, an initial agreement confirmed that autonomy was "the contribution of the Indian peoples to the necessary transition to democracy." The government had adopted the discourse of autonomy; with this the EZLN delegation achieved its first victory. Differences emerged, however, in the final document produced in this phase. Whereas the government stressed the right of communities and municipalities to join together only in connection with development or the optimal use of resources, the EZLN understood that this association could be undertaken to form autonomous entities.[12]

The EZLN's most important achievement in this phase was the consensus of its more than one hundred advisers on its explicit proposal of autonomy. From the very start it had been one of the goals of the Zapatistas to turn the negotiations into a platform on which representatives of civil society could debate the major national problems and pursue basic accords. The EZLN made a commitment to make those positions its own and to defend them. The resulting proposal of autonomy is probably the most elaborate and complete one made so far.[13] The general tone of this proposal was ratified at the National Indigenous Forum, sponsored by the EZLN, which took place January 3–8, 1996, in San Cristóbal de las Casas.[14]

PROPOSALS AND COMMITMENTS

During the third phase, which took place January 10–18, 1996, the parties formulated several joint documents that might eventually become accords. Among the commitments made by the government the most important was to set in motion the constitutional recognition of the right of the Indian peoples to self-determination and autonomy. This move reversed the official declarations of 1994 and 1995.

The main document includes the proposal to establish a "new relationship between indigenous peoples and the state," as well as principles for "the construction of a new social pact" in the context of a "profound reform of the state."[15] On the basis of these declarations, the federal government commits itself to (1) promoting "the recognition, as a constitutional guarantee, of the right to self-determination of indigenous peoples," as defined by ILO Convention No. 169, to be "exercised within a constitutional context of autonomy, ensuring national unity," (2) pressing for legal and constitutional reforms to expand the "political participation and representation of indigenous peoples at both local and national levels" based on "a new federalism," and (3) guaranteeing peoples' full access to the jurisdiction of the state, "with recognition of and respect for their cultural specificities and their internal normative systems."

These commitments are to be fulfilled within "a new legal context." The fundamental text in this regard, is point 5.2 of the document, which defines the "autonomous" status of indigenous peoples and sets the limits of self-determination. The government commits itself to working toward "the recognition in national legislation of the communities as entities in public law, their right to join together freely in municipalities with a majority of indigenous population, and the right of several municipalities join together to coordinate their activities as indigenous peoples." The appropriate authorities are to "transfer resources in an orderly and gradual way so that the peoples themselves may administer the public funds assigned to them and so that indigenous participation in government, negotiation, and administration in various areas and levels will be strengthened. State legislatures will determine in each case the functions and competences that are to be transferred to them."

THE CHARACTER OF AUTONOMY

The crucial issue is whether this "context" allows for effective recognition of autonomy in Mexico. Obviously, the content of autonomy has been substantially reduced. On the basis of the statement of the Indian peoples itself,[16] autonomy at any level assumes at least the following elements: (a) a *political-territorial* foundation and a corresponding jurisdiction, (b) *self-government* (autonomous government), and (c) *competences* that give shape to the *political* decentralization essential to the regime of autonomy. Do we find any of these elements in the joint documents?

In all of them, in contrast to those originally presented by the Zapatistas, when there is a reference to territory it is exclusively in the terms of Convention No. 169 (article 13.2), which stresses the "habitat" without any political or jurisdictional implication. Furthermore, the government objected to any reference to "juridical pluralism." There is no recognition of self-government at any level, including the communal. Despite declarations about "profound state reform" and "a new federalism," the present federal system remains intact. There is not the slightest reference to additional levels in the organization of the orders of government. The official delegation rejected the statement on "autonomous municipalities," and finally, the documents adopt the formula "municipality with a majority of indigenous population." The identification of the nature of the municipality privileges the character of the population instead of its political content and its position in a new federal and democratic regime. The reference to "indigenous" instead of "autonomous" has worrisome implications because of its *noninclusiveness*, contrary to the EZLN's insistence on this particular issue.[17] The danger here is the revival of the old "Indian towns" of colonial days, whose aim was precisely the separation of the native population from the rest of the people and the promotion of isolation and atomization. This *ethnic* emphasis would lay the basis for a segregationism that would harm indigenous peoples themselves, by cornering and containing them, and limit the democratic participation of nonindigenous people in the formation of autonomous and pluriethnic entities.

In brief, with respect to the demand for autonomy of the Indian peoples, the documents have serious inadequacies. There are indeed commitments whose effective fulfillment would bring about benefits for the indigenous people, but in the absence of true decentralization and other attributes of autonomy, we can reasonably doubt that these commitments can in fact be met. The central issue—the redistribution of *power* to confer the required amount of it upon the Indian peoples in the context of a decentralized and democratic system—has not been addressed. The "new" relationship between indigenous peoples and the state will continue to be based on a *heteronomous* logic. The proposed regime of "autonomy" is, paradoxically, *nonautonomous* or pseudoautonomous. There is no correspondence between the rhetorical acceptance of concepts such as indigenous self-determination, autonomy, territory, and people, on the one hand, and the rights recognized for indigenous people, on the other.

THE FORMALIZATION OF THE ACCORDS

During the fourth phase (the final plenary session), which took place February 13–16, 1996, the parties agreed to formalize the accords, including an addendum about which the EZLN had some reservations. In the meantime, there had been a debate over the documents among the EZLN's advisers. Quite simply put, two positions had emerged. The first considered the accords acceptable and, given the country's situation, sufficient. The second emphasized the limitations and political disadvantages that could arise from signing these agreements without any reservation. The main risk was that the EZLN might appear, particularly to indigenous peoples, to be reducing the scope of the proposals reached by consensus of its advisers and guests during the dialogue and the National Indigenous Forum. To avoid this it was suggested that, independent of the formalization of the agreements, the ELZN should issue a clear statement supporting the Indians' central demands. This discussion was held deep in the Lacadón jungle.[18]

The outcome of a poll of the Zapatista rank and file settled the argument; 96% objected to the "lack of a solution" to the serious national agrarian problem and to the demands for the right to information, justice, and political rights. They also objected to "the lack of juridical recognition of municipal and regional autonomies" and insisted on the fulfillment of the agreements of the National Indigenous Forum. The rank and file approved the formalization of the "minimal agreements" reached with the government but at the same time agreed that the ELZN and its advisers should issue "a statement on the demands that had not been met among the results of phases 1 and 2 of the 'Rights and Indigenous Culture' session and of the National Indigenous Forum" and that the EZLN should "commit itself to making those demands its own and continuing to struggle for their implementation."[19]

This direction was carried out by the EZLN representatives to the negotiations. The resulting statement spells out the fundamental elements to which the EZLN is fully committed. With regard to autonomy, it indicates that it is not enough "that indigenous communities may join together in municipalities in order to coordinate their activities. There need to be autonomous structures that, without being exclusively indigenous, form part of the structure of the state and break with centralism." Also, this document indicates the attributes of the regime of autonomy: recognition of the territory of the Indian peoples, establishment of governments of their own, the construction of a pluralist juridical system, and the redistribution of competences.[20]

Thus, the EZLN fulfilled its commitment, taking up and salvaging the Indian peoples' central demands. Apart from this, the arduous negotiations effected several meaningful achievements: the government accepted the nationwide character of the indigenous agenda, was forced to change its original position on discussing autonomy, and, finally, accepted the need for constitutional reforms (at least with respect to articles 4 and 27).

Up until now there have been only statements, proposals, and commitments. They have yet to be turned into legislative measures and put into practice. Only then will be clear to what extent autonomy will take root. We must wait for of this process to run its course without harboring too much optimism. However, whatever the outcome, it is foreseeable that both Indian and non-Indian people will continue working to create autonomous regions and municipalities in various parts of the country.[21] What the negotiations were about was conferring the status of a *right* on a historic demand of these peoples so that they would not have to continue swimming against the current, often on the edge of illegality or fully within it. As far as we can see, this option will remain open.

NOTES

1. Bartolome Clavero, *Derecho indígena y cultura constitucional en América.* Mexico City, Siglo XXI, 1994, pp. 187–189.

2. This line of argumentation can be found in Arturo Warman, "Chiapas hoy," *La Jornada,* January 16, 1994.

3. See *La palabra de los armados de verdad y fuego: Entrevistas, cartas y comunicados del EZLN,* 3 vols., Mexico City, Editorial Fuenteovejuna, 1994–1995.

4. Héctor Díaz Polanco, "Las voces de la autonomía regional en México (1994–1995): Recopilación," *Memoria,* no. 80 August 1995, pp. 18–27.

5. Interview by B. Petrich and B. Henríquez, *La Jornada,* February 4 and 6, 1994, p. 7.

6. Interview by journalists from the *New York Times, El Financiero,* and *Proceso,* cited in *Proceso,* no. 903, February 21, 1994, pp. 7–15.

7. CCRI-EZLN, "Compromisos por la paz," in *Perfil de La Jornada,* March 3, 1994, p. 1.

8. Alejandra Mereno Toscano has compiled Zapatista ideas on this topic in "Testimonio," *Proceso,* no. 956, February 27, 1995, p. v.

9. Federal Government, "Compromisos para una paz digna en Chiapas," in *Perfil de La Jornada,* March 3, 1994, pp. iii and iv.

10. "The bad government tried to restrict the demand for autonomy to indigenous communities, leaving the centralist scheme of power intact." EZLN, "Rechaza a las propuestas del supremo gobierno: Comunicado del 10 de junio," in *La palabra de los armados,* vol. 2, p. 203.

11. "Protocolo y bases para el dialogo y la negociación de un acuerdo de concordia y pacificación con justicia y dignidad entre el Gobierno Federal y el EZLN," MS, Mexico City, September 11, 1995.

12. See *Ce-Acatl: Revista de la Cultura de Anáhuac,* vol. 74–75, December 1995, pp. 12 and 18–19. There were also noticeable disagreements regarding other topics such as land and territory.

13. EZLN, "Propuesta general de los asesores del EZLN," in *Ce-Acatl: Revista de la Cultura de Anáhuac,* 74–75, December 1995, pp. 21–33. A proposal made throughout four indigenous assemblies between April and December 1995 is a background to this agreement; see Asamblea Nacional Indígena Plural por la Autonomía (ANIPA), *Proyecto de iniciativa para la creación de regiones autónomas,* Mexico, 1995. This process is described in Héctor Díaz Polanco and Consuelo Sánchez, "Las autonomías: Una fomulación mexicana," *Ojarasca,* no. 44, May-July, 1995, pp. 30–41.

14. The agreement emerging from this meeting can be found in *Ce-Acatl: Revista de la Cultura de Anáhuac,* 76–77, January 25, 1996, esp. pp. 16–24. Among the General Proposals (pp. 11–12) is the following: "Autonomy is the central demand that represents the spirit of all the proposals presented in this Forum: it is the strategic tool that allows the concrete expression of our right to free self-determination."

15. EZLN/Gobierno Federal, "Pronunciamiento conjunto que el Gobierno Federal y el EZLN enviarán a las instancias de debate y decisión nacional," MS, San Andrés, January 16, 1996.

16. See the texts quoted in the dialogue's second phase and the concluding remarks of the National Indigenous Forum; see also the document initially presented by the EZLN:

"Postura del EZLN para la Plenaria Resolutiva de las Partes, Tema 1: Derechos y cultura indígena," MS, San Andrés, January 10, 1996.

17. CCRI/General Command of the EZLN, "III Declaración de la selva lacandona," MS, Mexico City, January 1995, second item.

18. See the chronicle by Hermann Bellinghausen in *La Jornada*, February 14, 1996.

19. CCRI/General Command of the EZLN, "Comunicado," MS, Mexico City, February 13, 1996.

20. EZLN, *El diálogo de San Andrés y los derechos y cultura indígena: Punto y seguido*, pt. 3, MS, Mexico City, February 1996.

21. A survey of the strength shown by popular struggles in various parts of Mexico (for example, Chiapas, Guerrero, Jalisco, Morelos, Veracruz) for the construction of autonomous regions and municipalities can be found in Segio Zermeno, "¿La región contra el Estado? Un piso social para los mexicanos," *Revista del Senado de la República*, 2, no. 2, January-March 1996, pp. 85–92.

About the Book, Author, and Translator

This book deals with the perennial tensions between ethnic groups and the modern nation-state and does so from the perspective of a leading Mexican anthropologist with deep and long experience in these matters. As such, it is both a superb introduction to the basic issues and a presentation of the author's own original contributions. The appearance of this book in English gives North American readers access to these important scholarly and political currents in Latin American anthropology and political economy. It is required reading for anyone wishing to understand the current recrudescence of indigenous peoples at this moment in history—when conventional wisdom had predicted their demise.

Héctor Díaz Polanco is professor and researcher at Centro de Investigaciones Superiores en Antropología Social in Mexico City. *Lucia Rayas,* sociologist and translator, studied at the Universidad Autonoma Metropolitana and El Colegio de Mexico in Mexico City, and at the University of California at Riverside. She has translated several books and articles on social sciences and humanities.

Index

International Labor Organization (ILO), 70, 99,
    151
International Pact of Civil and Political Rights,
    99
International Pact of Economic, Social, and
    Cultural Rights, 99
International Symposium on State, Autonomy,
    and Indigenous Rights, 127–128(n37)
Ireland, 5, 80(n35)
Italy, 109

Jesuits, 52
Juchitán, 137
Just war, 25–26

Knowlton, Robert J., 67
Kohn, 10–11

Lafaye, Jacques, 15
Lagasca, Pedro, 40, 41, 58(n5)
Language
    equality of, 128(n42)
    in Nicaragua, 119, 122
    postindependence indigenism and, 71,
        79(n27)
Las Casas, Bartolomé de, 16, 23, 38, 42, 45–46,
    609(n28)
Latifundia, 67
Lenin, V.I., 102–103, 109–110, 114
Lerdo Law, 17, 67
Lerida, 117
Liberals
    centralism and, 13–18
    liquidationist of, 65–68
Liquidationist, 65–68, 72
Lithuania, 115
Llorens, Eduardo, 96, 97, 103
López de Gómara, Francisco, 28, 39, 40
López de Palacios Rubios, Juan, 26
Low-intensity warfare, 73

Macehuales, 48
Madeira, 109
Mapuches, 29
Marcos, Subcommander, 149
Marquesado del Valle, 41
Marx, Karl, 7, 75, 80(n35), 80(n36)
Marxism, 7, 75–76, 88
Maximal autonomy, 105
Maximilian, Emperor, 67, 139
Mayas, 53, 84
Meléndez, José Gregorio (Che Gorio Melendre),
    137
Mendieta, Gerónimo de, 46
Mesoamerica, 53
Mestizos, 9, 10, 84, 142
Metropolitan advisors, 100
Mexicas, 29
Mexico, 18, 76, 83, 84, 139

annihilation of population in, 32
constitutional reform in, 130–132, 133
disentailment of property in, 67
ethnocide in, 71
liberalism in, 17
nationalism in, 14–16
Porfiriato and, 68
religion in, 51
territorial division in, 133
Mexico City, 30
Minatilán, 138
Mindanao, 29
Minimal autonomy, 105
Miranda, Franciso de, 11
Miranda, José, 30
Miskitos, 119
Miskitos, Sumos, Ramos y Sandinistas Unidos,
    100
Missionaries, 38–39, 43, 44, 46, 57. See also
    Religion
    conflicts with officials, 51–52
    political and ideological role of, 49–52
Mita, 43. See also Repartimiento
Mixes, 136
Mixtecs, 134
Moctezuma, 29
Moldavia, 110, 114, 115
Montemayor y Cuenca, Juan Francisco de,
    146(n26)
Montesclaros, Marquis of, 52
Montesinos, Antón de, 38–39
Morgan, Lewis H., 66
Mosquitia Protectorate, 119
Mosquitia Reserve, 119
Motolinía, Toribio, 28, 30
Moya Pons, Frank, 30
Mulattos, 10
Multiethnic Assembly, 121
Municipalities, 139–140
Muslims, 114

Nagorno-Karabakh, 114
Napoleonic code, 4
Nation, defined, 3
National Commission for Autonomy, 87,
    120–121
National Commission on Justice for the Indian
    Peoples of Mexico, 130
National Constituent Convention, 85
National hegemony, 76–77
National Indigenous Forum, 150, 153
National Indigenous Organization of Colombia,
    84
National integration. See Integration
Nationalism, 13–18
Nationalities (nationality groups), 6
National sovereignty, 141
National struggles, 83–87
Nation building, 3–22